THE LIFE OF
SAINT PHILIP NERI

BY ANTONIO GALLONIO
OF THE ORATORY

translated by
Jerome Bertram of the Oxford Oratory

IGNATIUS PRESS SAN FRANCISCO

FAMILY PUBLICATIONS OXFORD

Credits for Illustrations:

*Frontispiece & Back Cover: St Philip Neri in Ecstasy,
by Pietro Antonio Novelli (1729–1804);
© Ashmolean Museum, Oxford.*

*All the following have been reproduced
by kind permission of the Oxford Oratory:*

*Cover: Painting of the Mass of St Philip
by a follower of Annibale Carracci.*

*Engravings on pp. xiv, 10, 14, 58, 68, 80:
drawings by Luigi Agricola;
engraved by various artists.*

*Engravings on pp. 20, 38, 141, 191, 205, 209:
drawings by Pietro Antonio Novelli;
engraved by Innocente Alessandri;
printed in Venice by Giuseppe Remondini & figli MDCCIC.*

*Engravings on pp. 26 & 217:
unattributed loose engravings.*

© 2005 by Family Publications, Oxford
ISBN 1-871217-55-5
All rights reserved

American edition published by Ignatius Press, San Francisco
ISBN 978-1-58617-150-6
ISBN 1-58617-150-X
Library of Congress Control Number 2005909728

Printed in Malta ∞

CONTENTS

TRANSLATOR'S INTRODUCTION v

BOOK I
I	Philip's early life, up to the age of 24.	1
II	His life until his ordination at the age of 36	13
III	After his priestly ordination, the Saint applies himself more diligently to the benefit of his neighbour	27
IV	What he did in 1555, 1556 and 1557.	43
V	The year of Christ 1558, when Philip was 43	59
VI	The year of Christ 1559, when Philip was 45	73

BOOK II
VII	What Philip did in 1560 and the three subsequent years	93
VIII	From the year of Christ 1564 to 1571	103
IX	What he did from 1571 to 1576 inclusive	117
X	The year of Christ 1577 and the five years following	131
XI	The year 1584 and the four following	145
XII	The year 1588 and the next two	157
XIII	What he did under Popes Gregory XIV and Innocent IX, in 1590 and 1591	169

BOOK III
XIV	The year of Christ 1592 and the two subsequent years	181
XV	The last year of Philip's life, and his holy death	195
XVI	On what happened after his death, and on his burial.	207
XVII	Various miraculous graces, granted to his followers after the burial of the saint	219
XVIII	Miracles performed in the year after his death, and the three following	233
XIX	A Summary of the virtues of blessed Philip	243

INDEX 251

The translator and the publisher wish to acknowledge with gratitude the generous sponsorship provided by several Oratories to help fund the publication of this book.

TRANSLATOR'S INTRODUCTION

It is curious that the earliest life of St Philip Neri, one written by a close friend and disciple, has never before been translated into English. This may be simply because no copy was available at the Birmingham and London Oratories in the first years of their foundation, when the Fathers were eager to promulgate devotion to St Philip in England. Of the older lives the only one they translated was the one by Bacci, which is available in many editions. It suffers rather from the time lapse between the saint's death and the compilation of the book, and also from the way Bacci arranged it, with innumerable miracle stories, making his life rather tedious for the modern reader. Gallonio is also keen to tell stories of miracles, but his have the benefit of being, in many cases, from personal observation.

Antonio Gallonio joined the Roman Oratory as a young man, and became the personal attendant on St Philip during his last years, including his final illness. Immediately on the saint's death, Gallonio began to collect evidence for his sanctity, and was prominent in the official Process for his Beatification. He wrote the first version of his life of St Philip (the one translated here) in time for it to be published during the 1600 Holy Year. This was an opportunity to spread devotion to the saint, who had died only five years before, and it is for this reason that Gallonio presents the life very much as if it were a case for the beatification. He tells the story in strictly chronological order, which was unusual for the time, and he is careful to give his sources for all the more astonishing stories. Whenever in a note he refers to 'sworn witnesses' he means the depositions made for the official Process of Beatification. These are now all readily available in the four volumes of *Il Primo Processo per San Filippo Neri* (being numbers 191, 196, 205 and 224 of the series 'Studi e Testi', edited by Giovanni Incisa della Rochetta and Nello Vian, Vatican Library 1957–63). In these volumes will be found the original evidence, often in quaint and ill-educated Italian, given by the many people of all classes who volunteered information for the Cause. Gallonio's remaining footnotes refer to stories in the lives of already canonised saints which are similar to the stories told of

Philip. Although many of these saints are obscure, and the editions of their lives difficult to find, the point is obviously that this recently dead Roman was just as much a saint as those recognised by the Universal Church worldwide.

The first edition of Gallonio's book was published in Latin in a large octavo volume, page size 203 x 150 mm, running to iv + 270 pages, and printed by Aluigi Zannetti in Rome. It carries the official approval of Angelo Velli, Provost of the Roman Oratory, and his deputies, who were Pietro Perrachioni, Germanico Fedeli, Tommaso Bozio and Blessed Juvenal Ancina, all of whom had known Philip intimately. It also carries a recommendation from Cardinals Paravicini, Borromeo, Tarugi, Baronio and Visconti, a dedication to Cardinal de' Medici, and an approbation from Pope Clement VIII, all of whom had also known and admired St Philip in his lifetime. The text is divided into paragraphs, each with a bold heading, and three dates are placed across the top of every page, being the year of Our Lord, the regnal year of the Pope, and the age of St Philip. The notes appear in the outer margin of each page. There are no numbers to the paragraphs, but the work is divided into three books. As a frontispiece there is an engraving of the saint surrounded by little vignettes from his life, and at the end is a colophon of Our Lady of the Vallicella.

The book was reprinted in 1606 at Mainz, in a smaller edition, 153 x 93 mm, but running to viii + 500 pages, printed by Hans Weiss. The introductory letter is addressed to the Abbot of Weingarten by Valentin Leuchter, who explains that he had visited Rome during the 1600 Holy Year, and learnt about St Philip, but was unable to purchase a copy of the new life by Gallonio because it was still in the press. Since then a copy had been sent to him, and he has undertaken to have it reprinted. It is not clear whether Gallonio had been consulted, but he had died in 1605. The layout, with paragraph headings, dates and notes, are all as in the Roman edition, and the dedication and approbations are all reprinted, though without the engravings. Although the title page claims that it is a better edition than the previous, *editio priore castigatior*, the text appears to be identical.

The life of St Philip, who was finally canonised in 1622, was first noticed in English by Henrie Taylor, who published a supplement to Ribadaneira's *Lives of the Saints*, under the title *An Appendix of the Saints lately Canonised and Beatified by Paule the fift and Gregorie the fifteenth*, printed in Douai in 1624. This rare book contains a section (pp. 104–43) entitled 'The Life of S. Philip Nerius of Florence, Founder of the Congregation of the Oratory; written in Latin by Antony Gallonius, Priest of the same Congregation; and translated into English', which has led the British Library catalogue into listing it as a translation of Gallonio. It is however a very short abbreviation, no more that 6,500 words, and omitting most of the miracle stories, presumably in the belief that English Protestant opinion would only make fun of them. The crypto-Oratorian Abraham Woodhead, who formed a community at Hoxton in the 1660s and 70s, possessed a 'Life of St Philip Nerius', which he strongly recommended to all his friends. That may have been Taylor's version, or a copy of the Latin, but unfortunately Woodhead's library was burnt following the Dutch conquest in 1688 (see *Oxford Dictionary of National Biography*).

The Latin version was reprinted in Rome in 1818, but only made widely available in the *Acta Sanctorum*, where it appears under St Philip's feast day, 26 May (volume VI, pages 456 to 519, Paris and Rome, Victor Palmé, 1866). Here it has been divided into nineteen chapters, and the paragraphs numbered consecutively, though ignoring the original paragraph headings. Gallonio's notes are grouped together at the end of each chapter, the dates are inserted in the margins, with occasional editorial comments. It is this version that we have followed here, retaining the chapter and paragraph numbers for ease of reference, but inserting the paragraph headings from the original edition, and placing the dates with these headings at the beginning of each new year. Our own new editorial notes have been given in italics.

Gallonio also produced an Italian version of the life, which appeared in 1601, from the same printer, only a year after the Latin, though it is substantially different. Some stories are omitted, others expanded, others added; names have been supplied and some parts are in a different order. The Italian version was reprinted in Naples in 1608, Venice in 1611, Benevento in 1706, and Rome in 1839, with a French translation already in 1606. It has recently been made available in a new version to celebrate the fourth centenary of St Philip in 1995, edited by the Secular Oratory of the Roman congregation, and annotated in great detail by Maria Teresa Bonadonna Russo. (Presidenza del Consiglio dei Ministri, Roma 1995). These notes have been very useful in providing a little extra information for our translation, though they contain a great deal more scholarly information which will be invaluable for future biographers of the saint.

The value of Gallonio's account is surely its freshness and immediacy: we hear stories at first hand, and the author makes it clear that he was intimately concerned in the events he recounts. He speaks often as an eyewitness, even though he admits that he couldn't quite cope with the post-mortem examination and had to leave the room. It is artless, naïve, repetitive, and prolix, with far too much attention to the aristocracy and the dignitaries of the Church, but all the more convincing for its lack of deliberation. It is certainly easier to read than Bacci. There are of course many modern lives of St Philip, in Italian, French, German and even English, which have the benefit of modern methods of scholarship and organisation, but there are few sources to which Gallonio did not have access, and the primary information remains the documents of the *Processo*. We can and should read the lives by Capecelatro, Ponnelle and Bordet, Türks and Trevor, but this primary source has been neglected for too long, and we therefore make it available at last in an English guise.

Jerome Bertram, Cong. Orat.
2 February, 2005

THE LIFE OF THE BLESSED
FATHER PHILIP NERI
OF FLORENCE

Founder of
THE CONGREGATION OF THE ORATORY

SET OUT CHRONOLOGICALLY
BY ANTONIO GALLONIO OF ROME,
PRIEST OF THE SAME ORATORY

BY PRIVILEGE OF THE SUPREME PONTIFF
PRINTED AT ROME
BY ALUIGI ZANNETTI
JUBILEE YEAR 1600
WITH THE PERMISSION OF HIS SUPERIORS

TRANSLATION BY
JEROME BERTRAM
OF THE OXFORD ORATORY
MMV

ORIGINAL IMPRIMATUR

We, Angelo Velli of Palestrina, Provost General of the Congregation of the Oratory, and the Deputies, have asked two priests of our Congregation to examine three books on the Life of the blessed Philip Neri of Florence, Founder of the same Congregation, written by Father Antonio Gallonio; they have approved them, and they have also been approved by the Eminent Cardinals of the Holy Roman Church whose names appear below; we therefore also approve them for publication, saving the authorisation of the most reverend lords the Vicegerents and the father Master of the Sacred Palace.

Given at Rome on the feast of the holy martyrs for Christ, Papias and Maurus, being the 29th January, A.D. 1600.

I hereby attest that I have either witnessed with my own eyes, or learnt for certain on the evidence of the most reliable witnesses, everything that is written below about blessed Philip Neri,

Ottavio Paravicini,
    Cardinal Priest of the Title of S. Alessio

Federico Borromeo,
    Cardinal Priest of S. Maria degli Angeli

Francesco Maria Tarugi,
    Cardinal of the Title of S. Bartolomeo, Archbishop of Siena

Cesare Baronio,
    Cardinal of the Title of SS. Nereo e Achilleo

Alfonso Visconti,
    Cardinal Priest of S. Sisto

Angelo Velli,
    Provost

Pietro Peracchione, Germanico Fedeli,
Tommaso Bozio, Giovenale Ancina,
    Deputies

Imprimatur   Rev. Bishop of Ravenna, Vicegerent

Imprimatur   Frà Gregorio Servanzio, associate of the most reverend Master of the Sacred Palace.

TO THE MOST ILLUSTRIOUS AND REVEREND FATHER AND LORD ALESSANDRO DEI MEDICI, CARDINAL OF FLORENCE, MY WORTHY PATRON, GREETINGS FROM ANTONIO GALLONIO

Peter Damian, Cardinal of the Holy Roman Church and Bishop of Ostia, had a reputation for learning and sanctity, most reverent Cardinal Alessandro: he is said to have taken it ill that after nearly fifteen years, no one had appeared who could write a book on the life of St Romuald, who was so illustrious for his virtues. He was right to feel thus, for he knew that it is most pleasing to God that the lives of the saints be written, as well as bringing joy to the saints themselves; there are many well-known indications of this in the history of the Church. Hence it came to pass that it has been found that reading such lives has been the first step towards salvation for many, and has brought very great benefits for many more in their progress in the spiritual life. Certainly St Augustine, the virgin St Demetriades, St Romuald, St Dominic, St Thomas Aquinas, and many others have gained great benefit thereby. Also Blessed Giovanni Columbini is recorded as having imitated them and so changed his life for the better. This being so, it is not remarkable that many holy men, the most weighty writers from the beginning of the Church until our own times, have given much time and effort to composing the lives of men who were outstanding in holiness. I have therefore attempted to follow their example, though with little hope of being able to equal their erudition, and undertaken to write the life of our blessed father Philip, relying on his grace and on the strength given me by holy obedience. By the help of God I have now finished it, and our Congregation believes it should appear under your name, not only because you have supervised it every day that you were able to do so (and you were usually able), but also because you held the said founder Philip Neri of Florence in the greatest affection while he was on earth, and now that he lives in heaven, you hold him in equal honour and veneration as a saint and friend of God. Accept, therefore, this token of my gratitude to you and my devotion to our holy Father, with the same gracious generosity as you have been accustomed to show to our Congregation. That you may continue to favour us with your patronage, with the same enthusiasm, and ever-increasing charity, and that long life may be granted to you, is the prayer we make, as is our custom and our duty, to Christ Jesus, the Son of God.

THE AUTHOR TO THE READER

Now at last, dear Reader, I have finished the Life of Blessed Philip Neri, not through my own efforts – for I am barely able to write at all – but by the help of Him who makes eloquent the tongues of babes. I have set it out chronologically, partly so that the various episodes might be less easily confused and be clearly distinct, but principally so that following through the sequence of the years I could show how the blessed man persevered in steadfast holiness, and his Congregation made progress. I have consistently used a style that is compact without being obscure. What I record in this history I have taken from reliable sworn witnesses, to the number of two hundred and fifty-two, who have either observed the facts themselves, or learnt them from those who were present. For each story I have cited the witnesses, as you will find in the footnotes, where I have also cited examples in the lives of the saints which are similar to stories told about Philip. Among the witnesses (to pass over the rest) are six cardinals of the Holy Roman Church, who were familiar with Philip and knew him well: these are Alessandro dei Medici, Agostino Cusano, Ottavio Paravicini, Federico Borromeo, Francesco Maria Tarugi, and Cesare Baronio. The witnesses were heard and recorded, observing all legal forms, by that respectable and reliable man Giaccobo Buzio, a priest of the Diocese of Gallese (or Cività Castellana as it is now called), Canon of the Lateran Basilica, and public Notary of the Apostolic See. They were recorded by him in the record office of the Roman Curia, in his capacity as notary to the apostolic visitation by His Holiness Pope Clement VIII, and secretary to Girolamo, Cardinal Rusticucci, Bishop of Sabina and Vicar of the Congregations (as it is called) to His Holiness. That is what I wanted you to know. Apart from that, if you find any benefit in reading what I have written, the recompense I ask of you is that in your prayers you will remember me before God, and deign to commend to our beloved Father, now at rest in heaven, me, his unworthy son.

BOOK I

S FILIPPO NERI

*Cadendo con un giumento in una cantina
è preservato da Dio.*

I : PHILIP'S EARLY LIFE, UP TO THE AGE OF 24

His birth and education
A.D. 1515–21; Leo X years 3–9; Philip's age 1–7

1.   Philip Neri was born in Florence under Leo X, on the 22nd of July, which was the day before the feast of St Mary Magdalen, a little before midnight, and in the year of the world's redemption 1515. His parents were Francesco Neri, and Lucrezia, daughter of Antonio de' Soldi.[1] The child was given the name 'Philip' when he was initiated into holy baptism, after his holy and respected grandfather. By the time he was approaching the age of five, he had learnt to respect his parents to the extent that he never departed from their orders by a nail's breadth, and never caused them any grief or anxiety.[2]

In about the twenty-second year of this century, or the following year, when Hadrian VI was Pope, it happened that a countryman was leading a donkey laden with apples to Philip's house from a farm belonging to his father Francesco Neri. Philip, who was then eight or nine years old, climbed on its back, whereupon both he and the donkey promptly fell down from a high place straight into a wine cellar. His parents were horrified, and ran to him, imagining that they would only recover a lifeless body, but found him alive and unharmed, with no injuries anywhere, which was a remarkable grace of God, who had destined him from birth to bring many to salvation. I remember that our holy Father used to tell this story, among the other great graces and favours he had received from God, about how he had escaped certain death because God had chosen him for great things.

Another time he was reciting the Psalms of David together with his sister Elizabeth, in the days of Clement VII, when their

---

[1] *In fact his mother's name was Lucrezia di Antonio da Mosciano; it was her mother who was called Maddelena Soldi. Francesco Neri (1477–1559) became a notary in 1524, but was more interested in chemistry than law.*

[2] At the beginning of our story, we will have to put several years together.

younger sister Catherine bounded up to them to annoy them. Our boy wanted to be rid of this nuisance to both himself and Elizabeth, and so pushed Catherine away gently, but their father was very cross when he heard about it. The holy child was so upset by this that he washed away his fault (if you could really call it that in one so young) with floods of tears.³

2.   You could not find anyone more decent, affectionate and good-looking than Philip. He behaved respectfully to grown-ups, got on easily with his contemporaries, and was kind to the little ones, apparently incapable of anger. The result of all this was that he was universally popular, and was commonly called 'Pippo buono', 'Good Pippin', a nickname which simply meant that Philip was a good-living boy. It followed that our boy, who had been called to serve the Lord, used to go to church regularly, and even at the age of eleven (around the year 27 of this century) was happy to sit in church and listen to the preachers of the Word of God. Among these the most notable was a friar called Baldolino, of the Humiliati brethren; he used to tell amazing stories about his sanctity, which for the sake of brevity I will omit. Yes, it must have been in the year of Christ 1527 that Philip attended the sermons of that servant of God.⁴

He spent his early years in learning to read and write well, and to good avail, for he gained much from those studies. His teacher was called Clement, who was quite good enough at Latin for the period.⁵ Philip did not only make progress in the humanities, but much more so in his religion. He was always devoted to his step-mother, and so kind to her when she grew old that she was deeply attached to him, and quite carried away with grief when he left his

---

³ Some of the most respected authors have told us how the saints began to be holy in childhood. See St Athanasius on St Antony, Paulinus on Ambrose, George the Monk on Theodore the Siceot, Pietro Ranzano on St Vincent Ferrer, and Surius on St Thomas Aquinas.

⁴ *Frà Baldolino da Francesco preached in the church of All Saints. 1527 was the year when the Imperial troops threatened Florence on their way to Rome.*

⁵ *Maestro Chimenti, lecturer at the Badia in 1535–6.*

⁶ *Francesco Neri only married again in 1532; it was in fact his step-grandmother, Maddalena di Michele Lensi, to whom Philip was so attached.*

native place, so sad and upset was she.⁶ When she fell into the disease from which she was not to recover, she constantly had Philip's name on her lips, and appeared to be looking at him from time to time as if he were there with her.

As a youth, he leaves his fatherland
A.D. 1530–1; Clement VII years 7–8; Philip's age 16–17

3. Our holy Father was eager for the perfection of the Gospel, even at the age of fifteen, and was encouraged by the example of the saints to endure all hardships with patience. When he caught a fever, he took it so lightly that you would not believe; he did not try to find any cure for the disease, and never told anyone that it was troubling him. Only one of his woman relations noticed that Philip was in need of help, and gave him the care he would not ask for.

As long as he lived in Florence, it was not possible that his virtues could be concealed behind the walls of his room or in the obscurity of his home; his reputation spread from the family dwelling into the light of Florence, and was spoken about in front of the leading citizens. Having called him 'Good Pippin' as a child, in his teens they called him 'Decent Philip'. It followed later on that when a few rumours reached Florence about the good he was doing in Rome, his fellow citizens talked about him, saying, 'Why should we be surprised about that? We saw what he was like when he lived here, and how he always behaved with decency, love and devotion in all circumstances.' This led them to ask for the help of his prayers.

When he was eighteen, his father Francesco sent him to his uncle Romolo, who lived in Campania in a town called San Germano, at the foot of Monte Cassino.⁷ He sent him there not only in order that he might join him in business, but in the hope that he might be named heir to his uncle's vast riches. Apart from Philip he had no other relation, and was so rich that the total of his capital amounted to twenty-two thousand gold pieces. But Philip only stayed there a few days, fearing to injure his conscience, for he had

---

⁷ *In 1531 the Medici recaptured Florence, and supporters of the Savonarola party, like the Neri family, might well have considered it better to leave the city if they hoped to prosper. Bartolomeo Romolo was actually a cousin of Philip's father, and was not particularly rich.*

in mind a much more valuable and influential line of business. He left his uncle and everything else, for the sake of Christ, for though he was rich, he wanted to make himself poor for our sake.[8] It was in the year of Christ's birth 1533 that he betook himself to Rome, where he could be free, and with an unburdened mind devote all his thoughts and concerns to God alone.[9]

4.   He entered the city, and lodged at the home of a Florentine citizen, one Galeotto Caccia, for a few years. Here he gave clear indications of his love for God.[10] He lived a strict life, sweetened by his constant prayer till it savoured of heaven; he ate but once a day, contenting himself with simple food and water to drink. Occasionally, or maybe even frequently, he abstained from food altogether for three days, in his determination to master his physical desires. He was always fond of making fun of himself, and held all worldly matters in contempt, so that he could enjoy a total dedication to Christ. Hating and despising selfishness, he longed to return the love of Christ, his beloved. Day and night he was eager for the constant contemplation of God alone. Not satisfied with that, as his love for Christ daily increased to an amazing extent, he was driven by that very love to ask in every prayer that he might do greater things, and suffer more, for the very love of that same Christ. Philip enjoyed night vigils, found consolation in tears, sought out opportunities for work: in short, there was nothing that he thought might please God that he did not embrace.

Now here is something that happened to him at that period, which I will not pass over in silence. He was travelling one day, and met some characters of very dubious morality. Prompted by an evil spirit, and perhaps attracted by his good looks, they cast

---

[8] *Later lives attribute to St Philip a stay of two to three years in S. Germano, but Gallonio is more likely to be right here. The story that Philip frequently visited the chapel hanging in the cliff at Gaeta during his stay at S. Germano cannot be verified: Gaeta is much too far for an evening's walk there and back. Possibly however it was a significant stage on his journey from S. Germano to Rome.*

[9] He appears in this to imitate the example of great saints such as Antony the Great, Hilarion, and Abraham the Syrian.

[10] *The house is now 11, via della Dogana Vecchia. Galeotto's elder son, Michele, became rector of the Florentine church in Citelle, and the younger, Ippolito, a Cistercian.*

modesty aside and invited him, chaste youth that he was, to join them in sin.[11] He did his best to get away from them, which is what he really wanted, but was unable to, which upset him greatly. But suddenly it occurred to him that the word of God, which is keener than a two-edged sword, has a great influence in softening the hearts of wicked men. He launched into them then, with a sermon about divine matters, and about the vileness of sin, and so enlightened their minds that the word of God had the effect of setting them free from all temptations of that sort, and quite put them off the sin they had planned; more than that, it turned them into reformed characters, as the Lord gave his assistance in the matter. Now there is a wonderful example of God's goodness. Those who came to entrap him were themselves trapped, for their own greater good, by an unarmed youth, simply by his preaching the word of God; they did not leave the scene before they had rid themselves of the virus of their iniquity.

At Rome he applies himself to philosophical studies
A.D. 1534; Clement VII year 11; Philip's age 20

5.　Since Philip was living in Rome, the idea of studying philosophy came into his mind, with God's prompting. During that time, however, he in no way neglected his study of piety, and never omitted any part of his usual spiritual exercises, on the pretext of being too tired to perform them. He applied himself to philosophy because he thought that would be pleasing to God, and in a short time made such progress that he was counted among the best in his class. But during the time he devoted to philosophy he never left out his frequent prayers, or the works of mercy that he usually did, although he spent a lot of time in prayer and pondering on the things of God. He became stronger daily, and more experienced in these matters, and as he grew older his virtue grew with him.[12] It is quite remarkable to see how he passed through the dangerous student age without losing his innocence and purity of thought. His tutors, a very learned man called Cesare Iacomello, and Antonio

---

[11] You will find a similar story in the life of St Bernardine of Siena.

[12] *During his stay in the Caccia home, Philip studied at the nearby university, the Sapienza.*

Altovito the Archbishop of Florence, had such a high opinion of his morals and integrity that they both called him by the old nickname, 'Decent Philip'.[13] He was endowed with a very acute mind for study, particularly in disputations. When it came to theology, in which he was well skilled, he always followed the opinions of St Thomas. He was very popular among his contemporaries and colleagues for his mild temper, his gentle manner, and his Christian humility: no one had a bad word to say about him. By the time he had gone sufficiently deep into philosophy, he was so clear of any vicious inclinations that his friends were all convinced that he was still a virgin. This virginal integrity of thought and deed was preserved to his very last breath, without the slightest suspicion of any fall, and his purity remained intact and unassailed, as I shall recount more fully in the appropriate place.

What he did as a student
A.D. 1535–7; Paul III years 1–3; Philip's age 21–23

6. While Philip was occupied in his secular education, he did associate with his fellow students from time to time, and had long discussions and arguments with them about obscure points of natural science, but he was at the same time extraordinarily fond of being alone, and spent long periods in nightly vigil.[14] As Saint Paul recommends, he discerned the invisible things of God through the means of visible things, and scrutinised His eternal power and divinity to the furthest extent possible for a mortal man doomed to die.

He often did the round of the Seven Churches of Rome, with no one to keep him company: these churches were the ones most distinguished for their liturgy and the indulgences granted them by the Popes. He was aware that Scripture says about a soul afire with the love of God, 'I will lead her into the wilderness, and I will speak

---

[13] *Cesare Giacomelli became Bishop of Belcastro in 1553; Antonio Altoviti (1521–73), too young to be a tutor, must have been a fellow student; he became Archbishop of Florence in 1548.*

[14] *Everyone agrees that the saints did the same: look at Osbert the Monk's life of St Dunstan, Archbishop of Canterbury (chapter 37), Bandomina in the life of Queen Radegund, Theodoric on St Dominic (book I, chapter 4) and finally Surius on St Elzear the Count (vol. V).*

to her heart' [Hos 2:14], and elsewhere, 'She will sit solitary and be silent, for she will lift herself up above herself' [Lam 3:28].

He practised poverty to the extent that he would never agree to accept anything from his family and relations. Once he got to Rome he accepted nothing even from his father Francesco, who was very fond of him, except, to begin with, a garment or two. He kept right away from anxieties about transitory things, particularly those relating to his family. He confined himself to a small room, which contained nothing but a bed and some books, and his clothes hanging on a rope along the wall. Whenever an opportunity occurred to curb the irrational desires and longings of his mind, he seized upon it eagerly, striving always to gain mastery over himself. That is why he was always advising his sons to try to conquer themselves even in the most trivial matters, if they wanted to be able to overcome in the greater struggles. His intention was to make every effort to follow Christ his leader in all things, Christ the lover of poverty and humility.

He dedicates himself totally to Christ
A.D. 1537; Paul III year 4; Philip's age 23

7. Once our dear Father had received sufficient education in the human sciences, to the extent that there were few of his contemporaries who could match him, he left secular learning behind him, to follow the call of Christ, giving himself totally to prayer and the contemplation of the things of God; this was, I think, at the end of the year thirty-seven of our century. In order to apply himself to this work above all else, he sold those books he possessed.[15] He began to be gripped by such a longing to find Christ, as can hardly be expressed in words, walking always afire with the Spirit. Philip found that prayer was more delightful, more refreshing, more joyous than anything else; he prayed by day, he prayed by night, and his thirst for prayer was never quenched by prayer, but ever increased. When he was meditating upon the bitter death that Christ died for the salvation of the human race, or the crimes and sins of the wicked, which bring the wrath of God upon themselves, he was quite overcome with weeping. He was glad to be harsh

---

[15] Theodoric says St Dominic did the same; see his life, book I, chapter 2.

with his own body, as the Spirit prompted. Constantly he begged for the conversion of the wicked, begging the Lord for this through the death of His only Son, not without copious tears. When he saw a figure of Christ hanging upon the Cross, he was unable to restrain his tears, so that even if he tried to apply himself to philosophy, he could not stop weeping at the sight.

He adopted the custom of visiting the Seven Churches of the city virtually every day, or at least one or two of them, without any companion, to make his devotions there. It is amazing to tell how much he profited from these pilgrimages, and what lasting fruit he plucked from the Will of God thereby. Often he spent entire nights in those places, lovingly contemplating heavenly things; even more often he spent the night in prayer in the catacomb called San Callisto.[16] Taking very little sleep, if he did find a little rest necessary he took it on the bare floor in the porches of those basilicas.

He acquired such a facility in opening himself in prayer to God that it was more a question of his being compelled by God's grace to pray, than having to force himself to kindle the flame of divine love by means of the new method of meditation on divine subjects. He was so saturated by the outpouring of heavenly joy during his prayers that he could hardly endure it. Because of this not only did he fall prostrate on the ground, but even had to call out to the Lord in such words as these: 'That is enough, O Lord, enough! Restrain the billows of your grace, I beg you.' It happened one day that he was more than usually overwhelmed by these delights, to the point of expiry, and so he began to beg for God's mercy with greater fervour than before: 'Leave me, O Lord,' he cried, 'leave me; I cannot bear so great a burden of heavenly delight: I am only mortal, I cannot! Lord, I shall die, if you do not relieve me at once, if you do not help me!' And after he had prayed in this manner for some time, the Lord did lighten the excessive fervour of his soul a little: this I heard from his own account. That is why we need not be surprised that he benefited from his own escape from these straits to teach us that for those who truly love God, there is nothing more difficult,

---

[16] *The catacombs of S. Callisto and S. Sebastiano form a single connected complex: it is with the area now known as S. Sebastiano that Philip is particularly associated.*

harsh and burdensome than the continuation of this life.[17] Saints are supposed to look on death with longing, and life with resignation.

His temptations

8. During these pilgrimages to the Seven Churches, which as I said he did very frequently, as well as receiving great gifts and blessings from God, he also in contrast had to endure much opposition from the devil, who was trying to frighten him away from his course of life. He would be attacked, now on this street, now on that; now he would be assailed with the burning torches of desires, which temptations he always overcame with prayer and compunction; now he would be savagely attacked in other ways.[18] But far from these troubles harming Philip, he actually profited from them, for they gave him ample opportunities to win a glorious victory over his malignant foe.

Here is something memorable that happened to him on one of these pilgrimages: it was a rough night, and he had no companion on his way to the churches we are talking about, when three demons presented themselves to him, at the place called Capo di Bove.[19] He was not alarmed by their terrible appearance, but simply passed them by with contempt, giving no sign of fear, for he was fortified by the powers of heaven, and sheltered under the shade of God's assistance. He continued on his way, courageously and without hesitation. When the evil spirits observed that they were foiled in every attempt to overcome him, they vanished at once.

At this period he had to endure many demonic attacks of that sort during his pilgrimages, but every new temptation from the devil served only to strengthen him. He was well aware in himself

---

[17] See the Register of St Gregory the Great, book IX, epistle 27, and book XI, epistle 24; also Augustine, Tract 9 on the First Epistle of St John.

[18] Saints have been attacked by the devil with similar temptations. See Osbert the Monk's life of St Antony; St Jerome's life of Abbot Hilarion, and Pope St Gregory on the life of St Benedict (*Dialogues*, book I).

[19] That the devil is accustomed to afflict the saints with terrors is shown in their lives: see Metaphrastes in the life of Dominic the Stylite, George the Monk on Theodore the Siceot, Osbert on Dunstan, and Theodoret on Philotheus. *Capo di Bove is the Tomb of Caecilia Metella near S. Sebastiano: the tomb has a frieze of bulls' skulls.*

S. FILIPPO NERI

Non paventa a vista di tre orribili demonj di notte presso Capo di Bue seguitando animosamente il suo viaggio, e la sua orazione

of the gifts that God had given him, but wanted to keep them hidden from anyone else, for he remembered what St Gregory said, that anyone who carries his treasure about openly in the streets is asking to be robbed. He constantly repeated to himself the phrase, 'my secret is my own, my secret is my own' [Is 24:16]. Everyone who knew him intimately agrees that they have never met any man who was as averse to human praise as Philip, or who had such a low opinion of himself, and said so. He did his best never to let anyone see either his learning, which was considerable, or his holiness of life, but in what he said and how he behaved tried always to keep his sights on modesty and contempt for reputation. He always cultivated the spirit of mortification, as they call it. No one should be surprised, therefore, if there is little more that can be said about his more hidden activity. What can safely be said is that these pilgrimages not only brought him a great advance in virtue, but also gave him the chance of many significant victories over the enemy.

He goes to visit the sick in the public hospitals

9. Meanwhile, Philip was not content with all this, but began to visit the public hospitals and convalescent homes, applying himself unreservedly to caring for the sick.[20] He did the rounds of the patients in their beds, gently cheering up the depressed, rallying those who had given up with the hope of heaven to come, and encouraging them all to be patient and well-behaved. He sat with those who were dying, looking after them night and day with alert attention, which amazed everyone, nor did he leave them until they had passed from this life. This work was not without results, for he gathered a rich harvest of saved souls. In this way he restarted the custom for lay people to tend the sick who were lying in the public hospices; for a long time this practice had fallen out of use, but now it began again. It was impressive how he persevered with this work.

He never visited Florence again, where he had been born and educated, neither in his father's lifetime nor afterwards; indeed he

---

[20] *Specifically, he is associated with the hospitals of S. Giacomo in Augusta, S. Spirito, S. Giovanni in Laterano, and the Consolazione.*

never left Rome except for the sake of visiting the Seven Churches.[21] Throughout his life he was constant in disparaging himself, encouraged by the example of Christ Our Lord, and the saints. For several years he lived almost like a hermit, refreshing himself more with tears than food. Every day he flogged himself briskly; he often slept on the bare ground. For his meals he took ordinary bread with some olives, vegetables or fruit, and he drank plain water. This frugal and simple regime lasted with him until the very end of his life. Once he had become a priest, he used to have a light breakfast, and a simple supper in the evening to sustain his body, with a little wine, much diluted, or frequently just water to drink. Supper consisted of a couple of soft-boiled eggs, or broth, or vegetables, followed by a salad with salt and vinegar; he hardly ever allowed any more dishes to be brought to his table. He very rarely admitted meat to his diet, and he was never greedy for any food even if he had been fasting for three days. All his life he tasted neither milk nor anything made from milk; fish he consumed very occasionally, polenta never.

---

[21] The great Archimandrite Nicephorus did the same, as we see in his life by Theosterictus.

II : HIS LIFE UNTIL HIS ORDINATION AT THE AGE OF 36

As a layman, he works energetically for the salvation of his neighbour
A.D. 1538–43; Paul III years 4–9; Philip's age 24–29

10. As a layman, he led the most admirable life on this earth: you could see in him an amazing detachment from things that pass away, with the greatest submission of soul, a burning desire for prayer, marvellous austerity in food, and tremendous love for God. By these steps he rose to the summit of Christian perfection, until he felt himself called to assist his fellow men, in about the year thirty-eight of our century. It was time for that light of his to be kept no longer under a bushel but to be placed on the lampstand of the Church, to give light to those who were in the house of God.

Every day he used to go to the part of the city where the Florentine merchants lived, where by talking about holy things he encouraged the young to think about the pursuit of virtue, and so converted several of them to adopt a life of devotion.[22] With the same purpose he began to frequent the schools. Philip aimed in particular at striking up friendship with the most depraved among them, reckoning that he ought to provide the most assistance to the ones who needed it most. Nor was he disappointed in this aim, for with the help of God he brought many to leave their dissolute life and adopt a better one. It was surprising how Philip's holiness was such that he could mix with the most sinful of men without himself contracting any evil, but rather doing them a great deal of good. However he was sufficiently wary of the threat to his own chastity that he did not associate in this way with women.[23]

---

[22] *The area around the Via dei Banchi Vecchi, between the Campo de' Fiori and the Ponte Sant'Angelo.*

[23] Saints avoided the company and conversation of women as far as possible, to ensure their chastity. See the life of St Bernadine of Siena.

Luigi Agricola inv.e dis.   Luigi Fabri inc.

S. FILIPPO NERI

Ragiona delle cose celesti à Giovani de' Fondachi traendoli dalle mani del Demonio a Cristo.

He tried to get as many people as possible to join themselves to Christ, and through frequently speaking at length about the things of God, combined with an example of frugal holiness, he brought many to join various religious families. Blessed Ignatius, the founder of the Society of Jesus, used to call our father Philip by the familiar soubriquet of 'the Bell' or 'the Signal', because while he summoned others to enter religion, he himself remained in the world outside. Let no one be in doubt that this was God's work, for the Lord intended to make use of his labour to establish a new form of religious life (as was proved in the event) which would be beneficial to the salvation of the whole Church and all mankind. From this institute, which continues to bear undoubted fruit to this day, men have emerged who are distinguished for their holiness and their learning. But I must not omit to mention that Blessed Ignatius was of such holiness that Philip used to say of him that the interior beauty of his soul shone outwardly, for he told us that he often saw sparks of light glittering in his eyes and face.

He is attacked by the devil with new temptations

11. One day he was passing by the amphitheatre built by the imperial Flavian dynasty (which we now call the Colosseum), intending to visit the Lateran Basilica, when he saw a demon in his way, in the guise of a beggar, completely naked. An impure thought did cross his mind at the sight, but he took refuge in prayer, and the temptation ceased at once; the demon, ashamed to be thus overcome, fled away. I remember the holy Father telling us that this temptation was caused not by human nature, but by the devil, and that he was quite convinced that the beggar was indeed a demon, not a man, even though it presented itself to him under the attractive form of a man – that was how he used to speak, in such an ingenuous way. We know the devil often does attack holy men in this or a similar manner, the most famous example being the story Pope Saint Gregory tells in the biography he wrote of Saint Benedict, the great Patriarch of the monks of the West.

After this, since the enemy of the human race realised that by no means could he induce Philip to fall away from his position of virtue by his own choice, and determined to overthrow him by violence, forcing him against his will. To this end he stirred up a jealousy of Philip's virginity in certain particularly depraved young men. When Philip was inside a house which he used to visit from time to time on an errand of kindness, they seized their opportunity to assail his integrity with the most seriously immodest attack. Not thinking that one woman's lust would suffice to oppose one man's self-control, they found two women, both utterly immoral as they thought, and locked them into the room with him without his realising it, so that there was no way he could escape: a wicked thing indeed![24] But our loving Lord, for whose sake this had happened to him, did not abandon his servant, although he could see no way out, all the doors being locked. He delivered Philip from all danger, unstained by any shadow of sin. He prayed most earnestly for the assistance of God, putting his trust in Him who had preserved the bodies of all those virgin saints from any defilement, even when they had been exposed publicly to the leering gaze of all, and hoping for the same deliverance for himself. Our loving God did not abandon His servant in his danger, and provided the assistance needed by frail human nature. Hardly had the shameless hussies cast eyes on Philip when they shrank back into the corner of the room, either because they were terrified of some divine punishment, or struck by a sense of shame, or (what is more likely), were moved by the air of authority borne by the youth whose innocence they were about to assail. Far from setting their hands on his chaste body, they did not dare so much as to set eyes on him. How great is the strength of virtue, which is a light in darkness, shining by its own brilliance, and undimmed by any stain brought upon it by others! How splendid is that integrity which does not only brighten the one whose own it is, but can reflect also upon the most evil of men who come into contact with it! But let us return to our Philip.

He is endowed by the Holy Spirit with great gifts
A.D. 1544; Paul III year 10; Philip's age 29

12. Every day Philip used to pray to the Holy Spirit, with all the ardour at his disposal, to endow him with His holy gifts. No day

---

[24] Similar stories are told of St Vincent Ferrer, in his life by Pietro Ranzano (book I, chapter 13), and William's life of St Bernard the Abbot (book I, chapter 3).

was suffered to pass without calling on the Spirit's aid. And this was not without result. While he was yet a layman, and not thirty years old, (in other words in the year of Christ 1544), he suddenly felt himself filled with such a violent inrush of the divine Spirit that his heart began to bound within his breast, and to be inflamed with such heat that, as he told us, his nature was utterly unable to bear it, as his heart began to palpitate in a strange way.[25] For that reason, so that he might be preserved longer for the salvation of so many, the Lord in his kindness enlarged the space around his heart in a wonderful way, so that it could beat more freely: two of the ribs on his left side, specifically the fourth and fifth, were broken and expanded outwards to the width of a fist or slightly more. This break was in the front of his chest, where the ribs join onto the cartilage. From that moment on, for more then fifty years, his heart used to palpitate violently, to a greater or lesser extent, as soon as he was mentally attentive to God, so that not only his whole body shook, but even the bench or whatever he was sitting on shook during his prayer as in an earthquake. This happened to him without any noticeable pain (his body was neither fat nor thin but well-built), and continued until his last breath, without causing any suffering, for he could not feel any pain, neither sharp nor dull, neither inwardly nor outwardly. All the doctors who either tended him while he was alive, or took part in his autopsy afterward, were agreed that this was quite beyond any natural explanation, and certainly miraculous. It was remarkable to see a man of his advanced age, still after fifty years or more, experiencing continuous involuntary tremors and palpitations of the heart. You would think it was the sign of a man who was already weary of this world, one who could say to the Lord, like David, 'O that I had wings like a dove! I will fly away and take my rest. Alas for me that my sojourn is prolonged: when shall I come and appear before the face of the Lord?' [Ps 54:7, 119:5, 41:3]

---

[25] *This inrush of the Holy Spirit, accompanied by a feeling of heat, is a phenomenon recorded of several mystics: we can recall the 'incendium amoris' of Rolle, and the Transverberation of St Teresa. St Philip confided some of the story to Gallonio, but it was only Consolini who heard the detail that the Spirit descended in the form of a globe of fire; this fact Consolini only revealed on his deathbed in 1543. The occurrence took place in the catacomb of S. Sebastiano, on the vigil of Pentecost 1544. (See frontispiece to this volume).*

13. The effect of this heavenly visitation was that he was so filled with the Spirit in an abundance of divine delight, as long as he lived, that he often had to be forced to apply his mind to earthly matters, even so that he could say Mass: this we learnt not only from what he admitted himself, but from what we actually observed. Although he took every measure he could to draw himself back from this absorption in God, when it came to preparing to celebrate Mass, as he informed one or other of his close associates, he was still barely able to complete the sacrifice, as I noticed thousands of times with my own eyes. How amazing the power of the Holy Spirit is! Other holy men, after spending some hours readying themselves in prayer, and having made the accustomed preparation carefully, still have to make a great effort to summon up devotion to God when they are about to say Mass: Philip alone was so saturated with devotion that he needed no preparation, but on the contrary was so incapable of sustaining the great influx of divine ardour that he did everything he could to withdraw his mind from this contemplation, and to beg God not to increase it daily. What is yet more remarkable, is that the power of the Spirit worked on him so that he was lifted up while he was praying.

In the middle of winter, which is a season when Rome can be very cold indeed, his heart and his whole body were so warmed by divine fire during his prayer, that to the end of his life (would you believe it?) he needed to be cooled to stop him dying of the heat. Thus at the age of eighty, and content with only the smallest amount of food, without any natural source of heat at all, he had to use every means to quench the fire of love within him: he would uncover his chest, open the doors and windows of his room all night, and use fans and other means of creating a draft so as to cool him down. Surely he would have died at once had he not been quick to relieve his heart in this way when it was consumed by the divine fire within!

14. Perhaps I should mention this, while I am on the subject: one day Cardinal Federico Borromeo asked him the reason for this remarkable and unprecedented agitation of the heart, and asked as well whether it caused him any pain when it happened. Philip replied modestly that it was the work of the Holy Spirit. 'When

I was a layman,' he began to say, 'I used to pray to the Holy Spirit, as fervently as I could, to come to my aid, and to fill my soul up with his gifts. One day, when I was praying like this, he answered my prayers. It is by the will of the Holy Spirit that this agitation of the heart you were asking about began to happen, but it has never caused me any pain.' And then he added, 'I can certainly put a stop to it, but it means that I would have to withdraw my mind from thinking about God and apply it to checking the motion of my heart, and so I do not bother to do so.' I should add that his heart was so heated by the force of this palpitation, that the high temperature deriving from it permeated his whole body.

He gains new sons for Christ

While Philip was planning his institute for the salvation of his neighbour, he brought to Christ (in the year forty-seven of our century) both Giovanni Manzoli, a Florentine, and Henrico Pietra from Piacenza. The latter became a priest, at Philip's suggestion, and afterwards founded the Congregation of Clerks of Christian teaching.[26]

He becomes one of the founders of the Fraternity of the Holy Trinity
A.D. 1548; Paul III year 14; Philip's age 34

15. Since Philip was greatly enamoured of the idea of helping his neighbour in whatever way he could, he set out to establish a Fraternity dedicated to the most Holy Trinity, along with Persiano Rosa, a priest of noted holiness.[27] Their plan was that the brethren should open a house to offer hospitality to the poor who were convalescent from a recent illness, and to pilgrims. The group began in the church of San Salvatore in Campo, in the year of our

---

[26] *Giovanni Manzoli came to Rome in 1543 to work in the bank of Donato Bonsignori: he became a leading member of the Company of Mercy. Enrico Pietra was also a banker, who came to Rome in 1547 to work in the Bettini bank. He came under the direction of Buonsignore Cacciaguerra, and devoted much of his life to the work of Christian teaching. He died in 1590–1.*

[27] *Persiano Rosa (1503–58) came from Genezzano, and was a member of the community of priests at S. Girolamo della Carità from 1547. He was Philip's confessor until his death, and responsible for persuading Philip to become a priest and live at S. Girolamo.*

Pietro Antonio Novelli inv.e diseg.no   Innocente Alessandri sculpsit in Venezia 1787

GIOVANE IL NERI ANCOR CO' SUOI SERMONI
A DIO L'ALME CONVERTE, E SUA CONQUISTA
SONO IN UN SOLO DI TRENTA GARZONI
AMPIO TESOR DI MERTI IL NERI ACQUISTA

(*) Nella Chiesa della Confraternità della Trinità in occasione della Esposizione delle 40 ore.

HIS LIFE UNTIL HIS ORDINATION

salvation 1548, in the fifth week of August, on a Tuesday. The first to be enrolled in the confraternity were poor in human resources, but rich in the grace of Christ; there were fifteen of them in all. They met frequently in the church of San Salvatore, where all went to confession and were fed with the Bread of Heaven, to give them new zeal in their quest for holiness. They all respected Philip as their father, and held him in great affection.[28]

On the first Sunday of each month, the brothers decided to make the Forty Hours Devotion, during which Philip used to give them much encouragement by his presence, strengthening everyone there by the example of his life and his devout words, which inspired them towards virtue and religion. He would pass virtually the whole night there sleepless, and would wake the brothers himself for their period of prayer. When they had finished their devotions, he would say, 'Your hour of prayer has passed, but you still have time to regret your sins and pursue religion.'[29]

In the same church Philip often gave sermons about holy matters, which were attended both by the brothers and by strangers. The fruit he gained from these discourses was that his listeners were so inspired by the strength of his words that they found themselves remarkably compelled to purify their minds. He had such facility of speech that although he was the only one of the brothers with the ability to discourse about holy things, he could pass whole days and much of the night talking about such matters, all but oblivious of himself. Certainly this work produced great results, through the goodness of God; with a single cast of the net he hooked thirty young men, who worked as jewellers or tradesmen, catching them on the word of God and calling them back from depravity to decent living.

This I can not pass over in silence, how those who first enrolled in that fraternity were of no ordinary degree of sanctity. The cook

---

[28] *This confraternity still survives, settled in the church of S. Benedetto alla Regola (now known as SS. Trinità dei Pellegrini). St Philip continued to assist in its work all his life, and a remarkable painting there shows him dressed in an apron, and ladling out soup to the poor pilgrims.*

[29] *The Forty Hours Devotion, begun in Milan by the Capuchins in 1527, was first introduced to Rome by St Philip in 1551; it remains a characteristic of Oratorian practice.*

for the house, as our holy Father used to tell us, attained such a purity of life that, through God's help, he attained great facility in prayer, and by looking at the sky and the stars (which was his great interest) he would be immediately caught up into the knowledge and love of God. There was another who was lying seriously ill in bed, and said to his sister, Margherita, 'Write this down: I will die on Friday, at this specific hour', and so it came to pass.

Prospero Crivelli joins Philip
A.D. 1549; Paul III year 15; Philip's age 35

16. In the year forty-nine of this century, Philip strained every nerve and worked hard to acquire new sons for Christ. One that he gained was Prospero Crivelli, a citizen of Milan.[30] When he first felt himself inspired to love God, at Philip's urging, he went straightaway to Giovanni Polanco, a priest of the Society of Jesus, with the intention of confessing his sins. He refused sacramental absolution to Prospero, because he was unwilling to stop visiting the house of a certain nobleman, with whom he had great influence, but where many opportunities for serious sin were put before him. Prospero went at once sadly to our holy Father, and told him the whole matter in detail, asking him earnestly to pray for his soul's salvation. Philip saw that he had the right intention, and so promised him his help, which was not unrewarded. Soon afterwards Prospero was enabled by our holy Father's prayers to find himself free and released from all the obstacles and difficulties which prevented him quitting that house.

Further developments of the Fraternity of the Holy Trinity
A.D. 1550; Julius III year 1; Philip's age 35–36

17. During the fiftieth year of this century, which was marked by the celebration of a Jubilee, the brothers decided that they would invite pilgrims to stay in their house, since they were previously having to sleep in the open street. This was needed during the

---

[30] *Crivelli came to Rome in 1549–50, and remained one of Philip's devoted followers, giving testimony at the process of his canonisation. Juan Alonso Polanco (1516–77), was one of the strictest followers of St Ignatius, displaying already the contrast in spirituality between the Jesuits and St Philip.*

Jubilee, for there was no hospice for the poor in the city, and no refuge, so pilgrims were compelled to sleep in public, subject to cold, hunger and other disadvantages. Philip was moved by seeing this, and thought he should do all he could to prevent such suffering. He conferred with the others about it, so they sought out anyone they could find lying in extreme poverty, and brought them to the hospice, either giving them a hand, or carrying them on a litter; when they arrived they were received with every courtesy, and supplied with everything they might need to live. The charity of the brethren towards the poor was such that they used all their resources to help them, and the one who happened to be the first to greet them was considered the most fortunate. I cannot tell you how loving the brothers showed themselves towards these poor people. You could see some of them washing the pilgrims' feet, others regaling the recent arrivals with comforting conversation; some cooking the food, others serving dishes, some making beds and others sweeping the floor. The companions were so prompt and cheerful in this work of charity that all were astounded at their goodness. Moreover, the power of example was such that there was no shortage of men wanting to be enrolled in this newly founded fraternity.[31]

The brothers decided that some buildings should be constructed to receive pilgrims, where at any time of the year they could be kindly entertained for three days, and this holy and admirable custom has survived till now. Not content with that, they observed that poor patients were being discharged from the hospitals as soon as they began to improve, before they had fully recovered their strength, and that lack of proper food and shelter meant that they relapsed into the same illnesses after having briefly tasted recovery; therefore they decided to do what they could for people in this situation too. They agreed together that the buildings used for receiving pilgrims should also be open to such convalescents until they had fully recovered their original health and strength. This and other works they did with the greatest assistance from

---

[31] *The reception of pilgrims during Jubilee Years became the most characteristic work of the Confraternity of the Trinity: during the 1550 jubilee they received up to 500 pilgrims a day, totalling some 50,000 during the year, and this was exceeded in subsequent Jubilee years.*

Philip; he himself passed whole days and nights there in ministering to the poor, and encouraging others to take up the work.

That was the origin of the Fraternity, which from small beginnings has grown into the great institution you see today. As time passed, men of noble families gave their names to it, and it was decided to move it from the church of San Salvatore in Campo to that of the Holy Trinity. Here it quickly grew until it became well known throughout the Christian world, and gave great glory to God. The devotion of that fraternity, and its generosity to similar fraternities all over Italy, became particularly prominent during the next Jubilee under Pope Gregory XIII, and now again it is conspicuous during the present Jubilee year of Clement VIII.

He falls into a deep ditch one night, and is rescued by God

18. Philip grew from day to day as the gifts he received from God increased, and he felt himself impelled to an even greater degree of service; accordingly, at the dead of night, when all were sunk in sleep, and a left hand could not even see what a right hand was doing, he used to go round the dwellings of the poorest people, and provided them generously with what they needed to live on.[32]

One night he was busy about this practice of his, bringing bread to a nobleman who had become very poor, when it happened (through the devil's work) that he stepped aside to avoid a carriage that was speeding down on him, and he accidentally fell into a deep ditch. But the Lord helped him out, for as he fell an angel held him back by the hair of his head, and he was brought out unharmed, in no way injured by the fall. This happened in the year of our Lord 1550.[33]

An angel accepts alms from him

Another day, when he was performing his works of charity with greater fervour than usual, an angel appeared to him in the form of a poor man, asking for help.[34] Philip gave him what money he

---

[32] St Marcian the priest used to do the same, as Metaphrastes tells us in his life, which you will find in vol. I of Surius.

[33] Cardinal Cesare Baronio swears to this story.

had with cheerful generosity, whereupon the angel said to him, 'I revere you for the work I know you are going to do', and promptly vanished. Because of that, Philip began to attend to the poor with such deep compassion that from then on he never refused anyone who asked alms of him. He provided abundantly for the needs of poor men and women; money, books and clothing were provided for young men who wanted to study; no week passed without him sending contributions to those who were in prison.[35]

He refused assistance to no one in need. Once he heard that a poor woman had nothing to wear, so he pulled off his own coat to give her. When he met poor teenagers who were eager to join religious communities, once he had examined their intentions, he would give them enough money to buy the habit necessary for the institute they wanted to join.[36]

We can say about him with every justification that he had nothing, and possessed everything: he possessed no income from the church, and was notably scornful of money, like no one else, but all through his life he was never short of what was needful for his own use as well as for the relief of others.

St John the Baptist appears to him in prayer

19. Philip during this period was eager to learn the divine will, and continually prayed that the Lord would show him what manner of life he wished him to follow. He had it in mind to embrace a solitary life (unless God thought otherwise), but he was uncertain whether that would lead to the greater glory of God, so he applied himself to earnest prayer to discover God's will, ready to embark on whatever course of life the Lord should indicate.[37] After long

---

[34] You will find something similar in the life of John the Deacon by Pope St Gregory (book I, chapter 10). This story was told by Philip to two priests, when it pleased God to give him the occasion to do so.

[35] *Gallonio himself, along with Zazzara and others, used to take Philip's alms to the prisons at the Tor di Nona and the Capitol.*

[36] Metaphrastes tells similar stories of St Marcion, as Audoen does of the Blessed Bishop Giles.

[37] Passing over other witnesses, it was Cardinal Federico Borromeo who gave public testimony to this.

meditation on this point, he at last was found worthy to hear an answer. One day, when he was praying at dawn, St John the Baptist appeared; Philip was greatly encouraged by that sight, and felt himself impelled by God to the decision, with no further hesitation, that he should apply himself not to his own salvation alone but to that of others.

On another occasion someone asked him why he lived so frugally, and he replied, 'Once when I was praying, two souls appeared to me, already resplendent with the glory of the saints: one of them appeared to be holding in his hand a dry crust of bread and eating it. When I was concerned to know what they might mean by this, I heard a voice saying, "The will of God for you, Philip, is that you should pass your life in the midst of the city as if in a desert." I took these words to mean that I should live simply and frugally.' Because of this, in his simplicity, he used to say that he hardly ever had meat to eat, because it was bad for him, pretending that what he did out of virtue was really out of concern for his health.

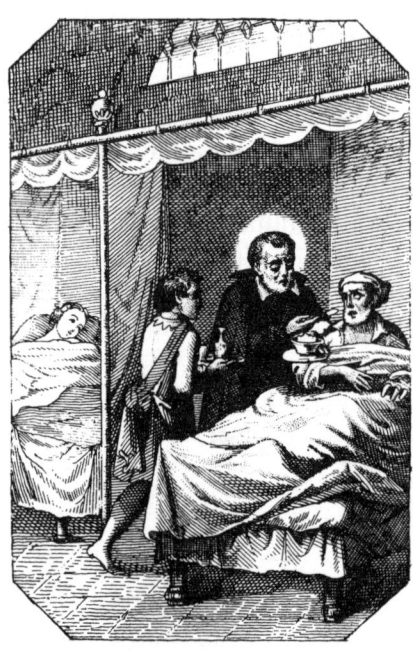

III : AFTER HIS PRIESTLY ORDINATION, THE SAINT APPLIES HIMSELF MORE DILIGENTLY TO THE BENEFIT OF HIS NEIGHBOUR

He is initiated into the Orders of the Church
A.D. 1551; Julius III year 2; Philip's age 36

20. Since our holy Father displayed every sign of sanctity, his confessor, Persiano Rosa, considered he should not so much encourage but actually impel him to be initiated into the Orders of the Church as soon as possible. Until that time he had held back from accepting any of the grades of Order, on the model of Saint Saba and other men distinguished for their holy life, whom he knew had done this out of humility.[38] All he wanted was to remain a layman, not because he failed to respect the dignity of the priesthood, but because he considered himself quite unfit for that responsibility, however untrue that might be. But when he understood that Persiano was of the opinion that he ought to be ordained priest, he at once set himself to obey that wish, not wanting to seem reluctant to accept the burden laid upon him by God.

In the year 1551 of human salvation, therefore, in the church of San Tommaso in Parione, in March, when he had nearly completed his thirty-sixth year, he began by being admitted to the First Tonsure, then the four Minor Orders, and the Subdiaconate. Not long afterwards he was admitted to the Diaconate, in the famous ancient Basilica of the Lateran, on the Saturday of Holy Week in that same year, which fell on the 29th of March. Finally he was ordained Priest in the same church of San Tommaso, on the 23rd of June. What preparation he made, and what thoughts he had, when he was ordained to these Orders, I had rather leave for others to imagine than include in my account. Our holy Father was elevated through all the grades of holy orders to the summit, which is the

---

[38] He seems to be imitating those saintly men Saba and Pachomius, Archimandrites of monasteries, as well as St Francis and others.

priesthood, in the proper solemn ceremonies, by Giovanni Lunellio, Bishop of Sebaste, when Filippo Archinto was vicar general to Pope Julius III.[39]

21. As a priest, he retained his former custom of living frugally, admitting to his diet nothing but eggs, vegetables and beans, though if he happened to be eating with others, as he often did for the sake of winning souls, he did all he could to avoid any sign of ostentatious singularity. He preserved this custom for many years, with the intention of making himself all things to all men, that he might gain them all for Christ.

After his priestly ordination he thought at once of living at the church of St Jerome, called 'Of Charity', and spending the rest of his life there if it should be pleasing to God. There were several distinguished priests at that church who were pious and devout, namely Persiano Rosa, Philip's confessor; Buonsignore Cacciaguerra, a nobleman from Siena who had been a rich trader but became a priest of Christ; Francesco, from the city of Arezzo, a learned man, who combined deep knowledge with angelic purity, and who heard our holy Father's confessions after the death of Persiano; and another Francisco, from Spain, who was equally learned and devout, and remarkable for his charity to the poor and his austerity towards himself. All these priests lived in the same building, but although they all had the same burning desire to help others, each one lived in his own style, as the Holy Spirit prompted him. Each looked after his own affairs, and they ate separately.[40]

Philip was, therefore, admitted to this church, and used to celebrate Mass every day there. He would accept nothing from the

---

[39] *Filippo Archinto (1500–58) was Governor of Rome 1536–9, and Cardinal Vicar from 1542; on being nominated Bishop of Saluzzo (the home of Blessed Juvenal Ancina of the Oratory), he appointed the French Cistercian Jean Lunel to be his vicegerent, as titular Bishop of Sebaste.*

[40] *The church of S. Girolamo della Carità had been the seat of the Fraternity of Charity since 1536; this was an association of laymen who paid the stipends of the group of priests who lived there. The priests did not form a proper college, since they had an exterior superior, Vincenzio Teccosi, and as Gallonio says, they did not even eat together; but they retained a limited degree of the common life which had for centuries been a familiar*

Fraternity of Charity except the use of a single room, and that was small. There he settled, quite uninterested in money, and very contented with lodgings where he could freely and easily apply himself to the salvation of his neighbour.

22. That year, although the price of grain was exceptionally high in the city, Philip was allotted six loaves. What did he do? He accepted the bread, thinking it was not meant for his own use, but was to be distributed to the poor, and gave it to a penniless Spanish priest, with a cheerful expression, giving thanks to Christ our Lord. Since he did this, they asked him why he had given his entire allowance to a priest in need, and he replied modestly that he thought it would be easier for him to get food from his friends than for that priest, being a native of a strange country. So what happened? On that particular day he tasted nothing more than a few olives.

Through Philip's efforts, Henrico Pietra of Piacenza, (whom he had brought to Christ when he was a layman himself) and Theseo Raspa were both ordained priest, and came to live at San Girolamo.[41] Here, under the guidance of Buonsignore, they made great spiritual progress, especially Henrico, who was afterwards of great benefit to the entire city through his long, freely-given labours, in reforming nuns and carrying out other ecclesiastical tasks, including the reform of the morals of the clergy and of the liturgy in the churches. After them there followed Pietro Spadaro, a priest of mild disposition, beloved of God and man; he was to be the last of the priests of that church who heard Philip's confessions, after the death of Francesco.[42]

---

feature among the secular clergy. The reformed bandit Cacciaguerra (1495–1566) was the dominant character, and after a reform of the community became its internal superior. Francesco Marsuppini of Arezzo (1512–68) succeeded Rosa as Philip's spiritual director; the 'other Francisco, from Spain' was in fact named Juan Valdez: he must have been the penniless Spanish priest mentioned in the next paragraph.

[41] *Raspa, who renounced his title to be a canon of Vercelli in order to join S. Girolamo, lived under Philip's guidance until his death around 1590, and was prominent in a number of the pious fraternities of Rome.*

[42] *Spadaro remained at S. Girolamo until his death in 1589, and held various offices there.*

Philip's ardour, piety and ecstasy while saying Mass

23. As a priest, Philip never let a day pass without celebrating Mass, unless he was ill; when ill he received the Bread of Heaven daily. When he was first ordained and celebrating Mass at San Girolamo, he would suddenly be so filled with the Holy Spirit that he could hardly pour the wine and water into the chalice in the usual way; his hands would be raised up so that he looked as if he were dancing or jumping up. Unless he was able to continue the action he had begun by pressing down on the altar with his arm, and applying all his concentration, he would never have been able to finish. He was more eager and passionate about this divine Sacrament than I can say; even if he was only holding an empty chalice, he would be flooded with indescribable joy. When the time came for him to elevate the sacred Host, his mind would be so rapt in God that he was unable to bring down his hands when they were stretched upwards. He told us afterwards that it seemed to him as if someone were taking him up, and lifting him off the ground by some marvellous power. Because of this occurrence, he later on developed the custom of elevating the Host and putting it down again very quickly.[43] While he was saying Mass, particularly after he arrived at the Offertory, he would be affected with such delight that his whole body shook and quivered as he proceeded with the ceremony. To check this effect, he used often to look aside, now to the right, now to the left, and from time to time he would rub his head with his hand.

24. There is one thing I must not pass over without mentioning, which shows the powerful effect of God's love on him. In order to celebrate Mass without interference (being very much afraid of raptures and ecstasies) he used to do anything he could to restrain that violent ardour of spirit which usually affected him, before putting on his vestments. Since he would never have been able to complete the Mass if he were suddenly abstracted from his senses and totally rapt into heavenly contemplation, he set himself to concentrate on

---

[43] Cardinal Francesco Maria Tarugi has given sworn witness to this, and many others have also affirmed it on oath.

AFTER HIS PRIESTLY ORDINATION

turning his thoughts away from God. Despite doing this, he still received those assaults of divine love, pierced by those darts of grace, so that his whole body burned with the divine flame, the fire of heavenly love, and he was quite consumed in tears. He broke out into constant sobs, as he contemplated the joy of his heavenly homeland, and saw so clearly how frail was the human nature of his soul; he seemed to dance, just as in the Old Testament, David danced before the Ark which contained a heavenly treasure. Thus it happened that he was often compelled to pause in the sacred action, until he could collect again the physical strength which the love of Christ had taken away. What a man he was, filled with God! What a man, in whom the breath of the Holy Spirit blew, to take him out of himself! Truly you could say, with full justification, like the Bride in the Canticles, 'The King has brought me into his wine cellar, he has ordained charity in me; stay me with flowers, encompass me with apples, for I am faint with love.' [Cant 2:4–5]

25. When he had completed the Sacrifice, he was often so abstracted from his senses that you would think he was more dead than alive. While I am on the subject, I must say something about the delight he had in drinking the Blood of Christ, and in eating His Body. Those who stayed close to his side believed that he was able to perceive the actual flavour of the Blood and the Body, as if he were tasting simple flesh and simple blood. He used to lick his lips most eagerly, and we could see that he brought the Chalice to his mouth again and again, although he would not allow anyone present to stand too close to the altar, or to be in such a position that they could see his face. When he was consuming the Precious Blood, you could hear a sound from his throat which made you think he was tasting something so thick and glutinous that it stuck to the priest's palate. The marks of his teeth remained on the side of the chalice where he drank the Precious Blood, and the gilding in that part was quickly worn away, however recently it had been done. He did not like what are called the purifications to be administered to him until he was ready to ask for them. He was so taken by delight in the divine Sacrament that he would retain the sweet flesh of Christ and His most precious Blood in his mouth, not swallowing it at once but letting it pass slowly, drop by drop, into

his stomach. His devotion in celebrating Mass, and in distributing the Body of Christ to others was no less than in his partaking of it, but not to expand pointlessly on a matter which is well known and familiar to all, I will pass on to something else.

He applies himself to hearing confessions

26. When he had been ordained priest he was put in charge of hearing confessions, and although he was reluctant to do this, he agreed, ever ready to obey others before suiting himself, for he knew how pleasing to God it was to conform himself to the will of others. Amazing, isn't it – Philip longed for nothing more than a solitary life, but rather than please himself, he put what others wanted before his own desires, following the example of Christ, who said, 'My food is to do the will of the Father who sent me.' And elsewhere, 'I came down from heaven, not to do my own will, but the will of Him who sent me.'

He was very assiduous in the work of hearing confessions, to the extent that he hardly ever left the church, forgetful of himself. That in itself is a great thing, but to tell you something more remarkable, he would pass the greater part of the day in this work, without ever becoming tired. He was so eager to summon wandering souls back to their senses, that merely being seated in the chair which he used to hear confessions gave him the greatest refreshment and delight. You would not believe how many people, and what great ones, he enabled to bring forth ample fruit from the manure of their sins, and how many men and women were encouraged by his efforts to embrace the monastic life. There was no institute of the religious life that did not acquire several of Philip's disciples, though of them all it was the Order of Preachers that most particularly flourished thus with his penitents. How many more were there, whom he led from the most terrible sins and heinous crimes to amend their lives, and who afterwards, at his direction, abandoned all frivolous matters and devoted themselves entirely to a serious life!

27. At the time when he first began to hear confessions, he was more ready to hear the sins of men than of women, and as far as he could, avoided hearing the faults of the latter. Cautious of any threat to his virginal purity, he was well aware that the demons

never cease from troubling the servants of God, even when they are engaged in good works, particularly those who trust too much in their own abilities. I will add that he was so strict and vigilant in guarding his modesty that if he was obliged to hear womens' confessions, he would receive them in church, speaking abruptly rather than gently, and from time to time showing his annoyance in his looks. He used to say that he behaved like that until he was granted the singular grace of God to be able to receive them in whatever manner he pleased. I think that what he meant by these words was that he had by the gift of God received the remarkable ability of not being in any way affected by impure thoughts, so that from then onwards to the end of his days he appeared to be as impervious as a marble statue.

Moreover, because he was so busy with hearing confessions every day (a noble work, which he continued until his death), he would often hear his sons if they came to him when he was still in bed, for he spent most of his nights in contemplation and devout prayer. Early in the morning he would get up and go to the church, not leaving it unless some really important and necessary task occurred which could not possibly be deferred until another time. No one ever failed to find him in church – maybe not all the time, but he was certainly very accessible and readily made his services available at once. He lived most of the time either in church or in his room, and was not much given to going out, unless he was summoned by some necessity or some work of charity.

The first beginnings of the Oratory and the spiritual discourses

28. Philip became ever more intent on bringing sinners to a better outcome, and to preserve the chastity and integrity of the sons he had so gained, lest they fall again into vice and so turn back to Egypt. In the year 1551 since the Virgin gave birth, he began to teach them about the things of heaven, as the best means to achieve his end, gathering them in his room every day after dinner, and often reclining on his bed, for he was exhausted by the love of God. Amazingly, during these conversations, he experienced the force of divine love to the extent that sometimes his whole body trembled, or was lifted up a little from the bed – you would think that someone was lifting him up. At times you could see the bed itself

shaking and quivering, or indeed the whole room, giving the impression of an earthquake.

Those who attended went not only for confession, but in order to be inspired with the love of God and detachment from all earthly matters. When these meetings first began there were very few who came to listen to him, though two of them are still alive as I write,[44] but the number soon grew until the place where these discourses took place was unable to contain the audience. He left it, therefore, and moved to a larger one, where he continued to speak with such a conviction and sensitivity to the spiritual that there was no one, however deeply sunk in vice, who could not change his life and turn to a better state on hearing Philip speak.[45]

He is afflicted in various ways for the sake of Christ
A.D. 1552–3; Julius III years 3–4; Philip's age 37–39

29. When the devil observed that this newly ordained priest was winning so many for Christ through his private discourses and administration of the sacraments, he determined to resist those pious endeavours with all his might. At the church of San Girolamo, the sacristans were two priests, men of depraved morals, who had abandoned their religious orders: these, in order to ingratiate themselves with Vincenzio Teccosi, of the Confraternity of Charity, began to persecute Philip, in the year 1552.[46] They used to make fun of him, and snarl like dogs, heaping insults on him, but he endured it all with an untroubled heart, never uttering a word to defend himself. They did not stop there, but seized eagerly upon any occasion that was offered of wounding him with accusations and curses, and disturbing him in whatever way they could: their

---

[44] *Probably Ottavio Ricci and Monte Zazzara, who gave testimony in the canonisation process.*

[45] *To begin with they simply met in Philip's room; the second location was an upper room over the aisle of S. Girolamo, and it was this place that was first called the 'oratory'.*

[46] *Similar things happened to several saints, as their lives bear witness. Read, for instance, the life of St Daniel the Stylite and St Vincent Ferrer. Teccosi was the external superior of the community; the two 'renegades' were members of religious orders from Calabria who had fled to Rome. Paul IV was later to take severe measures against such men.*

AFTER HIS PRIESTLY ORDINATION

aim was to force him to leave the place, since they could not abide his presence. Hence, when they knew that Philip was heading for the sacristy, with the intention of celebrating Mass, they were delighted at the fresh opportunity this provided for bullying him; they sometimes blocked his access to the place; or if he had got in, they used various means to obstruct him. To force him to leave without celebrating, they would sometimes hide the Missal, or the priestly vestments, or even his own Chalice; not stopping there, they would often order him to unvest after he was all prepared for the Sacrifice and was stepping out of the sacristy. But not even this treatment could provoke Philip to anger.

Meanwhile, though he had never received the slightest harm from him, Vincenzio Teccosi was so hostile, through nothing but the devil's envy, that he resolved never to cease from this persecution until he had compelled Philip to change his abode. Philip yielded nothing to this temptation, and never complained about his enemies; he was unwilling to leave San Girolamo as it was a suitable base to work for his neighbours' salvation, and he refused to fly from the crosses God had prepared for him, so with a calm mind he endured the attacks they hurled at him. Courageously he remembered the words of Saint James, 'Consider it all joy, my brethren, when you fall into various trials.' [Jas 2:12]

30. One day when he was celebrating Mass, after the usual abuse from those jealous priests, he held this anxious conversation with God during the Sacrifice itself: 'Why is it, O good Jesus, that when I ask you so often, so earnestly, to give me the gift of patience, I am confronted with so many things that are liable to make me angry?' And when he had said this, he heard an inner voice say clearly: 'Why do you ask me for patience, Philip? I will strengthen you with patience, but my wish is for you to strive as hard as you can to acquire it by means of these attacks.' And on hearing that, he felt himself wonderfully refreshed.

After two years of this, one of the sacristans was weighing into him in his usual manner with grumbles and curses, and would not leave off his foolishness, but Philip received it with such a cheerful expression and strength of character that he seemed exultant with joy. The other of the two renegades noticed this, and reflected on the unshaken patience with which Philip endured the insults, till he was struck with remorse and flew at the priest who was shouting curses; he could hardly be restrained from killing him in defence of our holy Father's innocence. Hardly had he done that when he began to mellow in the recollection of the community he had abandoned, and so came to his senses. Through the example and prayers of the blessed Philip, he was at once filled with shame, so that he not only resolved to do penance, but even to seek admittance again to his monastery, which in fact he achieved.

Vincenzio also, who had instigated the persecution, was affected by Philip's gentle patience, and came spontaneously to fall on his knees before him, asking his forgiveness. Philip forgot his injuries at once, and readily forgave him, accepting the man in the most friendly manner as one of his sons. From then on, Vincenzio was one of the leading disciples of our holy Father, and hardly a day passed when he did not visit him, for nothing gave him greater joy. He remained in this way of life until his dying day, eager to store up riches in heaven through the use of the sacraments. He eventually died in March of 1589.

How he behaved when being attacked
A.D. 1554; Julius III year 5; Philip's age 39–40

31. Philip was delivered from this annoyance through the kindness of God, and so deeply pierced by the love of Christ the Bridegroom, that he could devote himself totally to the salvation of others, hearing their confessions, and nourishing them with the Bread of Heaven. Thus it soon came to pass that his frequent use of Confession and Holy Communion renewed him again, and the devil's deceits were virtually extinguished. He was so kindly that everybody held him in the greatest affection. He was so determined to rescue the devil's prey that it is amazing how much he would do or suffer in order to bring even one soul back to Christ. Cheerfully he would hear the confessions of all who came to him, and he incited them wonderfully to piety and the love of heaven, partly by what he said on spiritual matters, and partly by his prayers. He constantly displayed the greatest zeal to make himself all things to all men, because in this way he could be more accessible for the benefit of others. The advice he gave to his sons in Christ about

the salvation of their souls was such that those who attended to it made great progress in virtue, and eventually became perfect in every way. He always wanted his room to be open, day and night, because of his longing for the salvation of others. He was so diligent at hearing confessions that in those early days he often heard the confessions of around forty men during the night, before daybreak.

32. It was a singular proof of Philip's charity that any of the crowds who came to him at night to be reconciled to God through confession always found his door open. This was not without results: first of all they would reveal to him their sins in confession, then at Philip's advice they would go to pray, remaining in prayer until it was time to celebrate Mass, at which Mass all communicated. Then at our holy Father's bidding, they went in silence to the various hospitals in the city, of which the most important were those called the Ospedale del Santo Spirito, and that of Santa Maria della Consolazione. In these places they gave a remarkable degree of comfort to the sick, mostly by their religious conversation, not to mention other means; thus they encouraged them to be patient, to confess their sins, and to put their hope in the mercy of God. They also brought them food to build up their bodily strength. All these matters were much neglected in those days, so that it is difficult to tell the extent to which they helped the patients and their attendants towards salvation.

One day in 1554, they were setting out with this intention in mind, with Father Philip accompanying them, and they were just passing the Colosseum, when they came across a man lying in the mud, so seriously ill, emaciated and despondent that he neither could nor would stand up, but had resolved to lie there and so to die. When Philip saw this, he asked one of them called Francesco to take him up at once on his shoulders and carry him to the hospital of San Salvatore, which is where they were going.[47] Although it was still a long way to the hospital, he took the burden on his back without hesitating, and carried him on his own to their destination,

---

[47] *This is another name for the hospital of St John Lateran, up a long hill from the Colosseum.*

VEDE IL NERI UN INFERMO E CHI IL CONFORTA
DICE RIVOLTO A' SUOI? UNO CON RARA
PRONTEZZA ALLO SPEDAL SUL DORSO IL PORTA.
NEI FIGLI IL PADRE SUA PIETA DICHIARA.

S. Filippo passando pel Coliseo incontrò un infermo, e comandò ad uno de' suoi figli spirituali, che lo portasse all'Ospitale.

to the great edification of his companions, and the benefit of the sick man.

Predictions

33. One of Philip's followers called Prospero once brought a Jewish friend along with him. They went together with the holy Father and a large gathering to the Lateran Basilica, but when the Father and the others knelt down before the high altar, the Jew stood alone in the throng, with his head covered, and his back straight. When Philip noticed this he approached him and said, 'Brother, why don't you pray to the Lord in these words, "If you are truly God, O Christ, I would ask you to bring my soul to turn away from my ancestral religion and accept the Christian faith."' But the Jew replied, 'I cannot, and should not, pray to God as you suggest, for if I did what you say I would appear to be in doubt about my religion and my belief, which would be wrong for a Hebrew man.' Then Philip turned to the others and said, 'Pray to God for the salvation of our Jewish brother here – for, believe me, he will give his name to Christ soon enough.' The outcome proved the prediction true; a few days later the Jew not only accepted belief in Christ but joyfully received holy Baptism.

At that period a devout woman called Fulginia Aneria used to confess to Philip very regularly. When her husband Maurizio discovered this, he at once forbade her to presume to approach the sacraments so often: being then very ignorant of the ways of Christ, he ridiculed the idea of the servants of God making any spiritual progress. He told her, following the common opinion of the mob who were so rapidly going to the bad, that she ought to abstain from frequenting the sacraments too much. But the powerful love of God strengthened that woman, giving her the courage to continue the course she had begun. Philip said to her, 'Do not worry, continue as you have been doing, and Maurizio will soon bring himself to a better mind.' And so it happened, and Maurizio came to confession to Philip for the rest of his life.[48]

---

[48] *Maurizio Anerio (died 1595) was himself a musician, and the father of Giovan Francesco Anerio (1567–1630), a well-known exponent of the Roman school of polyphony.*

Some miracles of Philip

34. In that same year, 1554, Prospero Crivelli became unwell, and as the disease increased daily, he appeared to be so ill that the doctors all gave up hope: these doctors were Alessandro Petroni, Giovanni from Munich, and Francesco from Lucca, all very skilled medical men.[49] He was accordingly fortified by holy Viaticum, and anointed with oil, for they all considered he was at death's door; indeed the priest was commending the dying man to God and the saints in the usual manner, and sprinkling him with holy water, when Philip arrived and found all this was going on.

'So why is it,' he began, 'that I have not seen you for the last two days?'

'The doctors assure me that I am dying, and will do so the next time that the fever I have been having recurs.'

'But', said Philip, 'I have heard that you have made me the heir to your property. I can think of nothing I should like to hear less, so I renounce your inheritance. Give it to someone else.' Then he added, 'And to make you understand this, I am going now to the Vatican Basilica where I shall ask God to have mercy on you and deliver you from death on this occasion. If I can't obtain that, I shall gladly offer my own life to God in exchange for your life and health, which I trust will bring it about that I get what I want.'

Having said this, he then prayed, with tears running down his face, and laid his hands on the dying man, who immediately fell into a sound sleep, astonishing as it is to relate. Philip took the occasion to make his visit to the Vatican Basilica, and knelt there for half an hour in prayer, pouring out his entreaties with all the submission of mind he could muster, and wearying God's majesty with his effective prayers for the life of the dying man. Nor was his prayer in vain, for even while he was raising his hands and voice to heaven, the dying man woke from his sleep, having slept for about a quarter of an hour, and discovered that his health had returned, to the astonishment of the doctors.

---

[49] Cardinal Tarugi and others have sworn to this. *Of the three doctors the only one recorded elsewhere is Petroni, a Neapolitan, who had lived in Rome since the end of the 15th century.*

35. It was around the same year that Domenico Saraceno came to Rome to study medicine, but began to suffer greatly from heart disease. He tried all the medical remedies for a long time, with no results, and so commended himself to Philip's prayers, putting his trust in him alone. Philip said to him, 'Be of good cheer, you will recover from this present illness.' Since he relied upon what Philip had said, he used no further medicine for his disease, but soon afterwards felt that he had recovered his former good health. The man is still alive, and remembers the occasion; he considers that what happened was a miracle.[50]

Now let us pass on to tell what Philip did in the time of Pope Paul IV – since we can omit the reign of Marcellus II, the successor to Pope Julius, which only lasted three weeks. Paul was elected Pope on the 23rd of May 1555, and reigned for four years, two months and twenty-seven days.

---

[50] *Actually Saraceno died in August 1599, while Gallonio was writing this book. He had been the personal physician of Cardinal Bonelli.*

IV : WHAT HE DID
IN 1555, 1556 AND 1557

Philip meets some demons
A.D. 1555; Paul IV year 1; Philip's age 41

Around the year of Our Lord 1555, Philip was walking with a crowd of followers near the Baths of Diocletian, when he saw a demon in the form of a man, standing on an ancient tumble-down wall. He looked at it more closely and saw that it appeared now as a youth, now as an old man.[51] Recognising by these changes that it was some wile of the devil, he ordered it in the name of Christ to reveal what it was. Abashed by this, it fled at once and quickly, but left the most terrible odour which filled the place, so that not even the animals could endure it, demonstrating clearly to Philip and his followers what nature of thing it was.

Here I must not omit to mention that the devil was so keen to disturb his peace of mind that it used to appear visibly to him at night, the time he spent in more intense prayer. With all its might it would strive to obstruct, or at least hinder, the fervour of Philip's attention to God. One night in particular (I am not sure at which period this happened), while Philip was offering his accustomed prayers to God, the demon appeared in order to terrify him. When the holy man noticed this, he immediately directed his prayer to the most holy Mother of God, dismissing the terror as something of little consequence, and defeating his enemy's design by his courageous devotion, being able to pray no less well, but rather better. You see, the devil is cowardly if you confront him, audacious only when your back is turned. But I digress.

The devil attacks his virginal purity

36. In the same year, when the enemy of the human race saw what a harvest of souls was being gathered in day by day through the

---

[51] The story comes from Vincenzio Teccosi, an excellent witness, who was present. Compare what Osbert says in his life of St Dunstan of Canterbury (chapter 18).

efforts of Philip alone, he was as jealous as usual, and determined to drag him away from his purpose through the lure of the flesh. Using an immodest women, he attempted it thus. There was a whore in the city, entangled in the devil's nets, named Cesaria, who had no good qualities apart from her looks.[52] At the devil's suggestion she began to boast in front of the entourage of young men who shared her life of shame that she could win Philip's attentions and entice him into lust. They wagered her a large sum of money to attempt that, and the wretched woman accepted the wager. She was however afraid that she would be able to achieve nothing with such a holy man (being, after her own fashion, cunning enough about the destruction of others) and so worked out that the only possible scheme would be through deceit. So what did the woman decide, what did the devil suggest to her? She sent to him, using a messenger who appeared respectable but was one of her devotees, with the message that she was dying, in peril of both body and soul, that she wanted to return to a good outcome, and expiate her previous life of crime through confession. She begged him not to refuse help to a soul in danger, and Philip, being full of an incredible charity for the salvation of all, was exceedingly delighted with the occasion offered for bringing one of Christ's lost lambs back to the sheepfold. He left his house and went to her, suspecting nothing. But hardly had Philip climbed the stairs before the woman, that instrument of the devil, cast off all modesty and shame, and exposed herself to him naked, save for a veil drifting across her body, hoping that it would fall off attractively in front of him and so achieve her object. But as God willed, and as He provided His assistance, Philip's simplicity overcame her cunning, his chastity her lust. Being a holy man, he detected the assault on his chastity, and since he alone was at risk, he at once seized his opportunity to escape. Thus he frustrated the wiles of that woman, so impudent, impious and vile, thus the devil's attempt came to nothing, and his power diminished, proving what Philip had so often told us,

---

[52] The devil often attacks the chastity of the saints, as their lives record. Among others, see Palladius on Lausiacas, and the lives of Sts Daniel the Stylite, Bernard the Abbot, and Vincent Ferrer. There are several sworn witnesses to our story, one of whom is Cardinal Cesare Baronio.

that other types of temptation should be resisted by confronting them, but in this case alone it is best to fly and not to engage. As for the scheming woman, once she realised she had been foiled, she was enraged as well as deeply shamed, and grabbed the first piece of furniture she could lay her hands on to hurl at his back, hoping to kill him. God looked after his champion, and he was unharmed, escaping with his health and his virtue intact, which was surely something of a miracle. As a result of this atrocious attempt, Philip discovered that God had granted him for the future complete immunity from the urges of desire and pangs of sensuality, for the thirty years that remained until his death.[53]

37. Now you cannot deny that these were great things, but there is more to add. From that time onwards, the Lord endowed him with a more distinguished virtue yet, namely that while he was asleep his body was never stained with any impure emission, of the sort that happens to us from time to time however little we want it. It is the more remarkable, because he used to sleep on his back, so that his face was turned towards heaven. By these accumulated gifts, he obtained a state of tranquillity, so that he did not seem to be living a mortal life among mortals, but already among the heavenly ones the life of heaven; if it be right to say so, he was close to the state of primaeval innocence and purity.

All libidinous desires were extinguished in him, and his body was subservient to his spirit; his virtue was strong enough for him not to fear any attack of impure desires, and his sense of touch was so controlled that his flesh seemed to be quite without any feeling, as if he were a stone. He did occasionally say (though he spoke of this to only a few of his followers), that it would be the same to him to touch a woman or a rock, so restrained was any instinct in him, so completely quenched was any desire for sensual pleasure.

There are firm and unquestionable witnesses to these remarkable statements. Above all it was his confessor, Cesare Baronio, who affirmed it, and he heard his last confessions at the very end of his

---

[53] According to St Gregory (*Dialogues*, book I, chapter 4), St Equitius felt no urge of the flesh. You could also compare what Leontius says of St Simeon Salus, and Cassian's 12th Collation, *On Chastity*.

life. He related, under oath, that a few days before Philip departed this life, he was making his confession and burst into violent tears and sobs, unable to restrain his weeping, and he said that he was afflicted with this great sorrow because he had received so many gifts from God without any merits of his own, and of them all the greatest was that God had preserved his virginity to that day, and for more than thirty years he had been quite without any urge of the flesh, so that even when asleep he was free from all that tyranny of desire, and yet he remained so ungrateful towards the generosity of God that he had never done anything worthy of the life of the blessed, and had in no way responded to his divine vocation.[54] What an example of perfect integrity! How amazing the humility of a holy man! And this is what he used to confess with so many tears, with such deep lowliness of soul.

38. It was from these virtues, as from a copious spring, that his ardour flowed, so that he never ceased to encourage his disciples to love chastity, in words that were all but divine. Our heavenly Bridegroom desires, as Philip knew well, that the souls He has called to share His dwelling for ever should be free from any taint of bodily impurity. Hence, when Philip knew that someone was tempted in this way, he used every means to save him, by advice, prayers and encouragement; those who were not so affected he tried to preserve untainted, being as careful in defence of the chastity of others as of his own.

I will also add that Philip's virginal chastity used to radiate in such a way that no one could be long in his company without beginning to think about embracing a life of purity. As everybody thought, and it was commonly believed, he was a virgin. Such was

---

[54] Apart from Baronio, the witnesses to his virginity include Cardinal Agostino Cusano, and other reliable men. Also Cardinal Francesco Maria Tarugi has given public evidence about the holy Father's chastity, and others have sworn to it, as something they learnt from the holy man himself. It was God's desire that there should be ample witnesses to such an unusual gift, such as Girolamo Pamphili, the Auditor of the Rota, Alessandro Fedeli and Germanico Fedeli. To these can be added the author of this work, and four other priests, who are very trustworthy, all of whom enjoyed his company every day, greatly edified by his kindness and decency.

the beauty of this virtue in his soul, that it was visible in his body as well, in his face and in his eyes, the signals of his mind. Thus not only in his conversation and in all his actions but even in his face was the beauty of his virginity apparent.

What can I say about the man's modesty and cleanliness? Whether he was well or ill, he never allowed anyone to see his chaste limbs, his bare flesh.[55] I myself can witness to that, among others, for I was close to him, night and day. Nobody ever noticed anything in him that could be offensive to the eyes or thoughts of anyone; he never even thought of using abusive or obscene language. Throughout his life he so conducted himself that from his first flower of youth he appeared in the eyes of all to be an example of chastity and Christian modesty.

39. One of the many remarkable things about Philip was that, through God's aid, he could detect virginity and other virtues by their scent, just as he detected impurity and all that sort of thing by its stench.[56] Several of those who went to confession to him have given sworn witness to that, after Philip's death. There were some who were addicted to this vice, and had not confessed it to him, but he would explain to them first the nature of their problem and its causes and then the appropriate remedy. 'My children,' he would say gently, 'you smell bad to me, you have fallen into some sort of impurity. Clear your consciences of the poison, eject the venom of sin by confessing, admit your fault and confess.' And having heard that, they were so astonished that they revealed everything in the sacrament of Confession, whatever each one regretted to have done in his life, and accepting penance, their hearts turned to the love of heaven.

How strong his purity of thought and cleanliness of heart was, you can judge from this fact among many others, that when he was

---

[55] St Athanasius tells the same about St Antony the Great and St Ammon; see also Cyril on John the Silent, and Pietro Ranzano on Vincent Ferrer.

[56] Cyril gives the same information in his life of Blessed Euthemius, and we read the same about other saints; indeed I myself am aware that there are people who can detect the sins of others by their smell. You can, if you like, look at the life of St Pachomius (in the Latin translation by Dionysius Exiguus), and St Jerome's life of Hilarion, Athanasius on St Antony, and finally Surius on St Birgitta.

hearing the confessions of men involved in these kinds of sin, he was so affected by the foul and pestilential stench which emanated from their unclean desires that he would put his hand or his handkerchief before his nose, and have to turn slightly away, though he did this with great subtlety to prevent anyone noticing. He used to say that he detected such an unpleasant smell arising from this vice that he could think of no other to be compared with it.

In this context, here is something that happened which is worthy of the greatest admiration, though it dates from a different stage of his life.[57] There was a woman who began to come to him; the holy Father saw with the eyes of his mind that there was a devil residing in her, and therefore put forth his hand, at God's instigation, to cast the devil out of the woman, but the moment he touched her, she exhaled such a sulphurous and pestilential stench that he was unable to bear its intensity. The smell remained afterwards in his nostrils, and could not be got off his hands, so that it was not until three days later, though he had used every means to rid himself of the nuisance, that he seemed to be restored to normal. He assured us afterwards that the smell came from the devil.

Philip falls ill
40. In that same year, '55, he was going round the Seven Churches of the city on foot when he fell into a violent fever, exhausted by the walk; it gripped him for many days, but did not take his life.

A Prediction
Massimiano Borgo was invited by a certain great man to live with him, and although he was unwilling, he accepted, on condition that he might never be involved in commercial business, for he desired to be intent only on God. However the man broke his word, and tried to use his guest's services for his own ends, though Massimiano remained steadfast in his purpose. As a result the rest of the household began to act very offensively towards him, to please their master. Being a man of discernment, he realised what was

---

[57] Cardinal Federico Borromeo swears to this, as do several others. Compare Athanasius' life of St Antony, and what Palladius says of Abbot Pachomas in his life of Lausiacas.

happening, and decided to remove himself from the house as soon as possible. But when Philip heard of it, he persuaded him not to, and warned him, in a spirit of prophecy, that if he did so, trying to escape from the Cross, he would ever afterwards have to live with a troubled soul. And what he said was certainly true: Massimiano ignored his advice, and from then on felt himself anxiously tossed between pondering and deliberation, as by the billows of the sea, though his life was still praiseworthy in the service of God.[58]

Great crowds flock to him

41. Philip's reputation and virtue grew from day to day, and through his labours the harvest of souls increased wonderfully. Every day very many gathered in our Oratory, and Philip explained the Word of God to them to fire them with devotion, so that they adopted a more worthy way of life, and abandoning all vain futile concerns, they gave their names to Christ. In his daily discourses his principal aim was to inspire the hearts of his followers to prayer, to frequent the sacraments, and to do other works of devotion. Through Philip's patient efforts, Giovan Battista Salviati, a man of the highest nobility, made great progress in piety.[59] He was a relation of Catherine de' Medici, the Queen of France, and a cousin of Cardinal Antonio Maria: he attached himself to Philip in the first year of Paul IV, and died showing remarkable signs of holiness. Another nobleman, Francesco Maria Tarugi, began to go to confession to Philip; when he first came to him he felt such a flame of divine love entering his heart, that it drove him to the point that his soul was melted by Philip's constant tears and prayers, and he gave himself over entirely to Philip's direction and rule, even though he was a man of high rank and dignity: this was in the year 56 of our century.[60] I must not omit to say that since Philip desired to form Christ in this man I have mentioned, he used to receive him in his own room, and in his presence gave himself to prayer till he began

---

[58] Cardinal Tarugi tells this story, on oath.

[59] *Salviati was a Florentine, whose family had been supporters of Savonarola. He had quite a reputation for leading a dissolute life until he met St Philip, after which both he and his wife Porzia de' Massimi became diligent hospital visitors.*

[60] *Tarugi, who came from Montepulciano, was to become one of Philip's most prominent*

to instil a spirit of mildness in his soul, so that he seemed to be tasting something of heaven, while still on earth, and in these heavenly joys was totally melted into delight.

42. Costanzo Tassone, a gentleman entangled in worldly pleasures, accepted the instructions of our holy Father, to the astonishment of the entire city, and under Philip's direction achieved such progress in virtue that he frequently received the sacraments during the week.[61] He gladly accepted the practice of mortification, and began to visit the hospitals; then at Philip's advice he was ordained priest and celebrated Mass every day. He kept up that fashion of life until his death, unchanged and inviolate, and died a holy and edifying death, which was in accordance with his life. Apart from these, there were many others of the highest nobility who followed Philip, but I purposely pass over their names, lest this passage be too long extended.

It was Philip's custom on weekdays to divide his children in Christ into three or four groups and send them to the city hospitals. To begin with, he would himself go after dinner to visit the sick in hospital, to enkindle by his example in his followers a greater desire to do this work; he would speak to the patients, tend them and do all sorts of things for them, which encouraged in his disciples an ardent desire to do the same. One example will serve to show you how devoted they were to the sick. Giovan Battista Salviati, being very dedicated, was in the hospital called the Consolazione, and headed straight for a patient intending to make his bed, asking him politely to get up so that he could do so. The patient thought he was being mocked. 'No, my Lord,' he said, 'don't make fun of me, I'm a poor man.' He knew all about Giovan Battista's licentious way of life, but was unaware of his marvellous change of character, by which he had wholeheartedly turned away from material concerns to the love of heaven. But what next? Giovan Battista urged him most earnestly, and the sick man was struck not only by his air

---

followers; he was ordained in 1567, and was appointed Archbishop of Avignon in 1592, created Cardinal in 1596, and translated to Siena in 1597.

[61] *Tassone was one of several courtiers brought to a better way of life by Philip. Although*

of authority but even more so by his humility, and got out of bed, lost in admiration. Giovan Battista retained that style of life with an unwavering intent until the day of his death, and having once put his hand to the plough, he never looked behind him.

While on this topic, something I must not pass over in silence is that Philip governed those who put themselves under him with such prudence and skill that they were overjoyed to perform what he told them to do, however tedious or difficult. No one ever went to him in search of spiritual advice without coming away happy; those of his sons who were cold in the love of God he warmed by his prayers; those who were unsure he confirmed in their faith.

Predictions

43. In August of that same year of Christ, 1556, Guglielmo Bucca fell ill; when Philip heard of it he said, 'He will certainly not recover from his present illness.' These words were not vain: the sick man was indeed defeated by his disease, and died that same year, fortified by the sacraments of the Church. I think it was about the same time that Francesco Fortino, one of Philip's spiritual sons, entrusted three hundred gold pieces to Alessio Bettini (himself rumoured to be a very rich man) without Philip's knowing anything about it.[62] But when it did come to his ears, although he knew nothing about finance, he immediately ordered his disciple to reclaim the money he had deposited, with no delay. He obeyed the command, although he was embarrassed at going back in the afternoon to withdraw the money he had deposited with the banker only that morning; still he chose to obey Philip, aware of the value of obedience, rather than suit his own fancy. He took the money back from Alessio, and only a few days later the general rumour began that, although nothing had been further from men's thoughts, the banker had failed. In the event, through misfortune rather than anything criminal, I believe, he lost his inheritance and also his private means, and was unable to meet his creditors.

---

suffering from nerves and scruples all his life, he became secretary to St Charles Borromeo, returning to Rome just before his death in 1569. See paragraph 95.
[62] Cardinal Tarugi and others swear to this story too.

He twice snatches Modio from the jaws of death

44. In the same year, I think, Giovan Battista Modio from Calabria, one of the more prominent of Philip's followers, was twice in a short period called back from the point of death through his intercession.[63] He was a doctor by profession, learned and devout; his book on the water of the Tiber circulates with great credit to the author, not to mention his commentary on the poems of Blessed Jacopone da Todi. When a serious disease first attacked him, it was so threatening that both Pietro Antonio of Pietrasanta and Hippolito Salviani, leading doctors of the period, quite despaired of his recovery.[64] The disease increased daily, and they declared that Modio would quit this life within a few hours, diagnosing from his pulse and other signs that death was imminent.

He was virtually unconscious and very close to death when Philip arrived: he longed to snatch this man from the jaws of death, for he had gained a great harvest of souls from conversing privately with him, and so he shut himself into a room. There he began to implore the mercy of God for the sick man's health with such fervour of soul that his whole body was lifted up six feet off the floor, and his face shone in a wonderful manner. When he had been thus raised up in prayer for about an hour and a half, a woman called Margaret, who used to cook for Modio, came into the room where he was praying, and saw him lifted up from the ground by divine force, shining with light, and his face emitting rays like the sun. She was terrified at the sight, and called out, 'Miracolo! Miracolo!' Those who were attending the dying man heard this, and rushed in at once; they saw how, though it was quite dark, everything here was lit up, and the Father was levitated. He thereupon came to himself, and went to Modio happily, while those present were still stupefied at this miraculous occurrence; he laid his hands on Modio's head, and called him by name, 'Be of good cheer, you will

---

[63] *Modio, who came from San Severino in Calabria, first attracted attention as the composer of a licentious operetta, but coming under Philip's influence became a diligent hospital visitor, and gave many of the discourses on lives of saints at the Oratory. The two books mentioned were, 'Il Tevere' (1556) and 'Cantici di Jacopone da Todi' (1558).*

[64] *Antonio was physician to Pius IV, and Salviani to Julius III; he also attended St Philip himself in 1562.*

certainly not die of this illness.' After he had said this, the sick man soon recovered his speech and senses, and replied to the holy Father. They had a long conversation together, and a few days later he recovered totally from his disease.

After Philip's death this amazing fact was told to me as it happened, on oath, by Bernardino Corona, a Roman citizen, among others; he was an elderly man, devoted to his religion, and one of Philip's oldest disciples.[65] In fact, during Philip's lifetime he had revealed the secret to one or two people, but never presumed to disclose it to everyone publicly, for he did not want to upset Philip's modesty, which would have been deeply offended.

45. This was not the only occasion when Modio experienced Philip's help. Not long afterwards he had an attack of the stone, and a severe retention of urine; the seriousness of the condition again brought his safety into doubt, when all medical remedies had failed.[66] Philip visited him, and as usual exhorted him to be patient, before going off to the church to offer prayers for him. Here he prayed in fervour of soul, in ceaseless longing for his son's recovery, and tears began to show on his face[67]; at the very moment they were perceived to flow from Philip's eyes, the sufferer passed the stones, with urine, and immediately felt himself so much better that he completely recovered from the sickness that had been troubling him.

Our holy Father often asked this man to discourse about the stories of the early saints, to the great comfort and benefit of his hearers, for he was gifted with a facility in speaking so that when he spoke to a large crowd he could mix entertainment with instruction, and fill the hearts of his audience with a rare delight. He also displayed great charity to the poor, and was greatly given to works of Christian charity; a few years after he had been received into the household of God, he died a religious and pious death, in accordance with the life he had lived.

---

[65] Several others have affirmed this, on oath.

[66] I heard this from Cardinal Tarugi: it was also confirmed by the evidence given publicly by Gian Francesco Bordini, Archbishop of Avignon.

[67] The same happened to St Antony the Great, as Athanasius tells us.

Visions

A.D. 1557; Paul IV year 2–3; Philip's age 42–43

46. Vincenzo the 'Miniaturist' led a life of holiness under Philip's direction, and revealed himself again to Philip in the very moment of his death, when Philip saw him with his own eyes piercing the clouds.[68] This happened in the year of Our Lord 1557. About the same time a very pious man named Mario Tosino also appeared to him as he was dying, and after twice calling Philip by name in a loud voice, ascended in his sight into heaven, surrounded by a brilliant light.[69]

These stories remind me that I should briefly explain what Philip thought about visions. 'Visions', he used to say, 'may present themselves to the servants of God under various forms, but everything depends on the frame of mind in which a man perceives them.' He was constantly warning his pupils to be careful about visions, for you can be very easily and very dangerously deceived by them, given that the angel of Satan can appear to men under the form of a good angel. He was therefore very averse to any prurient curiosity about visions and revelations, which can be extremely dangerous for spiritual persons, and he would severely correct anyone who was interested in such things. He said plainly that there was no snare of the devil more perilous for men than these absurd demonic deceits.

He instructed us that we should apply ourselves continually with diligence to correct our behaviour, extirpate vice, embrace virtue, control our desires and the like, and for that reason taught us to repudiate visions; the Lord would not be angry if we did so, he said, even if it really was He who appeared.

---

[68] Saints have often seen the souls of God's servants ascending to heaven soon after they died, as St Antony saw Paul the first Hermit, and you will find similar stories about Sts Euthemius, John the Silent and Saba. You can find other examples in the *Spiritual Meadow* (chapter 57), the *Dialogues* of St Gregory (book II, chapters 33–5), and Bede's life of St Cuthbert. Vincenzo died on the 9th of February. *He was a miniature painter, a Frenchman called Vincent Raymond, who served Leo X, Clement VII and Paul III.*

[69] Cardinal Federico Borromeo told us this, on oath; so did six others, among whom were Vincenzo and Mario, of the Fraternity of the Holy Trinity.

WHAT HE DID IN 1555, 1556 AND 1557

47. While I am talking about visions, I think it not irrelevant to add a little about the facility which he had in discerning these matters, for he was able to distinguish true visions from false ones without difficulty. There was someone who during prayer was suddenly bathed in a marvellous bright light, so that in a moment of time he clearly perceived many things about God. He was anxious to know whether this were through the devil's agency, being afraid of the deceits of the evil one, and therefore consulted many distinguished religious. Not being contented with their answers, he came at last to Philip, and was not disappointed. Philip clearly explained to him at once which visions were false and which were true, so that he understood perfectly from what spirit that light had come into his mind.

One of his disciples called Francesco, who was familiarly named 'Il Ferrarese', saw a demon one night under the form of the Blessed Virgin, scheming to deceive a man of such quality by this apparition.[70] He told Philip about it in the morning, who replied, 'It was not the blessed Mother of God who appeared to you, as you imagine, but a demon presenting itself under her appearance. If ever such a vision should present itself to you again, I tell you to spit in its face at once.' The following night, as Ferrarese was praying devoutly, the demon appeared under the same form, and shining with the same radiance. Obedient to the holy Father's advice, he immediately spat in the demon's face, and it disappeared at once, confused, ashamed and defeated. But hardly had it gone when the Blessed Virgin herself appeared clearly, and told him to spit in her face, if he were able to do so, before leaving him wonderfully refreshed, as she departed on high.

Francesco was a man endowed with great concentration of mind; he could hear the voices of angels, and detect harlots by their scent; nor were these the only virtues in his soul, for rivers of tears used to flow constantly from his eyes, especially when he was present at sermons treating on matters of God, or was regaled with

---

[70] This story of Ferrarese we heard from Cardinal Tarugi, as well as other reliable men of good character. *He made a living selling plaster statuettes, and was a man of simple piety.*

the Eucharistic sacrament, which he used to receive daily. One day he was suffering from the stone and finding it impossible to pass water: he turned to the Lord and said, 'Grant me, O Lord, the ability to relieve myself', and hardly had he said that than at once, without any feeling of pain, the urine flowed freely.[71] On another occasion as he was walking along he met a Jew, and felt himself suddenly seized with such a strong desire for his conversion to Christ that for the next three years he never stopped praying for him. Three years later to the day, as he was entering the Basilica of Saint Peter to beg for God's mercy, he suddenly became aware of the sound of a noisy throng. Going outside, he saw the Jew we have mentioned on his way to receive holy Baptism, and Francesco was more delighted at this than I can say, quite unable to restrain his tears of joy. But that is enough about the holiness of one of Philip's disciples.

He desires to travel to India to convert the pagans to Christ

48. It was in that same year of this century, '57, that in the evening, after prayers, they were reading the newsletters from India. Philip began to be so excited with zeal for bringing unbelievers to the truth of the Gospel, that he decided to set off for India himself, ignoring the many difficulties and dangers which presented themselves so abundantly, together with Francesco Maria Tarugi, Giovan Battista Modio, Antonio Fucci, and about twenty more of his disciples. However, as he always did in questions of this nature, his first thought was to place the matter before God in constant prayer, for he never undertook anything, great or small, without first submissively consulting the Lord. He further decided to consult men of holiness, to be more certain about the will of God, and also to have those who were capable of the priesthood ordained, before going to the Pope to ask for a blessing and permission to commit themselves to a long and perilous journey. They were all so eager to go that they thought nothing of the terrors, dangers to life, temptations of the devil and other hardships involved, happy to suffer all these things for the sake of spreading the Gospel of Christ.

---

[71] This we also heard from Cardinal Tarugi.

WHAT HE DID IN 1555, 1556 AND 1557

Philip being of such a disposition, God put it into his mind to go to a certain monk of St Bernard's order, who was famous for his holiness, to learn the divine will through his intercession and advice. This monk was superior that year in the Abbey of Saints Vincent and Anastasius, martyrs, at Tre Fontane. His parents, as I have learnt from Francesco Maria, were gifted with notable holiness, and among their many practices appropriate to a Christian life, they used to go to confession and receive Holy Communion two days before applying themselves to the procreation of children according to the most sacred rites of matrimony; after these sacraments they would beg God earnestly to grant them such a child as should be worthy to be enrolled in the number of His servants. When they died their reputation for holiness was such that everyone agreed they had attained the place reserved for those who die as saints. Their sons and daughters also made such progress in the practice of holiness that they lived and died in the greatest sanctity.

But to return to Philip: when Agostino Ghettini (that was the monk's name) heard what was in his mind, he asked for time, saying, 'This is a matter which must be asked of God in prayer.' When he had completed his prayer, he told Philip that he was called to Rome, not to India, and Rome was to be his Indies. He also told him that Saint John the Evangelist had appeared to him, who said it was God's will that Philip should remain in Rome to cultivate his own vineyard, where he had already gathered him many sons, and that God had determined to use his labours and those of his disciples for the salvation of many in Rome. He continued that he had seen the waters of the three fountains (hence the name Tre Fontane) changed to a blood-red colour, which he said clearly signified another storm was threatening the city.[72] This too he said he had learnt from the blessed Apostle, and he recounted the whole vision in order to Philip.

When Philip heard this, he showed himself ready as always to obey the will of Christ, and yielding to the advice of that servant of

---

[72] *The storm in question was either a great flood in September 1557, or the threat from the troops of the Duke d'Alba who were encamped around the City in August that year.*

God, he determined to stay in Rome, where no one can be ignorant of the efforts he made for the salvation of souls, and the abundant harvest he reaped.

S.Filippo Neri viene esortato per ispirazione di S.Gio.Evang. all' Apostolato di Roma, e non delle Indie

V : THE YEAR OF CHRIST 1558, WHEN PHILIP WAS 43

More designs of his for the salvation of his neighbour
A.D. 1558; Paul IV year 3; Philip's age 43

49. When more people began to attend than the place where the discourses were held could contain, they began to think about finding another place. In the year 58 of this century, therefore, Philip asked the Confraternity of Charity whether he could gather his people for the discourses in the space above the vaults of the right aisle of the church, a place quite large enough, and at that time not used for anything. Moreover, as he continued to form his auditors by these intense daily discourses about the things of God, he realised that the number of people coming to listen to the sermons was increasing every day, so he decided to appoint some of his followers to help with the work. He chose Francesco Maria Tarugi and Giovan Battista Modio, who were then laymen. Once these two had begun to speak to the crowds, they so inflamed the hearts of their hearers towards the love of God that they proved to the gathering that they were true sons of their great Father.

Philip later added to their number Antonio Fucci, and Cesare Baronio of Sora, and others who copied their father's example hand and foot, and assisted their brothers wonderfully in the work of God, to reap a great harvest of souls.[73] Philip worked out how to encourage the hearts of his audience with an even greater love of God, and those he encouraged he preserved whole and untainted from every sort of danger, damage or harm.

---

[73] *Antonio Fucci, a doctor, succeeded Modio in the task of speaking on the lives of the saints; he died in 1566. Baronio, the greatest of St Philip's companions, had trained as a lawyer, and was directed by Philip to speak, and later to write, on Church history. He succeeded Philip as superior of the Roman Oratory, which position he still held when Gallonio was writing. The Italian version also mentions Giovan Francesco Bordini here; he was a Roman, and a cultured man; after a mission to Poland in 1588 he succeeded Tarugi as Archbishop of Avignon, where he died in 1609.*

The Oratory was opened in that place every day when the bell was rung, in winter at the last hour of daylight, in summer at the last but one. Here the nobility and the poor came together to pray, and this was the manner of procedure. After half an hour of silent mental prayer (measured by the striking of the clock), on four days of the week, Tuesday, Thursday, Saturday and Sunday, they recited the Litanies, during which they commended intentions to God, either publicly or privately. On the remaining days, Monday, Wednesday and Friday, they put a light into a dark lantern, which had a paper image of Our Saviour on the Cross on its front, so that it was the only thing the brothers could see, and then all those present struck themselves with cords for a period of time, while a short account of the Lord's Passion was read (the one beginning *Recordemini, Fratres carissimi*), the whole of Psalms 50 and 129, and the antiphon *Salve Regina* or the one appropriate to the season, in a dignified but subdued voice. This custom is retained by our fathers to this day, being full of Christian devotion, and producing great spiritual results.

Philip does all he can to help his disciples

50. The concourse of people grew still greater at that period, and the work of the Oratory flourished, so he introduced a new custom for the daily increasing crowds: first of all he would read a book, or get someone else to read it, dealing with spiritual matters. Having done that, he would question one or two or even more of the gathering about the points raised in what had been read, such as the virtues to be cultivated, the vices to be avoided, and the like. When they had given their answer, with appropriate modesty, Philip would sum it all up very briefly, without any pompous or complicated language but very simply and straightforwardly. He was so ardent in speaking about divine matters that the hearts of his hearers were inflamed, and he was wonderfully effective in making

---

[74] *The Minerva was the church of the Dominicans, and had close links with S. Marco in Florence, where Philip had been educated. The Dominicans have always been close to the Oratory.*

them take up devotion, as well as strengthening the determination of those who had already given themselves over to Christ.

Once the divine discourses were over, like a wise and good shepherd, Philip used to lead his flock into fresh pastures; they most often went to the church of S. Maria sopra Minerva, and there with him they followed the Divine Office of the day, as well as sometimes attending Matins at night.[74] This custom was retained when the institute of our Oratory was transferred first to the church of S. Giovanni dei Fiorentini, and then to our home at S. Maria in Vallicella. At these places everything was done according to the set pattern laid down by our father Philip and it was carried out exactly.

Here I might add that Philip was so eager to incite his sons in Christ to apply themselves to prayer that through his own prayers he fired their hearts most wonderfully. Let me give an example: during that period one of them, called Simon, was praying in his bedroom, and since Philip was interceding for him, he was suddenly so overwhelmed with heavenly delight that the whole hour which he spent in prayer seemed to him but a minute, and he was filled with joy to the extent that he determined to pray without ceasing.[75] Nor should I omit to tell what Marzio Altieri used to say – he was a Roman nobleman who left this world to join himself to Christ with great fortitude, during the reign of Pope Paul III – that when he was in Philip's room he was bathed in such delight that the room no longer looked like a bedroom but an earthly Paradise. He was someone who attained such a degree of holiness that like Moses he was barely able to speak about the things of God, being overwhelmed by the spirit. He was moreover so kind to the poor that he would give them the blankets off his own bed.[76] He also followed Philip in this, that when he spoke to men's hearts he fired them with the love of God and impelled their souls to the desire of virtue.

---

[75] *Simone Grazzini himself told the story during the canonisation process.*

[76] This I heard from the holy Father himself. *Altieri was the nephew of M. Antonio, author of 'Nuptiali', an influential figure in early 16th-century Roman affairs. He also assisted St Ignatius in building the Gesù.*

He drives the devil away from a dying priest

51. It was in that same year 1558 that the priest Persiano Rosa, who was Philip's confessor, became gravely ill; when he was in the last extremity he began to be severely troubled by the devil in the form of the Black Dog. In this distress he implored the aid of God, with total submission, and frequently recited the Psalm, 'Judge me, O God, and distinguish my cause'. While he was contending with our common foe in this manner, Philip came in unannounced, and when he saw him, Persiano called out, 'Help me, holy Philip, the Black Dog is here who is trying to bite me; come and help, do what you can to stop me being eaten'.[77] Moved by these words, the holy Father immediately prostrated himself on the ground, after telling those present to recite the Lord's Prayer for the sick man at least once. As he did so, look, Persiano suddenly began to call out aloud, 'The Dog has fallen back ... the Dog has run away ... see, he is standing at the door.' Philip got up from his prayer, and drove the demon away from the doorway by sprinkling holy water, and brought great consolation to the dying man; he was overjoyed and would not stop giving thanks to God and our holy Father. He was delivered from that horrible apparition not only at that time but ever after, until he died very peacefully on the first of April.

A Prediction

52. In the same year, 1558 since the birth of Christ, two of his spiritual sons, Francesco and Giovan Battista Saraceno, decided to join the Order of St Dominic.[78] When Philip heard about this, he said, 'Giovan Battista, once clothed in the holy habit, will make such progress in virtue that he will persevere with praise to the end, in the way of life he has undertaken; Francesco, being frailty itself, will be overcome in the struggle and at the devil's urging will put off the religious habit and return to Egypt.' The event proved him

---

[77] I got this from an eyewitness.

[78] A Frenchman called Louis Ames who was present gave evidence for this on oath; it was moreover well known to our Holy Father's disciples. *Francesco Vipera was tested by St Philip with one of his remarkable penances: unable to cope with this, he went off and joined the Jesuits.*

true: in fact he told Domenico Saraceno about this Giovan Battista, that he saw his face shining with a remarkable light. He joined the Dominican community on the 29th of April, and took the name Pietromartire. He won great respect among his companions, he held the office of Vicar General in his Order, and after his retirement died in holiness and devotion.

He helps a disciple wonderfully at his death

53. During that year there was a young man among Philip's sons called Gabriele Tana, who came from Modena.[79] He lived very respectably in the household of Cardinal Giovanni Poliziani, went to confession twice a week and received the saving Eucharist regularly. When he was settled into this way of life, he fell ill, and could not be relieved by any skill of doctors or medicines; he began to feel his last hour approaching and was terrified as most men are, fearing death and longing for life. He said to those who were attending him, 'Let what God wants happen to me, I resign myself to His will, I commit myself totally to Him; all the same, since the flesh wars against the spirit, I really would like to recover my health and live longer upon this earth.' When Philip asked him about his health, he replied, 'I am glad to be hopeful of recovering from this present illness.' Philip, aware of the assaults of the devil, and being aware through divine revelation that he was going to die, first asked him to entrust himself to Philip come what may, and then requested the bystanders to pray for him. Then he began to pray himself, and with such a fervour of spirit that when he returned to the dying man after finishing his prayer, he found that his mind had changed, so that he was now saying, like St Paul, 'I long to be dissolved and to be with Christ'. While he was saying this with real sincerity, he caught sight of Philip and turned his face towards him; 'Pray, Father,' he cried, 'that I may be fit to enter Paradise as soon as maybe. I have begun to loathe my life; life is tedious to me,

---

[79] Iacopo Marmitta wrote an account of this matter in Italian; he was present and saw everything himself, as were a large number of Philip's following, most of whom are still alive. *Tana actually came from Parma, not Modena. He was eighteen years old, in the service of Cardinal Ricci, as was Jacopo Marmitta, and joined St Philip's circle along with Modio.*

because I wish to be with God.' Then he suddenly looked towards the bystanders and said, 'Give me that picture of the most holy crucifix; pass it to me, the one which my friend Giulio used when he was alive!' He took it, and at once dissolved into tears of sweetness; from time to time he exhorted those around him to serve God with their whole heart and set aside all the frivolities of this world. Then he would burst out with words like these, 'Believe me, this present life is a burden to me, I would rather die, so that I can contemplate God for ever.' And saying that, he turned to Philip, 'Until this day I have been begging you, Father, to pray that God would restore me to health; but now I entreat you by your prayers set me free from the prison of this body, let me go!'

54. His bodily strength continued to lessen until the following day, the first of September, and the last of his life. Already eager for what lay ahead, he was totally intent on preparing himself for a devout and Christian death. Many of our holy Father's following were with him continuously, and the Father himself was there, who intended to remain with him until the day declined into twilight. At that time the sick man began again to say, 'In heaven I wish to go, Father, that is all that now occupies my heart.' Philip replied to him, 'What if God were to will that you should endure this illness still longer, would you not put His will above your own desires?' Gabriele answered, 'What do you mean by that? I have told you many times that I really long to leave the restriction of this body for heaven; I am so afire with longing to see God that nothing could afflict me more than prolonging my stay here. Beg the Lord that I may fly to Him before five hours of the night have passed.' Philip replied, 'What you have asked for, you shall get. But I do warn you that the devil is preparing many traps for you, and will challenge your strength of mind with various different temptations (and he detailed them all). But believe me, he cannot harm you in any way if you keep firmly in mind that you have made your will over to God. Be sure that nothing can affright you, for Christ will overcome all things in you.' Philip then left, intending to go home and beseech the divine mercy for him; he commended the patient to Giovan Battista Salviati and Francesco Maria Tarugi, and told them to fetch him if it became necessary.

55. He had hardly been gone an hour, and Gabriele had been readying himself for a pious demise, when the devil put into his head the thought that he was already justified, and that there was no doubt at all about his eternal reward. Those who sat by him, keeping the night vigil, were reciting the Litanies for him, and came to the invocation, 'From an evil death deliver him, O Lord'; Gabriele smiled and shook his head slightly, saying to himself that he in whose heart Christ is dwelling can be free from any danger of an evil death. But having said that, although he had begun to be affected by that temptation, he came to his senses and realised what he had said. He did all he could to rid himself of the idea, saying out loud, 'What is this diabolical thought that has come to me? I beg you, brothers, help me with your prayers.'

That was not the end of the struggle: defeated by his virtue, the malicious foe plotted another type of challenge in the hope of destroying him. He began to use every means to prevent him from being able to utter the Holy Name of Jesus. Gabriele asked his friends to remind him of that Name as he was approaching his end, for he sincerely desired to invoke it. He cried out, therefore, and said, 'Brothers, help me! I cannot pronounce it, I really can't; help me, I am distressed, help me, I am in difficulties!' When they asked him, 'What was it you can't pronounce, was it the Holy Name of Jesus?' he nodded at once, and turned to Iacopo Marmitta, saying, 'What have I done wrong, that I cannot call on Jesus?' From this they realised how powerful the devil is, for although he spoke the Name out loud he still seemed to be unable really to express it. Those around him suggested that if he could not say it aloud he could speak it silently in his heart, and he answered, 'It seems so difficult, brothers, to call on the Holy Name of Jesus; I seem to be reduced to such a misery that I can hardly bear to hear the sound of it.'

56. He was greatly distressed by this terrible conflict, although the bystanders spoke to him and encouraged him to remain strong. The temptation continued to press upon him until he was bathed in sweat through anguish of mind and bodily weakness, and so his friends decided to send word to Philip. The patient was wonderfully refreshed at seeing him, and with the encouragement of that great man, called on the Holy Name of Jesus several times, together

with him, with no difficulty of speech. 'My Jesus,' he cried, 'My love, my spouse!' And after saying that, he complained to Philip, along with his friends, about the difficult struggle which he had endured from the devil's hands for nearly an hour. But being now happy, he began again to cry out a little later, 'O Father, help your son; I have the same difficulty as before in pronouncing the Holy Name of Jesus!' When he said that, Philip prayed earnestly for him, and he was quickly freed from the affliction and again called out the name of Jesus, speaking freely and quite clearly, as he gazed at the Crucifix.

His mind was put at rest, but now Satan, who had been unable to overcome him through the temptations we have mentioned, tried again to overthrow and destroy him under the appearance of lack of faith. He represented the articles of our religion to him in such a way that he put him apparently in doubt of the faith, and moreover suggested to him that he would after all recover from that illness. He was deeply troubled by these things, and revealed this new deceit of the devil to Philip, asking for his help to recover the peace of mind he had lost, and to be able to defeat the devil. Philip said to him, 'Despise these diabolical wiles, despise them: just say "I believe! I believe!"' He repeated these words several times along with the holy Father, but he still thought himself to be in doubt about the articles of faith, and called out again, 'Father, give me some assistance, I am in trouble, don't let me perish!'

Philip was moved by these words, and his heart burned with charity towards him. He spoke to the bystanders, and then to the sick man, telling them to recite the Apostles' Creed aloud, and that if he were unable to do so with his lips, he should try to recite it in his heart along with the others. Then he gave himself again to prayer, and immediately the whole of that devilish attempt came to nothing, to the great consolation of the dying man. He gasped a little, as he was freed from Satan's bonds, and then abused the devil with a clear mind in these words, 'I will believe, despite you; whether you like it or not, I will believe! I reject you, I will be faithful to my God as long as I live.' He said this, as the bystanders were just finishing the Apostles' Creed, and lay peacefully, free from that trouble, although his body was exhausted by the strength he had expended in combat with the devil.

57. Such is the hatred that the devil bears towards the human race that, despite being so defeated, he made a third assault on Gabriele, a serious and perilous threat, more terrible and intolerable than the last. So consider, the devil presented himself to sight in a foul and horrible form to terrify the dying man and drive him to despair, till he was all but reduced to the state that he had no hope of salvation. The young man was crushed by deep grief during these trials, and trembled all over through horror and fear. His face changed, and he looked severe and sad, with eyes full of dread, as he gazed around him, an object of wonder, demonstrating by his appearance that he could see the devil. He muttered to himself, 'Oh, oh, how wretched you are, Gabriele! What sins you have committed! What woe, oh Father, drive away those dogs, those Black Dogs that surround me! If you love me, Father, chase these demons away, drive them off!' [80]

Philip ran up to him as he suffered thus and gave him strength in his fears, aroused his faith, recalled to him the mercy of God and urged him to take refuge in Him. He reminded him that Christ suffered for him, and besought the Lord to take refuge together with his bride 'in the clefts of the rock, in the hollow places of the wall' [Cant 2:14] where there is true peace; and so he promised him the victory. After saying these things he knelt down on the floor to pray for him, and leaning on the bed rebuked the demon, 'I order you in the name of Christ to leave this place at once!'

The throng of terrors could not resist his virtue, and fled immediately, leaving the young man ecstatic with joy and crying out, 'Look, brothers, rejoice, the dogs have gone! Philip has driven them off, he has sent those dreadful hounds right away!' Then he pointed with his finger, 'Look, look, they have taken to flight, they are in full rout! I cannot tell you how ugly they are, but we will overcome, we will defeat the assaults of the enemy. You are running away, vile creatures, running away at last! I can now call on Jesus a thousand times against you, despite your hopes and intentions.'

---

[80] That the devil is accustomed to appear in the form of a black dog is recorded by Bishop Leontius' life of Simeon Salus, chapter 25; by Peter Damian in his life of St Romuald, chapter 67; and by Jacques de Vitry in his life of St Marie de Oignies, book 2, chapter 3; among other authors.

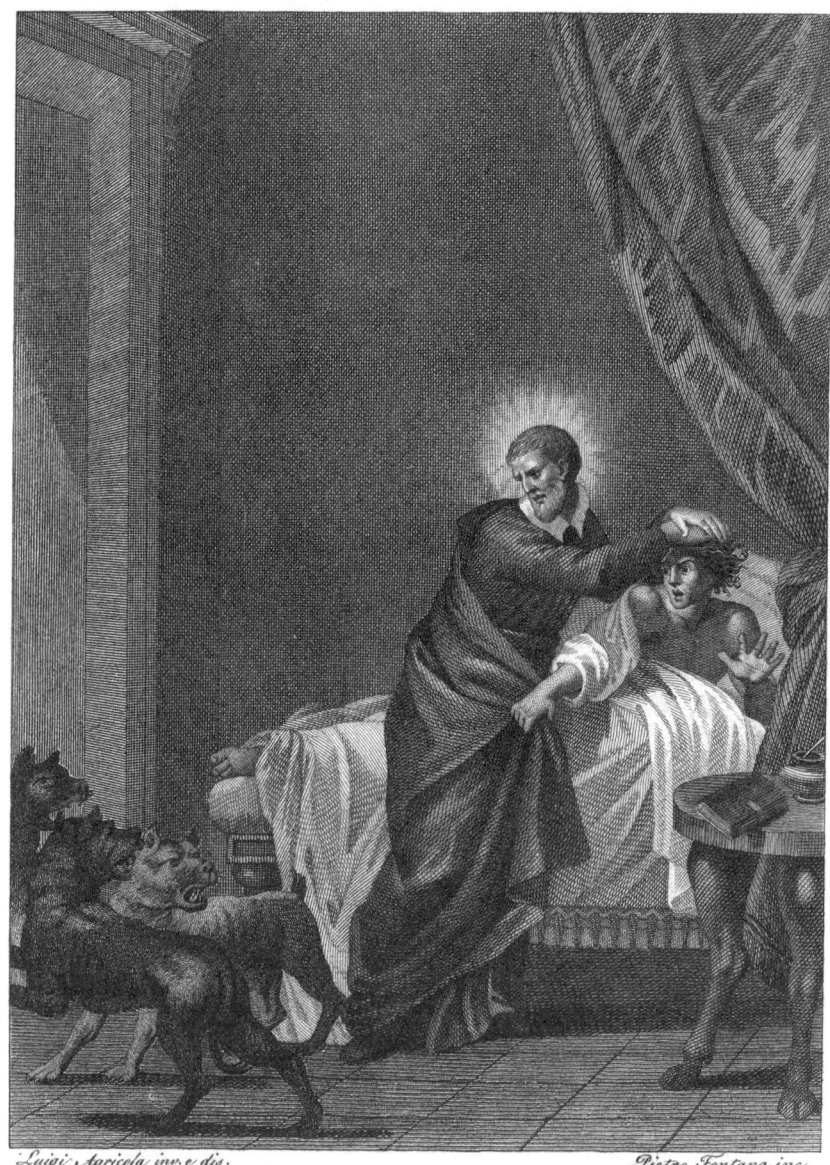

S. FILIPPO NERI

Conforta Gabriello Tana, che vicino a morte vede tre demonj in forma di negrissimi cani.

58. He exulted thus in the spirit, and then turned towards the holy Crucifix, which one of the party held in his hands, and prayed with such ardour of soul that none of those around him could restrain his tears. They could see how utterly grateful he was, how he welcomed the assistance he had received from God, as he said these words, 'O my Jesus, my sweet Jesus, my love, my creator, my redeemer! Who could ever tell the benefits I have received from you?' Then turning to his friends, 'What things I have seen with these eyes, brothers! Listen to my advice: make no delay in giving yourselves over totally to God, the Best and Greatest. Why is it, O good Jesus, that I can scarcely speak? Give me the Crucifix, I beg you, how I long to hold it in my hands, I can hardly tell you.' Then as he kissed it devoutly, he repeated these words, 'Long live my Lord Jesus Christ! Who can ever separate me from your love, O sweetest Jesus?' Then, wrathful against the devil, he continued, 'What was your design on me, you wretch, were you trying to seduce me from my faith in Christ before I die? How could that be, O God? Could I change the faith I have held from my childhood? Never! Depart from me, ye workers of iniquity!'

A little later he said, 'Have we not read Christ's word in sacred Scripture, "I am the Way, the Truth and the Life"? Now if Christ is the Truth, and He Himself has taught us His sacred law, how could it possibly happen that I should doubt about the certainty of that truth? O vile demon, O wretch!' He was unable to quench the thirst he felt for giving thanks to God and insulting the defeated demon, but rather the more he spoke, the more eager he was. The holy Father saw that this was tiring him excessively, and weakening his strength, and fearing that it would accelerate his death, said, 'That is enough, my son; put the deceitful and wicked fiend out of your mind, and rest your hope, I urge you, in God and in His Precious Blood, shed for you. It is He who has given you the victory, it is He who has overcome the evil demon in you, and through you.'

Hearing this, Gabriele fell silent for a little, but not long afterwards wanted more reassurance, and said to the bystanders, 'That traitor (meaning the devil) troubled me intolerably.' The men around him saw that Gabriele was speaking quite clearly, and seemed to be gaining strength, and began to think he might live until the following day. Damiano Valentini, who was tending the sick man, reported this to Philip, who replied, 'That will not happen; when he changes his position, then he will die.' His words were true: about half an hour passed, and then Gabriele turned himself over towards where Philip was, with his help called on the name of Christ, and breathed out his soul into the hands of Jesus, as if he were called to his wedding. This was at the third hour of the night, in the year 58 of our century. Watching all this had such an effect on all those who attended his deathbed that every one of them began to consider very seriously the final struggle in which our whole destiny is concluded.

He appears to one in peril on the sea

59. In the same year there were two of his disciples, an Italian and a Frenchman; the Frenchman was called Louis, but I forget the name of the Italian, who was chamberlain to Cardinal Guido Ascanio of Santa Fiora; only Louis is still alive, and he is eighty years old or over.[81] One day Philip took the opportunity to speak about them, during the period of discourses when there were many people present: the Italian, he said, would regret the enterprise he had begun and return to Egypt, although he appeared to be much better than the Frenchman (being a man deeply devoted to prayer and mortification, and demonstrating his piety openly); but Louis will be more fortunate in retaining the devotion which he has begun to practise. A few days later, the Italian was driven by the devil to request Philip's permission to travel to Naples, although he had no good reason to do so. In fact he intended to leave Rome in order to join in the war. The holy Father on hearing this suspected what was afoot, for he well knew how the devil deceives us, and refused his permission, so as not to bring the salvation of his son into danger. But he was unable to persuade him not to return, or induce him to change his mind in any way, and so failing in these attempts, Philip resorted to threats, warning him that he would either be drowned or be captured by the Turks.

---

[81] There are four sworn witnesses to this story. *One of them being Louis Ames himself, a native of Angers, who had known St Philip since around 1550. He happened to meet the Italian in the Banchi, and heard the story of his escape from him.*

THE YEAR OF CHRIST 1558

The prediction of the holy Father was not false, as the event showed. The Italian would not change his mind, but left the city and was travelling by sea when he realised he had fallen into the power of the Turks. He was terrified at seeing such a large force of pirate cutters advancing on him, and was on the point of being taken by the barbarians who were superior to our crew both in numbers and strength. Being paralysed with fear, and destitute of hope, he jumped into the sea to avoid capture by the Turks. He found himself caught up in rapid currents, and was unable to swim any longer, till he was on the point of certain death as the waters swirled round him. Then he remembered what the holy Father had said, and called out to him as best he could, though half drowned. Now here is a wonder! Philip was in Rome at the time, but was at once present to his son in peril on the sea; he held his right hand out, and although the sea was gaping, and the man sinking fast into the centre of the whirlpool, he held him up, and lifted him out; then across a great expanse of sea he brought him unharmed to land, and set him down on the dry ground.[82]

---

[82] It is well established that the saints can appear even when they are still alive. See the lives of St Euthymius, John the Silent, Theodosius the Cenobiarch, Marcellus the Archimandrite, Daniel the Stylite, Simeon Salus, Germanus of Paris and St Bernard.

VI : THE YEAR OF CHRIST 1559, WHEN PHILIP WAS 45

How he endured more tribulations for Christ
A.D. 1559; Paul IV year 4; Philip's age 44

60. Philip was not yet satisfied with all he had done and established as means to inflame the hearts of his followers to frequent the sacraments and do other works of devotion, and also to preserve what he had thus inflamed; he desired to do more, determined to remove from them any occasion of sin. Thus, on the day when men gave themselves up to the debauchery of the Carnevale, he used to lead them to the Seven Churches of the city, being concerned not merely to gather together a flock for Christ, but no less so to safeguard that flock.[83] To begin with there were only a few who went, no more than thirty, but not long afterwards the crowds grew until the number of men who assembled reached more than a thousand.

This was the way it was done: to begin with, all sorts of people were called together, then on the fixed day each one made his own way to the basilicas of St Peter and St Paul early in the morning. Once they had all assembled in the church of St Paul and in the surrounding buildings as arranged, the procession began when Father Philip gave the signal, and they set off for the basilica of St Sebastian with admirable and eager devotion. Then they went on to the basilica of St John Lateran, then to Santa Croce (the Sessorian Basilica), and to the others in turn. They were marshalled in perfect order, with regular intervals between them, and walked with composed expressions and such dignity that those who saw it were greatly impressed. As they walked they sometimes sang the litanies, and at other times hymns and psalms, very harmoniously. Either in the church of St Sebastian or that of St Stephen on the Caelian Hill, they celebrated divine worship, with delightful

---

[83] This whole matter I have gathered from those who took part, fifteen of them in all, and Tarugi confirmed it in his public testimony. *The three villas mentioned*

music, but following the proper ritual, and with appropriate devotion on the part of the servers. Everyone took part in the sacrifice, and after the priest had received the Body of Christ, at least eight hundred would communicate. When Mass was over they used to go to a garden, where there was plenty of grass, as well as vines and trees, and there the Fathers would distribute food, and everyone received as much food and drink as the needed, with good cheer. In those first days the villa they most often visited was that of Virginia Massimi, but sometimes they went to those of Mattea or Crescenzia. A table would be set up there, not with exotic dishes, but lots of bread, eggs, apples and cheese.

After dinner they thanked God as usual, and then they all went straightaway in silence to the Scala Santa, though at certain fixed intervals they sang as they went to encourage joy in their faith. It was after this that they went to the basilica of Santa Croce, and thence to St Lawrence in the Campo Verano, and then finally to the crib at St Mary Major. There a sermon was addressed to the crowd about some divine topic (as was also done in the other churches), to the great edification of the listeners, and then they sang a hymn beautifully, and everyone made his own way home.

These processions were so advantageous to souls that there were always some members of the throng who were touched by the Spirit of God with such devotion that they dedicated themselves to frequent the sacraments and live their lives under the direction of Father Philip.

61. Now, God does not wish his soldiers to grow sluggish in idleness, but rather expects them to be active in the dust and toil of the front, so that their valour may become more splendid through the peril of strife, as gold is tested in the fire: with divine permission, therefore, it happened in the year 59 of our century that the pilgrimage we have described, so well attended, so beneficial to all, a great example for upright and devout men, should become an object of

---

are those of Massimi on the Celio, near S. Stefano; Mattea nearby, now called the Celimontana; and Crescenzia, near the Porta S. Sebastiano. At times they also stopped at Cardinal Savelli's villa at the beginning of the Appian Way.

envy and hatred for the malicious, and gave them the occasion for a bitter attack on Philip.[84] As they observed an ever greater number of people flocking to him daily, they began to detract from his reputation, in private at first, then publicly. They said he was ambitious, and eager for public adulation, a man too pleased with himself, and trying to gather a following. Others claimed he was not only ambitious but greedy as well,[85] a great scavenger. So that their scheming might lead to popular dislike and offence, they added that he was collecting a sect, stirring up a revolution, and encouraging what he had stirred up, and so they spread every sort of slander you can imagine against an innocent man.

Not content with this, they filled the city with false rumours, saying that on his pilgrimage to the Churches he was not interested in the glory of God and the salvation of souls so much as in his own reputation, and that he banqueted splendidly on the most exquisite foods brought to him there in abundance. The devil saw to it that the matter reached such a pitch that the lies told about him were spread through the city, so that everyone was openly talking slander against him everywhere. Though Philip became aware of this, he was confident in his evidence of his own conscience, and in the promises made by Christ Our Lord, who said that he would remain always close to those subject to tribulation. Philip endured all the machinations of the devil and all his assaults with an undaunted spirit, quite free from fear.

62. Meanwhile his enemies reported the whole matter succinctly to the ecclesiastical authorities, the Vicar General of the city and the others who at that time were the custodians of the Faith. They accused Philip not only of ambition, pride and other vices, which they had made up, but also that he was gathering a cult, and was attempting to introduce a new sect, full of ambition. When the Vicar General heard this, he was stirred to great anger in his zeal for the faith, and his concern for peace in the city (which was indeed his

---

[84] Compare this with the story of St Daniel the Stylite.
[85] The same sort of thing happened to Saint Goar the elder, as in his life by Wandelbert, chapter 4.

responsibility); he sent for Philip, received him with severe words, rebuked him, threatened him with prison, and ordered him to abstain from such works, not to take any companions around with him, to appear for judgment promptly whenever he was summoned, not to hear any confessions for the next fortnight, and not to preach to the people until he had received a new licence issued by himself. All this Philip received with a cheerful countenance and gave the only answer he could, with a submissive and modest manner, saying that he was equally prepared to continue the work he had begun or to leave it off at his superior's request, for he had no intention in mind other than the honour of God and the benefit of souls.

The Vicar General became even angrier at these words, and after a few scornful comments sent Philip out of his house. Philip felt this vexation most severely because it was brought against him not just by men enslaved to this world but even more strongly by men dedicated to God, some of whom lived under the same roof as himself. Indeed there were some devout priests who, observing the huge crowds that followed him for their spiritual benefit, began to blame him for having an ambitious spirit. Philip had to endure these people who opposed him in his work for the Lord, and even went so far as to create a disturbance, although his soul was not troubled at all by what they said and did. Whatever harm they did him, under the pretext of religion, he bore with cheerful patience, and he did the best he could to conceal from his sons in Christ the unbearable insults directed at him, and also the names of the perpetrators. If it did ever happen that his disciples discovered them, Philip's charity was such that, where he could not conceal what had happened, he could at least put a very different interpretation on their words and actions, while they were present and listening, so that he was able to stop his disciples having any bad opinion of them. He besought God with tears for their salvation, for he followed the teaching that we should pray for our enemies, and return good for evil.

63. While he was assailed by these troubles, he begged help from God in his daily prayers, and his prayers were not offered in vain. During the specified fortnight, a priest came to our Oratory whom we did not know: he was girt with a rope, his shoulders were rounded, his face frank, his countenance neither pale nor dark, his

beard and hair naturally black. He said, in front of many listeners, that he had been sent by certain religious men to whom the Lord had revealed a great matter, which was that he should suggest the Forty Hours Devotion; he told this to Francesco Maria Tarugi, with no other witnesses. 'Great benefit will result from this,' he said, 'this whole diabolical attack will dissolve like smoke, and the work of the Oratory will prosper more than ever; those who follow Philip, if they persist in what they have undertaken, will die in holiness.'

Francesco passed this on to Philip: he was so totally reliant on God that he had never despaired of the divine help, nor let his soul become despondent, but was always ready to endure all these things with steadfastness, like everything else. Being exercised in this manner, he triumphed over it all through his patience, and said that the purpose of the attack was that he might acquire humility of soul, and since he had begun by reaping that harvest, he would be bound to make a good conclusion, and be found worthy of the consideration of the Almighty.

He replied to the judges with amazingly modest submission, showing that he was prepared to put a stop to his work just as readily as to continue it, and that he was in search of nothing but the glory of God alone, so that he would agree to the wishes of his superiors. This example of humility and this extraordinary constancy induced the authorities to kindly feelings towards him. Once they were convinced of his innocence and his moral integrity, the scheming of his malicious foes was brought to nothing, and he was granted full liberty to live in the manner he chose, and to use whatever means he liked to bring sinners back to God. Those who were with him at the time tell me that they never saw him in the least depressed; on the contrary he gathered strength day by day to further the glory of God. There was only one of those in authority, a man of great influence, who obstinately persisted in attacking the man of God, and he was carried off by a sudden death within the set period of a fortnight, on the 22nd of May, 1559.[86]

---

[86] *This was Cardinal Virgilio Rosari, who died of a sudden seizure while putting on his fascia in order to be received by the Pope.*

Delivered from these trials, he applies himself yet more earnestly to the salvation of his neighbour

64. Meanwhile, it had become public knowledge that Philip once again had permission to act as he pleased, so people began to come back regularly to his room to receive the sacraments and his direction, not only working people but also the aristocracy. The harvest reaped from his spiritual discourses was abundant, and steadily increased so that he was able to bring many to a happy union with Christ, as the Lord helped him to tear them away from their sins. He was so fired with love for his neighbour that you would think he had been born to benefit the world; he gave himself to everyone as if he were the father of all; he lived for everyone, so that he became all things to all men so as to bring all men to Christ.

It happened thus that he was so racked with pity for wicked men that he could hardly contain himself from bursting into tears whenever he saw them, clear evidence of the profound love within him. There was nothing he wanted more than the salvation of his neighbour. He would hear the confessions of those who came to him at any time, and helped them marvellously, either by consoling them or advising them, or in practical ways, with the overriding intention that they should be rid of all anxiety and become aware that God and all his saints cared about them and their salvation, till they were determined at last to use every means to free themselves of sin. He used to encourage them to live a good Christian life, by his frequently repeated words on devout matters, and never omitted to say whatever might be helpful even on minor points. Driven by his ardent longing to join them ever closer to Christ, he neglected himself and his own needs rather than leave them in want.

He always made himself available to everyone, and wanted his room to be open at all times to all comers. He used to say that he wanted no time for himself, no place to be alone. Enough for him if he could help others with whatever means he had. So it happened that he forbade those who later looked after him to stop anyone coming to his room, and they were never to say, 'Philip has gone to bed', or 'Philip has just gone to his room.' What a man, burning with love for his neighbour and the glory of God! He took no pleasure in rest, relaxation or any form of recreation, thinking that there was nothing worth having in this life unless it led to union with God and the salvation of men.

65. It happened often that, after he had finished Mass, many people came to him, and he would receive them all with great charity, thinking more of others than himself, even though that was a time when he preferred to devote himself to contemplation. He had a great desire for prayer and meditation, but for the benefit of others he would put their needs above his own convenience and his longing for holiness. Hence he used to say that for a soul who loves God, there can be nothing more pleasant or delightful than to leave Christ for the love of Christ. There was no toil he would not undertake for the sake of his disciples; he would think out every means that could benefit his sons, and strive to put them into effect, omitting nothing that might be useful in their spiritual progress. If it should happen that any of his sons was suffering temptation, words cannot express the efforts he made and his care to win back that soul.

He adapted himself to the character of each, so that like Saint Paul he made himself all things to all men most wonderfully. What would he hesitate to do, in order to preserve for Christ those he had begotten in Christ? He kept watch for them, with counsel to the best of his ability and labour even beyond his strength; he taught them to pray, warned them to shun the world, entreated them to give themselves totally to God. Even in those early days he used to take his frugal meal alone, so that he could unite them in a deeper love for each other; he was like the mother hen which is drawn by nature to gather her chicks under her wings; he was like the eagle, of which we read in sacred Scripture, 'As the eagle enticing her young to fly, and hovering over them, he spread his wings' [Deut 32:11].

He experiences a wonderful ecstasy

66. During Philip's frequent prayers he was able to keep his mind concentrated, fixed on God and the things of God, so that as we have already noted he was forced to avert his thoughts from the divine, in order to avoid ecstasies. It was easier for Philip to be rapt to God and experience the divine than it is for those of us in whom the fire of the Holy Spirit has grown cold to concentrate on mundane matters. He was often observed to be beside himself while

S. FILIPPO NERI

Rapito in Dio vede nell' Ostia Gesù Cristo benedire quelli, che sono all' orazione.

praying or saying Mass, as if his body might well be present but his soul was already in heaven. Several of us saw him on many occasions, even when he was already old, standing on the tips of his toes while elevating the Sacred Host in the usual manner. Many others saw him rapt out of himself while he was praying.

It was in the same year that the Fathers of the Friary at Santa Maria sopra Minerva, whose superior at the time was Angelo Diaceti, were keeping the devotion of the Forty Hours about some important matter, within the enclosure of their house.[87] Philip was present at the devotion, and was praying in a hidden corner, joining himself with God and quite rapt out of himself. He became like a stone, though still appearing to look at the Blessed Sacrament with his eyes open and a joyful countenance. Somebody noticed this, and they ran to him; finding that the vital heat had all but left his body, they called on him by name to come to himself, and touched him with their hands. All was in vain: he heard nothing, moved not at all, felt nothing. They guessed what had happened, and so carried him between them to a nearby cell, though he was like a dead man, quite without sensation. Here they left him until they saw that he had come to himself, all joyful with the ecstasy. Then Angelo Diaceti questioned him, as did brother Felice of Castelfranco from the same community, about what had happened to him. He yielded to their requests and said, with gentle modesty, 'My dear Fathers, the Lord has heard your prayers in his kindness.' Not content with this answer, they insisted that he should explain everything, to which he finally had to concede, 'While I was praying Christ showed Himself to me, and blessed those around me with the Sign of the Cross'.[88]

---

[87] There are three sworn witnesses to this, all of whom are priests. *The important matter was the attempt by the Jesuits to have the memory and writings of Savonarola condemned; as a life-long admirer of the Florentine prophet, Philip was naturally most concerned that his reputation should be vindicated. Angelo Dicati was also a Florentine, a relation of St Catherine de' Ricci, and had joined the convent of S. Marco only a few years after the death of Savonarola.*

[88] The saints do tell about their visions when they are forced to: see what Surius says of Saint Bernadine (chapter 6), and Theodoret of Philotheus (chapter 2), and George the Monk in the life of Saint Theodore the Siceot.

He is distinguished by the gift of prophecy

67. It was around that year that Cesare Baronio came to the holy Father one Sunday to confess his sins.[89] Philip said to him, 'Go at once to the Hospital of the Holy Spirit, I will hear you later, go at once.' Baronio replied that visiting hour was over, and anyway nothing remained to be done which could be of any use for their health or comfort (in fact he wanted some time to himself). 'Go on', interrupted Philip, 'do what I said, stop delaying over your own affairs which are of no importance. I will not say any more.'

He did obey then, without any further delay, and went to the infirmary, thinking to himself that Philip would not have sent him there without good reason. He started looking round to see who needed his help, and as he searched around the place he noticed a sick man on the point of expiry, with the usual lighted candle by his head. That made him guess this was the one he had been sent to find, so he approached the bed and addressed the patient, who had virtually come to his last breath. He began by asking whether he had confessed his sins and received Holy Communion. With a failing voice he said that he was dying without receiving either sacrament.

Baronio rushed to the Chaplain and asked him to hear the dying man's confession, warning him that any delay would be dangerous. Hearing this, the Chaplain began to make excuses to Baronio for his negligence. 'This patient, sir,' he began, 'came to our hospital last night at an inconvenient time after dinner. He was put into bed, as he had been once before, without having made his proper confession of sins, and then the nurses forgot about him and he was left without the benefit of confession; then he took a sudden turn for the worse and reached a critical point at once without our realising it. Once we did discover this he was virtually unable to move, and unconscious so that he could not speak – it was all over with him. I made sure to fortify him at least with the Anointing, though the other sacraments could not be administered since he was at death's door.'

He told Baronio this, but strange things happened. The Chaplain went to the sick man, warned him of his last extremity and asked if he would like to confess. He nodded, and then, amaz-

---

[89] Cardinal Cesare Baronio gives evidence of this, on oath.

ingly, was able to make his confession and receive the holy Viaticum at the Chaplain's hand. He then expired, in the presence of the astounded Baronio. Thus it happened that in an amazing way the life of the patient was prolonged even though his soul was on the point of departure, long enough for the holy Father to send him assistance, for God had made him aware of his condition, and so he concluded his life fortified by all the sacraments of the Church. After that Baronio returned to Philip and told him the whole story. He replied, 'Perhaps that will teach you to do at once whatever I ask you in future.'

68. I think it not out of place to write something here about the Annals of the same Baronio, since it was by Philip (at God's command) that he was forced to write them: I will tell you the whole thing as it happened.[90] When Baronio first began to give discourses to the people, he used to address them on the eternal punishments destined for the wicked, as well as the perpetual rewards which await the just in heaven, beyond all power of description, but it was on the severity of the divine judgment and the reminder of death that he spoke most earnestly. When our holy Father noticed this, he was led by the Holy Spirit to order Baronio to put an end to that sort of discourse, and apply himself to narrating the history of the Church. He replied that it would be difficult for him, because he thought the audience would gain no benefit from such a project. Philip listened to him, but insisted and told him again and again to carry out what he had been commanded. Finally after repeated orders from Philip, he tackled the Church History. The holy Father kept him at the work, and if he saw Baronio becoming even slightly weary of the task, he rebuked him very strictly and forced him to continue, burning with zeal (to quote Baronio himself) for the struggling Church.[91]

---

[90] Baronio told us this too, on oath. *The twelve massive volumes of the 'Annales' came out at intervals up to 1607, carrying the history of the Church up to the time of Innocent III. They remain an invaluable resource, in response to the notorious 'Centuries' of Magdeburg, which presented a badly distorted history of the Church designed to undermine the Catholic faith.*

[91] See Baronio's thanks in volume 8 of the *Annals*.

Philip had seen in his mind, revealed by the light of God, and breathing a spirit of prophecy, how the Satanic *Centuries* had emerged from the gates of Hell to imperil the Church; he rose to meet the foe, to fight the battles of the Lord for the house of Israel, realising that he had to array no less an army, or at least an equal one, to join the battle. Therefore out of all those who followed him he chose Baronio, and sent him alone to fight against so many enemies, though appearing to be asking him to do something irrelevant. Baronio rose to the task laid on him, and for thirty years has been working happily on what Philip once asked him to do: he has repeated the entire course of history in the Oratory seven times. It was marvellous to watch how Philip anxiously kept him at his work, encouraging him in person, and speaking so forcefully that Baronio thought he was a hard master at this work for God; he refused to let him apply himself even for a moment to any other project. Baronio did in fact often feel some resentment against him, little realising that it was by the inspiration of God that the holy Father was demanding this of him. But I need not tell you how much benefit all this was to the Church, for why need I say anything when the facts speak for themselves?

Through God's guidance he discerns the sacerdotal character on a seventeen-year-old boy

69. It was about that time that a youth called Thomaso came to Rome, aged around sixteen, certainly not more than seventeen. Although he was not of age to receive priestly orders, his relations had forced him to be ordained priest, keeping it secret from everyone else. This was so that they could secure for themselves a very rich inheritance, coming to more than fifty thousand gold pieces, which would only come to them as residual heirs if they could secure that Thomaso was got out of the way by accepting life as a priest. Now when he arrived in Rome, he was brought to blessed Philip about two hours after sunset. As soon as Philip saw him, he said, 'You are a priest, aren't you?' Thomaso replied, 'Certainly, that is true, I am a priest, you are right,' and he told him how it had happened. This discernment was all the more remarkable because the boy was quite unknown to Philip, and being seventeen or under was dressed in lay clothes. The holy Father told Francesco Maria

Tarugi that he saw Thomaso's face shining with the glow which derives from the priestly character. Do not think this story is a myth or a lie: I heard it from Cardinal Francesco Maria Tarugi himself, on oath, and he was very close to Philip.

Now I must pass on from the things Philip did in the reign of Paul IV, though I will insert here a few stories to conclude the chapter, since I do not know in which Pope's reign they took place.

Predictions

70. One day Francesco Maria Tarugi came early to the holy Father, and Philip said to him, 'What do you think has happened to that woman (and he named her)? [92] How long is it since you saw her? Do you know whether she is in good health? I am very concerned about her, so go as soon as you can and see her, and bring me back news straightaway.'

This was a very devout woman, who used to go to confession to Philip, and devoted herself to looking after sick women in St James' Hospital for the Incurable. Although a few days earlier she had been in excellent health, she had been struck down suddenly by an unexpected illness, and brought to death's door, so that the holy candles were already lit by her head, and she was about to depart. Tarugi found her thus on the point of death, and quite unconscious, uttering her last breath: he returned to Philip and told him everything, but he already knew by God's inspiration about her condition, though he had no previous knowledge of it.

A certain army officer began to go to confession to Philip,[93] but when he had not seen him for several days, he knew by God's power what was happening to him, and sent someone to go quickly and discover diligently where he lived, for none of Philip's disciples knew at all where his home was. They sought him out, and when they did find him he was, unknown to everyone, all but devoid of respiration and very close to death.

---

[92] Cardinal Tarugi himself gave this evidence on oath.
[93] The same witness.

He knows the secret thoughts of men

71. A virtue that was particularly noticeable in our holy Father at that period was his ability to detect the most secret thoughts of men very accurately.[94] We have a great many reliable witnesses to this fact, particularly that he could tell by looking at people what their secret sins were. God gave him the ability to look into the wounds of conscience of his disciples, and before his penitents could utter a word, he would explain things to them, in these words, 'You have been at risk in such a way', or, 'You have fallen into this fault; I discovered that while I was praying.' And after saying that, he would give them useful advice, so strengthening their souls in the fear of God and the love of himself that from then on he could direct them by his nod and bidding. He saw the innermost recesses of their souls and told his sons in Christ what their temptations were, while they remained silent in wonder.

Sometimes when he met people, he would give them a buffet, saying, 'I am not striking you, only the devil.' In this he followed the example of the saints who used to drive demons out of people by striking them.[95] There were many who were both learned and prudent who realised that Philip could clearly see their secret sins and thoughts, and were greatly astounded, revering him as a heavenly man of God. In this way he frequently revealed their thoughts and inner feelings to those who consorted with him every day, even those who did not go to him for confession; he did this the better to bring them to the love of heaven and hatred of sin.

72. A youth called Domenico was very troubled one night with actions of impurity, and in the morning was so ashamed that he had not resisted this as much as he should have, that instead of going to see Philip as usual, he remained at home. In the afternoon, however, he did go to the Oratory to listen to the discourses, for

---

[94] Cardinals Borromeo, Tarugi and Baronio have all given sworn witness that Philip could see and understand what people were thinking; as well as them, sixty men of good character have sworn to the same point.

[95] See Dorotheus on Bl. Dositheus; St Gregory's *Dialogues* (book II, chapter 30); Everhelm on Poppo in Surius, Kranz on St Evermodus (book V, chapter 42); Peter Damian on St Romuald, and Surius on St Edmund the bishop.

he never let any day pass without coming, but he was unable to look Philip in the face. He addressed him directly, 'Last night you suffered terrible temptations to lust,' and went on to describe the whole business, so that Domenico was dumb with astonishment. There was another occasion when he revealed some deeply secret matter, I forget what, to the same youth; Domenico alone knew about it, and he had never revealed it to a soul.

I will end this chapter with these last few points: Philip was so skilled in discerning the most secret thoughts, both of his close companions and of those strange to him, that just by looking at someone's face he could tell his state of mind.[96] It would often happen that somebody would come to see him and he would say, 'What is this change I see in your face, my son? Your disease, your vice, is written on your countenance.' By these words he indicated the internal change of character which had happened to those he was talking to. You could often hear him say, 'Now you are a little better, now you are getting well again, now your condition has changed.' I cannot tell you the degree of divine knowledge he had, for it could not be a human skill, this ability to know the inner character of a man just by looking at him. I must not fail to mention that with the same remarkable ability he could detect the inner holiness of people as well.

He predicts the future
A.D. 1559; sede vacante; Philip's age 45

73. There was another youth, from Portugal, called Francesco Basso, who began to go to confession to the holy Father when he was seventeen. Philip encouraged him gently to receive the sacraments frequently and devote himself to prayer, and trained him with various mortifications, with the result that he made great spiritual progress, and won the admiration of everyone, a shining example to others, with the rays of divine grace glowing on his face. When Father Philip asked him to give a discourse on some religious matter, he spoke with ardour and easy eloquence,

---

[96] On this point we have Cardinal Borromeo as a witness, not to mention others.

interspersing prayers to God and the Mother of God, so that he brought holy and devout consolation to those who heard him. He spoke so effectively about the beauty of virtue and the love of God that everyone who heard him was lost in admiration of his power, ardour and ability: the most learned Aluigi Lipomano, Bishop of Verona, was particularly taken by the lad.[97]

That was not the end of the story: he was so steadfast in mind that he could tolerate all sorts of difficulties, however serious, with cheerfulness, and was so eager to be obedient that whatever Philip told him he would do at once, with a good will, as if he had heard the command of an angel. Eventually, in the desire for a more perfect manner of life, he decided to enter the Order of St Dominic. When Philip heard this, he was grieved that the youth was departing from himself and his institute, but after examining the spirit of his vocation, he granted him permission rather than seem to be opposed to the will of God; and so he was clothed in the habit of that holy Order in the year 59 of our century, on the 24th of September. The holy Father was present when this happened, weeping copiously. Francesco Maria Tarugi asked him why he was weeping, and Philip replied, 'I am mourning for the virtue of this youth'.[98]

At the time, Tarugi did not understand what those words meant, or why Philip was weeping, and Philip who alone knew what he meant kept silent, but the outcome showed clearly enough what would be the result of the youth's attempt at adopting a better state of life. He, whom so many had admired for his integrity of life and his burning love for Christ, fell into such a negligent and idle state that, although he did not actually throw off the religious habit, yet he degenerated gradually to be so disturbed and anxious that he became deeply depressed by the way he lived, and considered abandoning the quest for a more severe discipline, and returning to the comforts of this world. He has therefore become a vagrant,

---

[97] *Basso was a typical adventurer of the period; after leaving Rome he was captured by the Turks, but somehow escaped. In 1583 Tarugi discovered him living in Naples. Luigi Lippomani (1500–59) was President of the Council of Trent in 1551–2, and Nuncio to Portugal and Poland.*

[98] *Tarugi himself is the sworn witness to this fact.*

THE YEAR OF CHRIST 1559

avoiding the demands of obedience, with no fixed abode; now he finds one home, now another, now a third, wandering about unhappily, living an unhappy life. He is still alive, detached from his Order and rootless, moving pointlessly here and there.

So now let us move on to the things Philip did when Pius IV succeeded Paul IV as Pope, on the 26th December 1560.

Here our author ends his first book.

BOOK II

VII : WHAT PHILIP DID IN 1560 AND THE THREE SUBSEQUENT YEARS

How Philip discerned the most secret thoughts
A.D. 1560; Pius IV year 1; Philip's age 45–46

74. It was in the year sixty of our century, I think, that a young man of respectable family, who devoted his life to the pursuit of pleasure, happened to bump into a friend while out walking, which friend greeted him very warmly.[99] The latter was a religiously-minded man, and followed the guidance of God in all he did. Pretending to be going somewhere else, he accordingly brought his friend to the discourses in our Oratory, and his friend followed, albeit reluctantly. He listened to the discourses, and afterwards wanted to go home, but his friend, who was eager to save his soul, took him to meet Philip, and then persuaded him to go to confession to him, though nothing had been further from his mind. Hardly had his friend suggested this than the young man imagined he was being ridiculed, and began to resent his good intentions. Nevertheless he was overawed by the appearance of the holy Father, and knelt down before him to make a show of going to confession. Invited to relate his crimes, since he had no intention of admitting anything, he told falsehoods about his sins. The holy Father discerned this, through God's agency, and asked him whether he had not committed any other wrong. Let him open himself in confession! He replied that he had already explained everything quite adequately, but Philip put his arm round him and said, 'It is all lies, my son; the confession of sins you have made is false and deceitful, but come, take my advice, confess everything properly, and if you do that you will be fit to be forgiven.' His words were not wasted, for what he said so influenced the man that he began to realise Philip's true holiness. He began his confession again, telling everything from his childhood, and surrendered himself totally to Philip's guidance. Soon afterwards he joined the Franciscan community known

---

[99] The principal witness to this is Beatrice Caetani, not to mention others.

as the Observants, and there he died in holiness: the name he took, Raffaele Lupi, is held in honour in the community he joined.

He helps a youth who was close to death
A.D. 1561; Pius IV year 2; Philip's age 47

75. In the year 1561, a certain spiritual son of Philip named Sebastiano fell gravely ill, and was likely to die.[100] As he was on the point of death, he began to be tried by grievous temptations from the common enemy of mankind. The devil showed himself under a dark and terrible form, in order to bring the man to despair, laying siege to his soul. The sick man was terrified at the sight, crushed by these afflictions that surrounded him, and brought near to desperation by the horrible apparitions around him. His face twisted with grief, he cried, 'Alas, I am lost! The Lord has abandoned me, wretch that I am! What can I do? I have spent my life to no avail, I am outside the way of salvation!'

For two hours he would say nothing else but that he was in despair, that no medicine could be found to help him, that it was all up with him. Things came to such a point that they gave up any hope of helping his body, for he was clearly dying, but had a faint hope of saving his soul. Being as desperate as that, they had recourse to his parish priest, who said all the right things to the sick man but with no effect. Indeed the moment he saw him, he turned away and shrank back from him as if he had seen some horrible monster, calling out that he had no hope of salvation, and was abandoned by God.

76. So Philip arrived: the moment he set foot in the front hall of the house, he called out, 'What's the matter?' Then he came into the bedroom and took Sebastian gently by the hand. At his touch the sick man was immediately raised from the deepest despair and depression to a great peace of mind, to the amazement of all who saw it. He began to call out aloud, 'Father Philip is driving the devils away – look, the demons flee from Philip! O how powerful

---

[100] There are four witnesses including two priests; all were present and gave evidence on oath.

Philip is! Long live Christ, long live Philip, who has helped me to escape the jaws of hell! Long live the Oratory! Long live my father Philip! I owe him so much – may he live for ever!'

Filled with the greatest delight, he would not stop singing the praises of God. 'My Jesus!' he would cry, 'Jesus my sweet one! Everyone call on Jesus!' As well as calling on Jesus over again, and wishing long life to Philip, he also broke out in these words, 'I can see the face of angels! I can see the angels, they are here, they will take me to heaven!' Then a little later, 'See, there are Archangels, and Thrones, look, there are the Dominations', and he enumerated all the other orders of the angelic hierarchy. Shortly after that, very happy and singing God's praises, he yielded his soul to God in the arms of our holy Father, on the 28th of September, being the vigil of St Michael the Archangel.

He liberates a dying woman from death

77. It was in the December of the same year that a worthy woman called Delia Buscaglia, being in her eighth month of pregnancy, unexpectedly began to give premature birth to her fourth child.[101] As the pains began, the midwife arrived; her name was Bianca. Although very experienced, she was unable to assist the birth, for when the child began to appear, she found that the difficulty lay in that it could not emerge completely, because, unusually, the infant lay in the womb with its feet foremost, ending up partly still in the womb, partly outside. The mother was reduced to the state that her heartbeat was so slow and feeble that she was hardly alive, and she lost consciousness, all but at the end of her life. The best doctors came to her, as she lay in bed, and they tried every means in vain to restore her to health. Bianca herself says that, and adds that if they had attempted to pull the child out by force, since the mother could not expel it herself, they would have torn it in pieces, and the mother would undoubtedly have died at once.

78. The woman lay unconscious like that for nine hours, till the doctors and her servants thought she was dead, but Gasparo Brissio,

---

[101] Both Delia herself and her husband Gasparo have told me this, on oath.

anxious over his wife, went to see Philip, and begged him as earnestly as he could, with total confidence, to come and help his dying wife. Philip was touched by his devotion, and came to the woman, finding her apparently dead. He came closer, and put the cap he was wearing over her stomach,[102] then raised his hands to heaven, weeping and sighing from the depths of his heart; then he knelt down and asked the women around him to recite the Our Father and the Hail Mary with him for the dying soul. After that he called the woman by name, and not without result: Delia awoke as if from a deep sleep, to the amazement of all who saw it, and answered Philip quite clearly, though it had been nine hours since she had lost the use of her speech. 'What do you want me to do, Father?' she said, and Philip answered, 'This is what I want: that you should give yourself totally to Christ, and love Him above all else with all your heart.' She replied, 'May God help me to love Him!' and then after a pause she added, 'Help me, Father, I am not well, I am dying in childbirth.' Philip said, 'Be of good heart, Christ will save you', and signing her body with the sign of the Cross, he went out. Now here is a miracle; he had hardly left the room when the woman was suddenly delivered of the dead child, with no human help, and with no pain. It happened so easily that she was instantaneously healed from her imminent peril, and feeling perfectly well she got out of bed. This too we should recall, that as Philip left the bedroom he met Gasparo, who was sad and in tears, but taking him by the hand he looked into his eyes so long that it made him blink. Then he let him go and said, 'Go to your wife: God has taken pity on you both, so be grateful and make sure that you always pay attention to keeping his commandments.' Gasparo immediately rushed into the room and found his wife, who had been dying only just before, now safe and in her full health, though the child had been born dead.

He helps those close to death in their last struggle

79. Now it remains for us to tell a few stories about his care for the sick and the dying. He was always concerned for the unwell,

---

[102] Compare this with book 4 of Godfrey's life of St Bernard; chapter 4 of the life of Peter of Asturia, bishop; and Abbot Gaufried on Peter, Bishop of Tarentas, chapter 33. Many miracles have been worked by the clothing of the saints while

especially those who were known to him for any reason; he would visit them every day and help them with money and service. He did not hesitate to spend the night with those who were in imminent danger of death, if it were necessary; he could strengthen them and encourage them for their last struggle. Those who trusted too much in themselves he would bring to a state of humility, while those whom the demons were driving to despair of God's mercy he would lead towards hope in God and divine confidence, in a marvellous way.

Let us turn to specific examples. In that year Philip displayed great charity towards Iacopo Marmitta as he was approaching his end.[103] He was secretary to Cardinal Ricci of Montepulciano, a man of intelligence, prudence and education. He used to confess his sins several times a week to Philip, who was very fond of him, and he received Communion at the church of San Girolamo. When he fell into the disease which was to result in his death a few days later, he became deeply depressed, for it was a serious sickness which brought him great pain. Iacopo did not bear this with the strength and constancy of mind which would have been appropriate, for the lower part of his mind rebelled, and he complained bitterly about the disease. The Holy Father warned him to trust in God, to recover the joyful heart he had lost and revive his soul, asking him to say with him, 'Our God is our refuge and strength: a helper in troubles...', and the sick man continued in a wavering voice, 'which have found us exceedingly' [Ps 45:2]. Then Philip gave himself to prayer, to drive temptations from Iacopo's mind, and so it resulted that the warrior found rest, his heart lightened. He was not so much delivered from fear as made so courageous that he sent forth his spirit with exultation, on the 28th December, when he was sixty-two years and two months old.

A Prediction

A.D. 1562; Pius IV year 3; Philip's age 47

80. In the year 62 of our century, a young man of good family called Giovan Thomaso used to attend the discourses every day,

---

they were still alive, as you can see clearly in the accounts of their lives.

[103] The sworn witness to this story is Giovan Francesco Bordini, Bishop of Avignon.

but more to make fun of the institute than with any intention of saving his soul.[104] When those near him noticed this, they told the Holy Father, and complained a lot about his irreverence. Philip replied, 'Let him behave as he pleases; put up with him, I beg you, with a tranquil mind.' But since he continued to be a nuisance, those who attended the discourses again complained about him to Philip, and heard the same answer as before. And eventually God worked the miracle. A short time afterwards, though no one expected it, he was so struck by the procedure and the way the Fathers behaved that he came to the point of reaping the benefit of the discourses being preached, and found understanding of the things of heaven, with contempt for the world. He abandoned his business, renounced his riches and honours, and determined to follow the counsels of Christ. He joined the order of St Dominic, and on the 10th February took the sacred habit at the friary of S. Maria sopra Minerva, to the astonishment of those who saw such a sudden change in him. He died after a few months of his novitiate, fervent with devotion and full of confidence. Another youth from Philip's group, Paulo, also joined the same community on the same day and month; he made great spiritual progress in a little time, and died, also full of faith and hope. When he became a friar he changed his name and chose to be called Giovanni.[105]

The Death of Giovan Battista Salviati

81. It was on 15th October that year that Giovan Battista Salviati died – we have mentioned him before, since he and his wife Porzia led a heavenly life on earth under Philip's direction, to the great admiration of the whole city, who were aware of their former wealth, rank, youth and beauty, and the luxury they had known.[106] When Salviati was stricken by a serious illness, and was on the point of death, he was visited by our holy Father, and by Vincenzo Ercolani, then prior of the friary of S. Maria sopra Minerva (he was

---

[104] *This was Giovan Tommaso Arena of Catanzaro, as the Italian version reveals.*
[105] *Gallonio must be recounting a personal memory here; the young friar may be identified with Paolo Grillenzoni, who had been in the service of Cardinals Sforza and Alessandro.*
[106] *All of Philip's disciples are very familiar with what is told of Giovan Battista.*

afterwards bishop, first of Sarno, then of Imola, finally of Perugia). As death threatened in the evening, he received Holy Viaticum, and then spoke aloud in a clear voice without fear, in great tranquillity and constancy of mind, and conscious that his death was imminent; they all heard him say, 'I rejoiced at the things that were said to me: We shall go into the house of the Lord.' [Ps 121:1] Not long afterwards he breathed forth his spirit, giving himself entirely to his heavenly homeland, with a joyful glance at Father Philip, his face shining and serene. After his death his wife became a nun at Florence, where she happened to be a year later; she afterwards returned to Rome for a change, and founded a convent on the Viminal dedicated to St Catherine; she still lives there today.

Philip is gravely ill

82. Philip often suffered from serious and dangerous diseases, as the Lord regularly gave his servant new opportunities for winning a crown of gold. Often he was gravely ill twice in a single year.[107] I myself cannot ever remember a year passing in which he was not seriously unwell, from the time that I first began to associate with him, that is from 1570 to 1595 when he died. When he was ill, no matter what suffering his fever would cause him, he never seemed to take the least notice; he tolerated the inconvenience of the sickness as if God had sent it, not just with resignation but even with joy, and no one could be more patient. Nobody ever heard him utter a word of complaint about his illness, or ever ask any of his friends to help. What words he did speak were such as displayed his great holiness and humility; he would speak with tears, to encourage the bystanders to think of religion, and indeed all the words, deeds and actions of this servant of God were to this end, revealing to us his greatness in pain and sickness, as eventually in his death. The only thing that grieved Philip, despite his calmness of character, was that he had squandered his life uselessly, without

---

[107] The saints are recorded to have suffered serious illnesses: see the Register of Pope St Gregory, book II, epistle 32; book V, epistle 61; book VII, ep. 16 and 127; and book VIII, ep. 35. You could also look at the lives of Theodore the Siceot and Bernard the Abbot.

achieving anything good in his own estimation. The only thing he wanted to do while he was ill was to continue to hear confessions, unless the doctors forbade it, for he was prompt to obey the orders of his doctors with regard to the care of his body.

83. In the year 1562 he fell into an illness so serious that he was close to death.[108] That was the beginning of Philip's debility. He began by being affected with a sharp pain located in the right arm, which was continuous and acute. The pain then spread through the arm into the nerves of his muscles, and became continuous there. To the pain succeeded a fever, which began by being slight, and then increased rapidly to the point that all hope of life was lost, in the opinion of the doctors Hippolito Salviani and Bartolomeo Eustachio of Urbino; all they could hope for was to delay his death.[109]

Meanwhile our holy Father's disciples, fearful that they would lose so excellent a father, besieged God with prayers, lamentations and fasting; they visited the most holy places in the city to pray, and climbed the Scala Santa at the Lateran on their bare knees. Others remained by him in turns, day and night, thinking their greatest privilege was to minister to their holy Father in his needs, if the sick man gave them leave. And so, when all had despaired of his life, he was given Viaticum, so that nothing would be missing to sanctify his death, and he was given the last Anointing, and his followers were lamenting the sad loss of their dearest mentor – but here is a miracle of God's power! Although all considered that he had virtually died, after he was fortified by the sacraments of the Church the fever suddenly left him to the astonishment of the doctors, the pain was greatly relieved, and within a few days he was quite restored to his former health.

I must not neglect to add that during his illness, when he heard others lamenting his condition, he said to them boldly and in full

---

[108] Cardinals Tarugi and Baronio are the sources for this. When Philip was ill he was attended by Angelo Velli and the bishop of Avignon we have already mentioned, as well as others.

[109] *The Italian version mentions a third doctor, Stefano Cerasio, a Neapolitan who worked at the Consolazione hospital. Salviani, a Roman, was in general practice near S. Girolamo, and Eustachio was professor of medicine at the Sapienza.*

consciousness, 'I am prepared, and not disturbed, but although the Lord has laden me with so many benefits, for some reason I do not find my spirit refreshed and strengthened enough for such an important step, which makes me believe that it is not yet time for me to pass from here.' Then he said to Francesco Maria Tarugi, 'It is not up to me to make myself ready for a holy death, for I am certain that this disease will pass away altogether.'

His Miracles

84. In the same year Maurizio Anerio fell ill, and as the disease increased, came into danger of death.[110] The doctors had given him up, and he was expecting the approach of death, and had already nourished himself with the Body of Christ for the new life he was to enter, and fortified himself for the struggle with the enemy with the anointing of holy oil. Philip came to visit him, when he was all but unconscious; he comforted his tearful wife and the neighbours who had gathered around, and then went to the dying man, urging the bystanders to implore the help of the Virgin Mary for his recovery. He made them all kneel down, and laid his hands on the dying man, and having done that he went out without anybody noticing. He had hardly left when Anerio, who had lain silent from just after sunset until late in the afternoon of the following day, suddenly opened his eyes as if recovering, to the astonishment of the others who had never seen anything like it; then as his spirit revived, he began to speak rapidly, and declared that he was entirely recovered from his illness, which astounded the doctors. Finally, as the next day dawned (Philip had come to see him late the previous afternoon) he got out of bed, healthy and strong, and never stopped telling everyone joyfully, all over the place, what a great grace he had received, and crediting Philip with being the cause of the wonder. He lived on until the year 1593, when he fell asleep in the Lord on the 28th of January.

---

[110] We have sworn eyewitnesses for this story too.

The death of the devout woman Bradamante
A.D. 1563; Pius IV year 4; Philip's age 49

85. In the year 63 of our century, it happened that Bradamante Aneria passed from this life in holiness and devotion.[111] She was a woman of extraordinary goodness, and by the example of her life brought many of her relations and others to Christ; she was tireless in performing works of mercy, and constant in prayer. But I must by no means pass over the good that Philip did to her when she was seriously ill.[112] Some years before she had been suffering from terrible headaches, of such severity that no medicines were of any use. Philip came to visit her, after she had tried doctors and treatments to no avail. He took her by the hand, and tore off the bandages she had around her head. 'Silly woman,' he said, 'what do you want with these bandages?' He had hardly spoken before the woman stood up, and found that she had been restored to her former health, to the extent that she never after felt any of the same pain.

She was one of those whom Philip had won for Christ in the year 1551. One day, around that year, Philip was walking through the Hospital of the Holy Ghost, and happened to be approaching the place where wounds were treated.[113] Suddenly inspired by God, he turned to his followers and said, 'Let's go in here, I feel God wants me to go in here.' Saying this, he went straight to a bed where someone was dying; he found him not only unable to move but unable even to talk, as his spirit failed him. Philip called him, with the marvellous effect that, to the amazement of those who saw it, the dying man was first able to speak, then to make his confession, then to receive holy Viaticum, and finally to end his life in a holy and religious manner.

---

[111] *She died in August, on the feast of the Assumption of the Virgin. The Italian version names her as Bradamante Pacelli, a member of a well-known Roman family. Her sister was Fulginia Anerio, whose devotion to St Philip caused her husband Maurizio also to become his follower (cf. paragraph 33).*

[112] Cardinal Tarugi told me the whole story, and swears to it.

[113] The sworn witnesses to this are Giovan Francesco Bordini and Domenico Giordano, a priest, both of whom were present. St Bernard tells the same story in his life of St Malachy the bishop.

VIII : FROM THE YEAR OF CHRIST
1564 TO 1571

The beginning of the Congregation
A.D. 1564–5; Pius IV year 5–6; Philip's age 49–51

86. Soon after Philip had recovered from the disease we have been talking about, the citizens of Florence [resident in Rome] sent a deputation to him to ask him to take charge of their church, which is famous under the name of San Giovanni de' Fiorentini. Philip replied that he would see about that, for he never undertook any important matter without consulting the will of God. However, after commending the matter to God for a long time, he did agree, and said that the idea pleased him, but that he first wanted to have some of his disciples ordained priest, and that he himself did not intend to move away from the church of San Girolamo.

The Florentines agreed to his suggestion, and allocated a house for them to live in and a stipend to support them. Meanwhile, Philip had three of his followers ordained. The first of the companions to reach the rank of priesthood was Cesare Baronio of Sora, who is now famous throughout the world because of his scholarly edition of the *Annals of the Church*. Not long after Philip died, our present Holy Father, Clement VIII, made him a Protonotary of the Holy See, very much against his will, one of those called *Partecipanti*. Then, despite Baronio's great reluctance, he promoted him from Protonotary Apostolic to being enrolled in the Sacred College of Cardinals, on the fifth of June, 1596.

The second of them was Giovan Francesco Bordini, who was appointed by our same Holy Father bishop first of Cavaillon, on the 10th February 1592, and then of Avignon, in '98. The third was Alessandro Fedeli, a Roman, a man of marvellous innocence and integrity. The Congregation enjoyed his gentle manner and outstanding virtues for thirty three years altogether, until he died of the stone in our house in October of 1596. These last two priests, Giovan Francesco and Alessandro, were ordained priest on the same day.

87. The community began in 1564. To begin with, even though they went to the church of San Girolamo every day, each one lived under Philip's individual direction, without any set regulations. The first of the Fathers who began to live together in community were Cesare Baronio and Alessandro Fedeli, shortly followed by his brother's son Germanico, who was at the time a promising teenager. He had come to Rome two years before, to study, and had put himself entirely under Philip's guidance and direction. After that Giovan Francesco Bordini joined them; the fourth was Jaime Salort, a Spaniard, a very straightforward man. The fifth was Giovanni Rausico, who was the first appointed to be the parish priest, because he had some experience of the care of souls.

With these first members, Philip started his Congregation. Not long after, Francesco Maria Tarugi joined them: he was still a layman, but shone like a star among his contemporaries, a man full of the Apostolic spirit, and worthy of great honour. He was a relation of Julius III, and had once been a chamberlain to Ranuccio Farnese, the Cardinal of Sant'Angelo. At the bidding of Pius V, he joined the train of his sister's son Michele Bonelli, the Cardinal of Alessandria, on his legatine mission to the kings of Spain and France. On this mission his companion was Hippolito Aldobrandino, who was then an auditor of the Rota, afterwards raised to the Sacred Purple by Sixtus V, and who is today the shepherd of the entire Catholic Church, under the name of Clement VIII. When Pope Clement first held the Keys of the Church of Rome, he determined to endow our Tarugi with ecclesiastical rank. Thus in the year of Christ's birth 1593, in December, he first appointed him Archbishop of Avignon, then in '96 he made him a Cardinal on the 5th of June. This new and highly exalted rank could bring no fresh honour to a man of moderation, already adorned with all virtues, save only that his position could be of benefit to many others. Finally, in 1597, His Holiness decided that he should resign the see of Avignon and undertake the administration and rule of that of Siena, as it has come to pass.

When Tarugi joined the community, he was followed by Angelo Velli of Palestrina, who later became the superior of our Congregation after Baronio: he is still our Provost, a man who does not need me to praise him. Tarugi and Angelo Velli, although they are considered among the earliest companions of our holy Father, were not ordained priest as early as the others.

88. The Fathers lived under the same roof, and had but one heart and one soul, loving each other with mutual affection. They all endeavoured to do what was pleasing to God in every way. Philip governed his disciples with gentleness and kindness, making himself all things to all men, for he was as a father to them, enabling them to carry out their duties more by paternal advice and encouragement than by imperious authority. What was remarkable in him, and worthy of imitation, is that he hardly ever employed commands and orders so as to get people to do things, but spoke to them in a mild and friendly manner. He was able to exact obedience in carrying out what was necessary, even if it were difficult or disagreeable, through his humorous and gentle admonitions, as if he were requesting rather than requiring, more easily than others attempt to do by direct commands. He won the minds of all in such a way that he could guide them as he wished.

Eventually he composed some Constitutions, in order to introduce structure and form to religious life, establishing them by common consent, so that everyone agreed to them readily and with enthusiasm. One of his wise principles was that there is no more certain or safer method of advancing on the way one intends to go than by following an experienced guide; on the other hand there is nothing more perilous than trying to govern oneself by one's own will, setting aside the authority of the Provost.

89. Now we must return to our Fathers, who walked together in harmony in the Lord, and began to labour vigorously, tending Christ's vine among the Florentines, harvesting a rich vintage of souls. They heard the confessions of all who came to them; those who were priests administered the holy Eucharist; after dinner they returned to San Girolamo where they gave the customary discourses to the crowds on sacred subjects. On Sundays, as well as the usual daily Oratory discourses, either Baronio or Bordini would preach extempore to the people, who came eagerly to listen to them in the church of the Florentines. It thus happened that in a short space of time the number of priests grew, as did the crowd of those

who gathered there to hear them. By their word and example, they inspired the people to virtue and to undertake every sort of good work; they recovered many whose lives had been scandalous so that not only did they become moderate and chaste, but turned away from all passing things and were gently brought to Christ's saving counsel and the frequent use of the sacraments. Others, by often hearing the discourses, were encouraged to join our institute and embrace our way of life.

Four of the Fathers, who were considered suitable for the task, were chosen in turn to deliver the discourses to the people in the Oratory, on every day of the week except Saturday, as is still the custom among our Fathers. They preached not themselves but Christ, and him crucified; their discourses turned on moral matters, in a straightforward manner, adapted to all manner of folk, particularly the common people. For this reason they avoided all subtle enquiries, and instructed the people about the necessary, not the spectacular, without any pomposity. Following the example of the saints, they spoke about what would heal the thoughts of men; of the four speakers, the first two would talk particularly about questions of morality, the next two on the lives of the saints or the course of Church history in chronological sequence, each one being allotted half an hour to speak.

90. For a long time the Fathers continued to instruct the people on the things of God in the church of San Girolamo, until the Florentines constructed a splendid building designed for the purpose, on the banks of the Tiber, and here they began to deliver the spiritual discourses. For several years the Fathers lived like this, sharing the same house, surrendering themselves and their property to the service of God and the harvest of souls. They had a single purse, a common table, and that frugal and sober. They prayed and meditated much. The priests celebrated Mass – there were five of them to begin with – and the others communicated on the Bread of Heaven either daily or on alternate days. This manner of life was generally approved, so that many intelligent and learned priests and laymen came to join the community of the Fathers, for not all were prepared to bind themselves with the vows of religious life. This, then was the origin of our Congregation.

91. It is now time for us to move on to discuss what Philip did under Pius V: already in the reign of Pius IV, Philip had foreseen that he would be Pope, and knew him already, for he had heard a voice in the very still of the night, saying that Brother Michael, Cardinal of Alessandria, would become Pope. He was elected on the 7th of January, 1566, and reigned for six years, three months and twenty-three days.

He liberates Pietro Vittrici from death
A.D. 1566; Pius V year 1; Philip's age 51–52

In the same year 1566, Pietro Vittrici of Parma was bedridden, suffering from a serious disease.[114] The illness afflicted him to the point that the doctors gave him up, and his family mourned him as one dead. Philip then came to him, laid his hands on the dying man, and prayed for him; the result was that he immediately began to feel much better, and two days later was able to get out of bed quite well. He is still alive, and comes to confession three times a week, receiving Holy Communion as frequently, in our church of Santa Maria in Vallicella.[115]

He helps Antonio Fucci make a holy death

92. It was in that same year that Antonio Fucci, a doctor, discovered for himself what Philip's care for the dying was like. Philip spoke about him one day, when I was among the company, and told us that Antonio once visited a certain maiden, who was very devout but suffering from a terrible disease, and found her in an ecstasy. He waited until the sick woman had come to herself, and as soon as she emerged from her ecstasy he heard her say, 'Hey, Tonio, how beautiful you looked among the angels! You looked splendid!' He was so scared by this, that he went straightaway to the holy Father, and told him everything that had happened. Then

---

[114] Pietro himself is the sworn witness to this story, among others.

[115] While this book was in the press at Rome, the said Pietro Vittrici was taken from us, fortified by the sacraments of the Church, on the 25th March, aged 79. *Vittrici, a servant of Cardinal Boncompagni who became Gregory XIII, contributed largely to the building of the Chiesa Nuova.*

he went home, but the same day fell into an illness from which he was not to recover. Philip visited him every day, with great affection, and strengthened his soul with talk about God, but as the disease took hold increasingly, and death approached, the devil appeared to him in the form of a doctor who bade him be of good cheer, promising him long life, and assuring him he would survive this illness.[116] The sick man believed this, although he did not know who the doctor was, but he was advised by the holy Father and his other friends to recognise that it was a devilish deceit, and so with a willing heart he accepted the death which came to him that same day. He died with every indication of holiness.

Now I must not pass over another thing about that man, who had been among Philip's earliest disciples. Because of the temptations of the flesh which the devil brought upon him particularly when treating women, he decided to give up his medical practice.[117] However, when he told Philip this (for Philip was then his confessor), he received the following reply, 'You cannot, and should not, give up your medical work, because you need the income you receive from your practice, to provide food and clothing for your family, who are in need. So carry out all your duties without anxiety, and believe me, you will not in future experience any difficulty of the flesh.' The fellow believed what Philip said, and shielded only with his obedience, he continued to practise medicine till the end of his life, without suffering any feelings of lust, whether he were treating men or women.

In that same year, Francisco Soto, a Spaniard from Osma, joined our community.

A new attack on the Oratory
A.D. 1567; Pius V year 2; Philip's age 52

93. At the beginning of the year of Christ 1567, a new storm blew up against Philip and his companions, for there were plenty of people who were suspicious about our institute and schemed day and

---

[116] I heard this part from Cardinal Tarugi.
[117] Cardinal Tarugi was also aware of this matter, not to mention other witnesses.

night to put an end to it. However, despite the vehemence of those who opposed our work, God assisted us, and all the schemes of our enemies came to nothing.[118]

He restores to health a youth whose eyes were bad

I think it was in the same year that a teenager called Giovan Battista Crescio was suffering seriously from ophthalmia, and had such a flow of hot tears that he could not bear either a draft or any light.[119] When he had been suffering from this complaint for many days, the doctors decided that the youth could only be helped by cautery. However his uncle Giovanni disapproved of this treatment, and brought Giovan Battista to Philip. 'Here is my sister's son who has bad eyes', he said, 'and he begs you to pray to God for him.' Philip listened to this, and placed his hands over the affected part at once. 'From this disease,' he said, 'you shall be free.' He began to feel better at once, and after a few days had passed with no extra medical attention, he quite recovered his previous health.

The harvest of souls
A.D. 1568; Pius V year 3; Philip's age 53–4

94. Now we must pass on to the harvest of souls reaped in the year 1568. It might be more decent for men to make their own silent assessment of the results achieved among those who attended the Oratory than for me to vaunt about them in this history: what I will say is that as many people used to flock to the discourses as the place could possibly hold. Some record of that period is preserved in the book which Giovanni de Rossi dedicated to Philip in 1569, and it is not inappropriate to quote in my history, as follows:[120]

---

[118] *During the pontificate of St Pius V, certain officials were greatly suspicious of any unusual devotions, citing in particular Philip's public processions such as the Seven Churches devotion. See paragraph 98 for the complete vindication of the Oratory in the eyes of the reforming Pope.*

[119] It is the said Giovan Battista who gives evidence about this, on oath.

[120] The book was published in Italian, under the title of *Esamine* [*et ammaestramenti cristiani, raccolti e ridotti dalla spagnola nella lingua italiana da Alfonso Ruspogiari*, Bologna, per G. Rossi, 1589].

Of all the things that impressed me at Rome last year [i.e. 1568], I was most delighted at the sight of such a crowd of pious people going every day to the Oratory at the church called San Girolamo della Carità. This remarkable form of devotion seemed to me to surpass in glory the splendour of all those ancient famous buildings, all those fine palaces of great men, all the marvels which were shown me. I was all the more pleased and impressed by seeing so many very distinguished men among people of all classes gathering together so eagerly to listen to the private advice and sermons on religious matters which were conducted by you [he means Philip] out of pure love for the Christian Faith and their salvation. As a result of this, very often your spiritual sons developed a holy longing to set aside all things of this world and to serve God alone; thus today they can be found in different monasteries and holy religious families where they have consecrated their whole lives to the worship of God in lifelong service. And so on.

That is a quotation from his dedicatory epistle, translated from Italian into Latin, which gives you an idea of what the attendance at the discourses was like, how many people came to us, and what a harvest of souls there was in those days. I know about this not only from the epistle I have quoted but from what people who were present at those discourses have told me, for my evidence comes from eyewitnesses who are quite reliable and trustworthy.

A Prediction
A.D. 1569; Pius V year 4; Philip's age 54–55

95. In the year of Our Lord 1569, Costanzo Tassone was invited from Milan to Rome by Pius V in order to be given an honour. He came to San Girolamo with the good intention of visiting Philip and greeting him. When Philip heard of this, he called two of his disciples, teenagers and younger than the rest, namely Ottavio Paravinico (whom long afterwards, in 1591, Gregory XIV made a Cardinal for his singular qualities) and Germanico Fedeli, and asked them to lie down pretending to be corpses on the threshold of the door that Costanzo was about to enter, and to keep on lying

there until he had passed through. Nobody understood at the time what Philip meant by this, but it all became clear from events that followed. Only a few days later, Costanzo, who had been in excellent health, was suddenly stricken by a serious and deadly disease, and died of it.[121]

He delivers a dying man from death

It was at the same period that a cleric of the Vatican Basilica named Lorenzo Cristiano, aged about twenty or a little more, fell ill. As his health declined the doctors gave him up, and after having received comfort through the sacraments of Confession, Holy Communion and Anointing, he was hourly expected to die. He was in bed and virtually unconscious when Philip came to visit him, an hour after nightfall. He asked those in the room how the sick man was, and then prayed to God. Rising from his prayer, he said, 'Enzo, you are surely not going to die of this disease!' and went close to him, laid his hands on him, and called his name out aloud. Nor was he disappointed: the dying man was woken by Philip's shouting and opened his eyes at once. He felt better, took a little food, and after a few hours recovered his senses fully, was able to speak, and as the fever left him, became perfectly well again. In the meantime his doctor, Pietro Crispi, was summoned by the attendants to come back to him in the morning, and feel his pulse. Realising from the state of the pulse that he had recovered, he was amazed. 'It was a greater hand than mine that saved you, Lorenzo,' he said, 'you have been cured by no human skill, but by God's agency.' [122]

He endures new difficulties for Christ
A.D. 1570; Pius V year 5; Philip's age 55

96. It is ever God's way to challenge his friends frequently, so that he might increase their merits, and so no one should be surprised that Philip was constantly permitted to be tried by new tribulations, some of them very severe, brought upon him either by men

---

[121] Both Cardinal Tarugi and Germanico Fedeli himself have given sworn evidence of this.

[122] Cardinal Alessandro Medici was the sworn witness for this story.

or by the very devils. We read about the just that, 'many are the afflictions of the just: but out of them all will the Lord deliver them' [Ps 33:20]. Philip embraced the afflictions laid upon him with an ever-constant soul and a cheerful countenance; not only did he not despair under them, but he never felt himself deprived of his peace of mind even to the slightest extent. He suffered persecution from strangers and from his own brethren, and refuted them through the power of the Holy Spirit with patience and kindness. Just as we read about the greatest of the saints, there was no lack of members of his own following who said the holy Father was over-endowed with stupidity (as they put it) and excessively uncultured. All this he treated with laughter, being ready to bear much more for the sake of Christ's love, and in this we can see a real resemblance to those great saints who were superiors of religious communities, such as Saba, Theodosius the Cenobiarch, Nicetas, Romuald, and Francis, not to mention those great bishops Martin and Gregory, and so many others about whom the same or even greater criticisms were circulated, though they themselves were men of great prudence and kindness.

97. Towards the end of the year 1569 and the beginning of the next year (which happened to be 1570), the Lord tested Philip in another way. The devil could not bear to see the harvest which was gathered from our Oratory for the benefit of souls, and having some intimation of what was to come, he put it into the mind of some of those who disapproved of the style of our institute to denounce Philip to the Supreme Pontiff, under the pretext of a concern for devotion. They accused him of being responsible for many foolish things being said in the daily discourses about religious matters which took place in the Oratory in his presence, at his bidding and request. Such things, they said, indicated great stupidity and incompetence, as well as extraordinary arrogance on the part of those who gave the discourses.

When this came to the ears of the Supreme Pontiff, he was afraid that some new outrage was about to break out, and thought the business should be carefully examined. He therefore summoned to him two of the most learned men of the Dominican family, Paulino, a citizen of Lucca, and Alessandro, who is now bishop of Forlì.[123]

He spoke to them privately, not only with no other witnesses but separate from each other, and told them what he had heard about our Oratory, with his fears that Philip, whom he considered to be something of a fool, might make mistakes in dealing with matters of Christian doctrine. He therefore required them in the name of holy obedience to attend the Oratory every week, pretending to be there for some other purpose, and to listen to the discourses; if they heard anything contrary to the true faith and morality, spoken by any of those present who might be unskilled in theology in reply to Philip's questions about the catechism, they should notice it, commit it to memory and report it back to him at once. (It was at that period our custom that during the discourses even laymen could be asked to give a reply on the matters treated in the Oratory.)

98. The Dominican fathers accordingly went to the Oratory several times a week, and applied themselves to investigating and recording everything that was going on, though each was unknown to the other. They observed what Philip's spirit was, what sort of doctrine he taught, what was his way of life. Along with the crowds they listened to the discourses, and took careful note of the manner of delivery and the purport of what was said. They found themselves lost in admiration for Philip's facility in speaking, his earnestness and his amazing confidence; he did his best to appear uneducated, in disparagement of himself, but in every question that was put to him he replied so appositely that he never failed to hit the target, which absolutely astounded the Dominicans.

Impressed by this, they gave the Pope a better report of our Oratory and of Philip's learning and devotion than had ever been delivered before, and assured him that they had found everything in order. Thus with the help of God the whole affair was rapidly concluded without any sort of judicial interference, and everything was as satisfactory as before. That Philip had foreseen this,

---

[123] *Paulino Bernardini (1518–85) was given responsibility for introducing the reforms of Trent in Naples and Chieti, and was a famous preacher and great friend of the Oratory. Alessandro Francheschi (1535–1601) was another famous preacher; he had actually retired from the diocese of Forlì by the time Gallonio went to press.*

through God's aid, we can learn from the following incident. The Pope complained one day about our Oratory and Philip's spirit to a certain important man, with no other person present.[124] That same day Philip met the man in question, who happened to be ill in bed, and told him all about what the Pope had said to him in secret about himself and about our Oratory. It was not long after this that the Pope was satisfied by the investigation, and thereafter for the rest of his life held Philip and his companions in the greatest esteem and affection. I ought to mention what many people have noticed, that God punished those who attacked Philip.[125] There are many examples of this happening, but I will pass over them so as not to offend anyone.

Predictions

99. In that same year, 1570, Giovan Angelo Crivelli came to Philip to confess his sins, as he usually did, on the Thursday of Holy Week, being in good health and strength.[126] He had hardly knelt down before him when Philip looked at him intently and said, 'Be prepared, have a firm heart and a strong will, fear nothing, but let your heart be bold. God wants something of you, I don't know what, for His greater glory.' Giovan Angelo replied, 'I am not afraid now, Father, I am ready for any eventuality: let God do with His servant as He wishes; I have placed my life at His disposal, I am entirely His.' Philip answered, 'And what if the Lord wishes to try you with the most severe affliction?' 'I conform myself to Him' he answered promptly, 'as always I will place His will before anything I might want.' Philip concluded, 'Be careful, then, summon your strength to sustain with a calm and willing heart whatever this great matter is that will come upon you with God's permission.'

Giovan Angelo returned home soon afterwards, still in good health, but as the day wore on a severe sickness suddenly afflicted

---

[124] It was Cardinal Alessandro de' Medici who told the story under oath. *He himself was the 'important man'*.

[125] There were several sworn witnesses to this matter, including Cardinal Baronio.

[126] There are three sworn witnesses to this.

him, so that he died four days later, a death he accepted with a cheerful mien, strengthened by the sacraments of the Church.

He delivers a woman from a demon

100. Philip used to be diligent in examining the true case of those who were reported as being possessed, and he was not easily convinced that anyone was being troubled by the devil. Any symptoms that might be taken as evidence for this, he usually referred to natural causes, for instance a disease arising from black bile, or an affection of the womb, or some damage to the brain. For this reason it was rare that he applied himself to the exorcism of one possessed, except when it was truly necessary, and he warned his disciples wisely about this, telling them that for their own safety they should never try to exorcise a woman unless there were many others present.

It was in that year, I think, that a noblewoman called Caterina came to Rome from Aversa, and she was possessed by unclean spirits.[127] Although she had never studied classics, she was speaking Latin fluently and accurately, and when questioned in Latin, she replied in the same language. You would think she had been deeply educated and polished in classical literature and Latin grammar, though in fact she had never been to school nor had any tuition.[128] Moreover, her mental and physical strength was such that is was hardly possible for four strong men to lift her up, restrain her or set her down, as the demon gave the woman strength, though she was naturally frail and weak. And so they brought her to Philip. He began to exorcise her, and had hardly finished the prayers of deliverance before the demon was driven out of her.[129]

---

[127] I have heard the whole story from Philip's disciples who were in his following at that period; one of these is Cardinal Tarugi.

[128] We hear that the possessed can speak in other languages from St Jerome's life of Hilarion, Gregory of Tours on the miracles of St Martin (book I, chap. 2), Abbot Einhard on the Translation of SS. Marcellinus and Peter (book III, chapter 13), and St Antony (part 3, title 23, chap. 14).

[129] The saints often spent a long time over delivering the possessed. See St Jerome on Hilarion, Palladius on Lausiacas (chap. 28), the lives of Sts Auxentius, Theodore the Siceot and Anastasius the Martyr, and Baronio's *Annals*, vol. VIII, year 713.

One day the holy man was chastising Caterina mercilessly with iron chains, and the demon began to cry out in a loud voice, 'Beat me, beat me, strike me, kill me!' and repeated those words again and again. It was remarkable to see how the woman never moved in the slightest during the whole time she was being beaten by Philip, but remained motionless in the same place like a marble statue. I should not omit to mention that whenever she realised that her family had called Philip in, she would be so wary of being found by them that she would rush off and hide herself in one place or other, fearing that she would be subjected to the customary exorcisms. If she failed in this design, she would fill the house with loud cries, and refuse to come so that it would be necessary to carry her to Philip, resisting with all her might, so that it took four men to bring her. When Philip saw her he was so moved with pity for her, and set to work chastising her with blows and adjuring her with exorcisms until at last by God's power the foul spirit departed from her.

This too I must not omit: one day Caterina, about whom we have been speaking, had been chastised at Philip's orders; but the same night when Philip was in his room and the doors closed, Satan appeared; with flashing eyes he glared at him and burst out with these words, 'Hey, hey, my good man, today you have chosen to frustrate my authority, but I will not forget my injuries!' And saying that, he vanished at once.

IX : WHAT HE DID FROM 1571 TO 1576 INCLUSIVE

Giovanni Animuccia, Philip's disciple, is called to the end of his life
A.D. 1571; Pius V year 6; Philip's age 56

101. In the year of Christ 1571, Giovanni Animuccia breathed his last in the presence of Philip, his mind entirely at peace.[130] He was one of Philip's disciples, a very devout man, who for more than fifteen years had abstained from consorting with his wife Lucrezia, a woman of equal devotion. After that time, through their desire for a still greater degree of perfection, his wife requested him to make a vow about what he had formerly done spontaneously; this was five years before his death. She then imitated his action by making the same vow to God, very gladly, and she kept this vow happily to the end of her life. They did this with the holy Father's permission, although he showed himself extremely reluctant to grant it, knowing well how many perils there are in this life, and what traps the devil sets in his jealousy of the good.

On the 9th of January in the year 74 of our century, a man called Alfonso came to our Oratory to attend the discourses.[131] As he was starting for home, an hour before sunset, he encountered Animuccia (the one whose death I have mentioned) in the corridor at San Girolamo. Animuccia asked him, as if he were still alive, what was happening in the Oratory. 'They have finished the singing', he replied, 'and the Fathers have finished their discourses.' He then added, 'Do you want to see Father Philip?' 'I cannot,' replied the dead man, 'but I came to ask his prayers, so if you are sympathetic to me, please ask him to give me help in my needs.' And having said that, he vanished.

---

[130] *Animuccia (1514–71) was a Florentine, who came to Rome around 1550, and divided his time between the direction of the Capella Giulia and the organisation of the music at the Oratory. He is noted as a leading exponent of the Roman polyphonic school, second only to Palestrina.*

[131] I heard this from Cardinal Tarugi.

That reminds me to say something about Animuccia's wife Lucrezia, that devout woman I have already mentioned, who was Philip's spiritual daughter. In order to encourage her to pray, Philip had set her a specific time during the night for her to devote to prayer, adding that if she failed to get out of bed at the set time, he would be sure to call her. Whenever she was overcome with sleep and did not get up at the time he had prescribed, she would hear Philip's voice in the silence, though he himself was far away, calling her to prayer, and encouraging her to get up and pray.[132]

When she was suffering from a fever, she did not get out of bed for many days, until one day Philip sent to tell her that she must come without fail the following day to hear Mass at the church of San Girolamo.[133] Amazingly, the following morning she found herself quite well and strong enough to leap out of bed and come to the Church, to attend Mass and come safely home. She was loud in praise of Philip's virtues, and continued to live for many years. It was she to whom Philip one day predicted that she would suffer great temptations to intemperance, during her morning confession, and indeed that same night she experienced these through the agency of the devil, but overcame them.[134]

Four others admitted to the Congregation
A.D. 1571; Pius V year 6; Philip's age 56–57

102. It was in the same year 1571 that the following were enrolled in our Congregation and joined themselves to us: Tommaso Bozio from Gubbio, many of whose works have been published; Niccolò Gigli of Troyes, a very devout man with great skill in resolving cases of conscience; and Antonio Talpa of San Severino, a learned lawyer. Oh, and Antonio Sala of Bologna also joined us that year.[135]

---

[132] Compare what Godfrey says in his life of St Bernard, chapter 1.

[133] There are two sworn witnesses to this fact, who had often heard her tell about it, and they are quite reliable.

[134] Lucrezia herself told me this before her death.

[135] *Bozio (1548–1610) was noted as a theologian and controversialist, who assisted Baronio in writing the Annales. Nicolas de Lys (1520–91) helped greatly with the administration of the congregation of the Oratory. Talpa (1536–1624) had already experienced life in a community of reformed priests before he came to Rome to settle various questions*

WHAT HE DID FROM 1571 TO 1576 INCLUSIVE

He restores the health of a priest, one of his disciples who was in danger of death
A.D. 1572; Pius V year 7; Philip's age 57

In the year 1572 since the Virgin gave birth, in early March, Cesare Baronio began to suffer from a dangerous fever.[136] The fever was so intense that on the eleventh the most experienced doctors gave up hope of saving him, and with no chance of any human remedy he was rapidly approaching death. Once Philip realised this, he set himself to pray for his recovery, and was not disappointed; he discerned that his prayers had been heard, and Baronio too discovered it by this sure means. At the very moment that Philip was begging the divine mercy, Baronio fell into a refreshing sleep. In his dreams he seemed to see our holy friend standing near Christ, and the Blessed Virgin in a white gown standing to Christ's right. Then he heard Philip entreating the Lord, saying, 'Save Cesare, restore Cesare to his former health; I want Cesare unharmed: give me Cesare, I beg you.' And he repeated these words over and over, like another Moses, showing his confidence in God. Philip was wrestling like this with God like a new Jacob for a long time, but did not prevail, until Baronio seemed to see him turning to the Blessed Mother of God, and beseeching her earnestly, so that what he could not gain of himself, he might attain through her. The Virgin nodded to his request, and at once asked her Son not to refuse what Philip was asking, and she continued to ask Him as long as Philip maintained his entreaty. And after seeing all this, the dying man awoke, gladdened by that sign from heaven, and began to feel better. On that same day he was declared to be out of danger, to the admiration of the doctors who considered it a miracle. Shortly afterwards he became entirely free from his bodily illness, which outcome showed that the vision was not false. Baronio is alive today, and famous throughout the world; he has not forgotten whose help it was that restored him to life and health.

---

about this form of community life. He was influential in organising the Oratorian communities both in Rome and in Naples, where he died. Sala (1525–1605) was the first Oratorian lay brother, who administered the fundraising for the Chiesa Nuova.

[136] It was Cardinal Baronio who told this story on oath.

He heals the sick

103. It was at about the same time that someone called Ambrogio was gravely ill, and the disease grew more virulent daily to the point that he was quite deprived of the strength to move at all except with the help of others. When it was necessary to lift him onto his bed it took four men to do so. When Philip heard of this, he immediately gave him an order, 'Ambrogio, get up at once!' He had hardly spoken when the sick man got up with no assistance; everyone who saw it was astounded and kept crying out that it was a miracle. Soon afterwards, as Philip continued to pray for him, he was restored to his natural health.[137]

So we must pass on, and come to what Philip did under Gregory XIII, the successor to Pius V. He was elected Pope on the 13th of May in 1572, and reigned for twelve years, ten months and twenty-eight days.

He sees the thoughts of men
A.D. 1572–3; Gregory XIII year 1; Philip's age 58

104. A young man called Muzio, who had resolved to follow the holy Father's direction, began to go to confession to him in October 1572, but human nature being inconsistent, he soon afterwards returned to his folly which had the effect of bringing him into depression. It was in early February the following year that he fell into a sin of impurity, and was so ashamed of revealing his lapse to the healer that when he told his other sins in confession, he kept silent about that one. God revealed this to the holy Father, who advised the youth to make a full confession and thereby put the devil to flight. The youth, however, closed his ears to the voice of counsel, and continued to keep back that sin. Philip then said to him, 'You have not told me all your sins, and because of that you are involving yourself in a greater sin.' Then he told him concisely what sins he had committed, saying, 'You did that, and then that, and you veiled them in silence because you were embarrassed.'

---

[137] The sworn witness to this is a priest, Father Giuliano Fuscherio, who was there, the only survivor of many witnesses. *Ambrogio was a servant of Pietro Spadaro, who lived in the Piazza Navona.*

No one knew these things apart from Muzio. Hardly had Philip mentioned them when the boy, both astounded and embarrassed, confessed his sin, and repeated the confession of all his sins from childhood, shedding many tears as tokens of true repentance. Thus he returned to where he belonged, and never afterwards deserted the way that leads to Christ.[138]

It often happened to many people that they had only just knelt down before the holy Father with the intention of confessing their sins when he interrupted them by telling them plainly what sins they had committed, what temptations they had endured, and the thoughts that had passed through their minds, which astonished them exceedingly.[139]

He restores health to a sick priest

At that time there was one of his spiritual sons, who is still alive, who was suffering from a *sarcocela* (what we call a hernia). He had applied many remedies for his condition, on medical advice, but eventually despaired of anything the doctors could do, having found by experience that they were useless, so he applied to Philip, and described his case to him. Philip listened to him, and then answered, 'Be of good cheer, you will soon be better.' And so it happened, and he never suffered from that complaint again.[140]

The Oratory is transferred to the House of the Florentines
A.D. 1574; Gregory XIII year 2; Philip's age 59

105. Meanwhile the Oratory increased, both in numbers and in effectiveness, and so at their own expense the Florentines constructed a new and splendid building more suitable for our purposes, on the banks of the Tiber. Here we began to give the discourses, with no less an attendance or fewer results, in the year '74, on the

---

[138] It was Muzio himself who told me this, on oath. *Muzio Achillei had left a position in a canonry to join the Oratorian community in S. Severino in 1588.*

[139] We have a large number of sworn witnesses to this fact.

[140] The priest to whom this happened told me the whole story, and swore to it; I also heard it from Cardinal Tarugi. *It was actually Germanico Fedeli.*

15th of April, which that year happened to be the Thursday after the great feast of the Resurrection of Our Lord Jesus Christ.

It was that year too that Fabrizio Mezzabarba joined us, the son of Politonio, an expert on canon and civil law; he died thirteen years after he joined us. Then there was Pompeo Paterio, a priest, from Pavia.[141]

Predictions

That year Giovan Battista Altoviti fell seriously ill, and the doctors gave up on him. Philip prayed for him, and when he had finished praying, called for Francesco Maria Tarugi and asked him to tell the sick man in his name that he was certainly not going to die from that disease, but in fact was going to feel better the following morning (it was evening when he said this). We have it on good authority that what he predicted came to pass.[142]

On the 24th of March that year, Lavinia, wife of Fabrizio Massimi, a lady of the highest rank, was expecting a child; when this was mentioned to Philip he assured them that she would have a boy. Having said that, he turned to her husband who was present and said, 'Your wife is going to have a son, and I want you to call him Pietro.' It happened; the child was born in April, and he has outlived his mother and is already the father of two boys.[143]

He delivers a dying woman from the jaws of death

106. That same year, in April or possibly May, a distinguished lady called Costanza de' Crescenzi had been brought to grave danger of death after losing a baby.[144] Suffering from various alarming symptoms, she began to reflect that no possible remedy for her

---

[141] *Both of these came to Rome in anticipation of the 1575 Jubilee; Pateri joined the community, while Mezzabarba remained a guest, but bequeathed all his property to the Oratory.*

[142] *It is Cardinal Tarugi who confirms this.*

[143] *The Massimo family were close friends of St Philip, and are mentioned again in the context of the raising of Lavinia's second son Paolo (paragraph 125). Pietro lived on until 1655, and eventually had ten children. For Lavinia's death, see paragraph 111.*

[144] *Apart from Costanza herself, there are two other eyewitnesses who swore to this story. She had four sons, all of whom gave evidence in the canonisation process.*

condition remained save Philip alone. She felt that if he prayed for her, the complaint would vanish at once, for she had heard so much about him, though she had never seen his face. He visited her, and laid his hands on her, praying God for her recovery. She was filled with great delight at his touch and began to hope still more that she would recover her former health through the prayers of a man like that. She was not disappointed: Philip visited her again and asked her if she would like to come to the church of San Girolamo. She agreed, adding that there was nothing she would rather be able to do. He replied, 'Be cheerful, you have nothing to fear, believe me; you will come and see me at San Girolamo.' His prediction came true; the woman shortly afterwards recovered her health as before, contrary to all expectation, and ever afterwards went to confession to Philip, who was still living then in the house at San Girolamo.

A Prediction
A.D. 1575; Gregory XIII year 3; Philip's age 60

In January of the following year, Agnesina Colonna had a miscarriage and became very ill; she was another lady of the highest rank.[145] She got worse steadily, until everyone expected that death was imminent. Philip visited her, therefore, since she was so ill, and the doctors had abandoned her to the grip of the infection. He brought her hope of recovery, saying, 'Agnesina, stop being afraid! Forget your fears and worries, you will survive this illness.' His words were not in vain; although they had despaired of the woman's life, she returned to her former good health, and lived on until 1578, when she finally died on 26th April.

The Congregation is established, and flourishes

107. Since every day the fruit won by our little flock could be seen to increase, our community began to consider moving away from hired accommodation, to acquire property of our own. In this way God's work could be passed on to successors who would be heirs

---

[145] It was the noblewoman Beatrice Caetani who confirmed this story on oath. *Agnesina was the sister of Marc'Antonio Colonna, the victor of Lepanto; she married Onorato Caetani, Lord of Sermoneta.*

to our spirit and manner of life, so that they would continue the same ministry, and perpetuate a work which was pleasing to God and useful to men. There was some discussion of this matter, to discern whether this was for their own interests or those of God and neighbour, and they talked about confirming and establishing the Congregation. Philip did not want to appear to express his own opinion in such an important matter, and commended the entire business to earnest prayer before God; the others did the same. After long application to prayer, they finally thought of the church of Santa Maria in Vallicella, in the region of Ponte or Parione, in the very centre of the city.

The rector of that church was named Antonino Adiuti, a priest from Messina; the Fathers asked him whether he would resign the church to them, while retaining the income from it as long as he lived.[146] He agreed to this, and once his agreement had been secured, Philip entrusted the responsibility for his parish to Tarugi. He accepted the responsibility, and went at once to the Pope, explaining to him what Philip and the others had decided and intended to do. He was not disappointed, for Gregory knew Philip well, and was aware of his devotion to God; he had heard much about the institute of our Congregation from Tarugi and the others. Not only did he grant them the church, but he also gave his apostolic authority for the proper establishment of the Congregation, which had also been requested. (Up to that time the Congregation had no official approval from the Pope.) We have Apostolic Letters about this matter, at great length, issued on the 15th July that same year.

He restores the health of a woman dying in childbirth

108. On the 27th of July a lady called Olimpia Troiani had been in labour for two difficult days, unable to bring forth her child, and was not far from the moment when death would put an end to her life.[147] While her household was mourning her as if she were

---

[146] *He lived on until September 1627, enjoying an income of 110 scudi from a parish in which he had actually only served for one year.*

[147] We have three sworn witnesses to this story, two of whom were eyewitnesses.

already dead, she thought of Philip, and that thought brought her new hope of recovery: she begged the women around her again and again to have him brought to her at once. He arrived, for his charity towards all was such that he could not refuse; he prayed for her, and laid his hands on the dying woman. Having done that, he withdrew at once, as if he knew that his prayers had been heard. And scarcely had he left the room when, amazingly, Olimpia gave birth to a live girl, and she herself was kept safe from the danger that threatened her. We know there were many other women who were given up for lost during difficult labour, but at Philip's prayers, or through contact with the reliquaries which he kept, were able to give birth safely and easily.

The Church of Our Lady of the Vallicella is rebuilt from its foundations

109. Now, since the church [of Santa Maria in Vallicella] was very small and in bad condition, the Fathers thought it ought to be restored, since it was ideally situated in the most suitable part of the city for the function of the Congregation. Much as they would have liked to build a new one, the limitations of their private funds made it impossible. But while they were considering this, God in His mercy responded to their devout wishes. They had hardly set about the work of restoration, when Philip, relying on nothing but his faith in God, decided to have it pulled down completely and to rebuild it from the foundations in a larger and more splendid style, though the Fathers had no money, or very little. The matter did not rest there: what he had decided to do, that he determined to carry out at once, confident in the providence of God. All his life long he had depended on that providence, and thought nothing too difficult or too great, never hesitating in the attempt at the most ambitious schemes.

At Philip's command the ruinous church was levelled to the ground, and in September Matteo [Bartolini] of Città di Castello was called in, one of the best architects of our time. He surveyed the site carefully, and was marking out the groundplan of the intended building, when Germanico Fedeli told Philip what he was doing. Philip was already vested for Mass, but told the other priest that nothing should be decided before he arrived. After Mass he came to the site and found Matteo there, who showed him the place where he had decided the foundations should be dug. Philip did not consent to his plan, for he said the building should be bigger. They went to the place which God had shown him, and he said, 'Dig here, the foundations must be here.' They did so, and lo, they brought to light an ancient and solid wall hidden under the rubble. It was ten spans wide, and so long that the length of the eventual building did not use it all, but it extended further. On this foundation the right hand wall of the church was completed, though for the remainder it was necessary to lay new foundations. For this purpose a foundation stone was laid in the usual manner, which was done with great splendour before a large crowd. The first stone was solemnly consecrated, and laid in the foundations by Alessandro de' Medici, Archbishop of Florence, to whom our Congregation owes a lot (he is now a Cardinal Priest of the Holy Roman Church with the title of Santa Maria in Trastevere).[148]

110. While the church was being built, the Fathers were never short of money both to pay the stonemasons and other workmen, and to buy up adjacent houses. The expenses were heavy, every day, during the building, and the total sum amounted to around seventy thousand crowns, apart from the money which Cardinal Pietro Donato Cesi contributed to the work, as we shall recount in due course. The project progressed well, aided by our excellent Pontiff and many of the citizens, who freely donated funds, in their devotion to our holy Father, and their reverence for God. Gregory XIII himself spontaneously invested seven thousand crowns in the building. Construction of the church proceeded without interruption, as the Fathers never ran out of money, and God kept them continually supplied. In a very short time, round about two years, it grew to the shape and size you can see today, splendid in its workmanship and its appearance. And so the church was dedicated to God, under the title of the Blessed Virgin and St Gregory the Great.

---

[148] *Cardinal de' Medici, who is so often mentioned in this work, became Pope Leo XI briefly in 1605.*

I must not omit to tell you what happened to the Fathers during the building of our church. Some of the locals could not abide our building a church near them, till the devil worked them into such a fury that they began to throw stones and other objects at Giovan Antonio Lucci, a priest who was clerk of the works, as well as through the windows.[149] God protected his priest, and Lucci suffered no harm, which he attributed to the prayers of the holy Father. There were some brothers, whose names I shall be careful not to reveal, who attempted to obstruct the building of the church. Philip said nothing, and merely prayed for them, but they paid the penalty for their malice: they all died within two years, acknowledging the justice of God, and not a single child of theirs remained to continue the family. There were others who attacked the Fathers, but since, as we read in Holy Scripture, 'to them that love God, all things work together unto good' [Rom 8:28], the malice of men, far from harming the Fathers, was greatly to their benefit.

The death of Lavinia, Philip's spiritual daughter, the wife of Fabrizio Massimi

111. It was in October of that same year that God called Lavinia to her reward; she was a noblewoman, wife of Fabrizio Massimi, and since she was one of Philip's penitents, it will not be out of place to say something about her here. At first she thought him comic, but once she had heard him speak about the things of God, she felt herself so fired with longing to worship God that under his direction she came to such a state of life that she dedicated herself totally to the love of Christ, and to works of charity, forgetful of herself. Philip assured us that during her meditation on divine matters, which occupied her for many hours, she was quite abstracted from consciousness. She finally died on the 30th October: as Philip said, her last hour was a journey to heaven, where the blest enjoy eternal life.

---

[149] We read of similar things happening to saints who built churches or monasteries: see the lives of St Pachomius, Deodatus the Bishop, and Malachy the Bishop.

It was in that same year, '75, that Giulio Savioli of Padua joined the congregation on 2nd April, as did Francesco Bozio of Gubbio, brother of Tommaso, on the first of November.[150]

He is warned in a vision of the roof that threatened to fall
A.D. 1576; Gregory XIII year 4–5; Philip's age 61–2

112. In the following year, 1576, something happened during the building works, which I must not pass over in silence.[151] When the old church had been demolished, along with other buildings on the site of the new construction, one little hovel remained roofed, after the others had been levelled. Suddenly one day Philip had Giovan Antonio, the clerk of works, summoned, and as soon as he arrived he told him to have the roof taken off the hovel immediately. 'Last night,' he explained, 'I saw the Holy Mother of God, who was holding it up with her own hands.' (The place was being used as a chapel to say Mass and administer the sacraments to the people, for the old church had the responsibility of souls attached to it.) Giovan Antonio went back and ordered the workmen to demolish the roof. As soon as they set to, they noticed that the beam which supported the roof had no support for itself; one of its ends (what they call the beam's head) was quite out of the wall, which quite astonished those who saw it.

He delivers a sick youth from death

In that same year, '76, Giovan Battista Cresci was suffering so much from frequent headaches and fever that he used to scream and moan day and night, in a pitiful manner.[152] The pain continued to increase for several days, and he never found any relief, till the suffering brought him to such a pitch that he often thought of putting an end to his misery by throwing himself down a well. Finally,

---

[150] *Savioli (1532–1618) wanted to remain a lay brother, but Baronio persuaded him to become a priest. Francesco Bozio, despite being a cultured man, remained fond of games, and excelled in that of 'piastrelle', which St Philip loved to watch.*

[151] I heard this from Father Germanico, and there are four other sworn witnesses to it.

[152] He himself gave sworn evidence of this story.

having exhausted all other means, it occurred to him, in desperation of any other remedy, to apply to Philip; for there was no doubt that his prayers would be beneficial. Philip visited him, and laid his hands on him, and spoke to him thus, 'Avoid sin; cultivate great devotion to the holy Mother of God: you have nothing to fear, this illness is not going to cause your death, you will be well enough soon.' As soon as had said it, the sick man began to feel better, the headache disappeared altogether, he was able to sleep, and soon afterwards got out of bed in good health.

He is marked by the spirit of prophecy

113. That same year, Girolamo Beier, who was a teenager at school with the Dominicans, was suddenly inspired by God to think of trying to join the order of St Dominic.[153] He became so eager to do this that he presented himself that very day at the Church of Santa Maria sopra Minerva, with the intention of telling the Novice-master (Brother Pietromartire) what he was thinking. He asked him how long he had had this idea. 'It was just today,' replied Girolamo, 'that I felt myself drawn to it by some inner feeling.' Brother Pietromartire was already vested, and the bell had rung, for him to attend a funeral along with his novices, so he asked Girolamo if he knew Philip, assuring him that he would be able to learn from him very easily what he ought to do in this matter. He sent Girolamo to Philip, therefore, and as soon as Philip saw him he asked him to wait, because he wanted to say something to him. Quite soon, before the boy had spoken a word, Philip said, 'I know what it is you want: Brother Pietro has sent you to tell me that the idea has occurred to you, this very day, of leaving the world and embracing the order of St Dominic. And I am to tell you whether the idea comes from God or not. Do what you intend to do: and give thanks to God for calling you to Himself by this means.'

Hearing this, the boy was so astounded that he could but stammer, 'You are right, Father', and was unable to utter another word. He went back to Brother Pietro, who had returned home from his

---

[153] Father Girolamo is the sworn witness to this story. *The novicemaster, Pietromartire Saraceni, eventually became Prior of the Minerva, and died in 1588.*

funeral, and told him what Philip had said, admitting that he felt like the Samaritan woman, in meeting a man who knew all the secrets of his heart. The Novicemaster accepted the boy when he heard this, and promised that he would shortly give him the religious habit. He added that he had sent him to Philip precisely because he knew about his sanctity of life, and his knowledge of spirituality. This all happened on the 18th October. Brother Girolamo put on the religious habit on St Martin's Day that year, and is still alive, performing the office of Master Preacher.

A Prediction

114. During that same year, four of Philip's disciples, all priests, were in Milan. They were Alessandro Fedeli, Niccolò Gigli, Pompeo Paterio and Pietro Perrachione. They were working for the good of others, but had hardly begun to labour in the Lord's vineyard before Philip suddenly wrote to recall them to Rome.[154] For when the Fathers had gone to Milan, Philip asked Francesco Maria Tarugi to write to them at once, telling them to return to Rome immediately with no delay. This seemed rather hard to Tarugi, because he thought the abrupt withdrawal of those priests would cause great offence to many people, but he had to be told again, 'It is your duty to obey my commands, just as all of them must obey me in everything without hesitation; as soon as they hear my command they ought to come here as I wish.' Now what is amazing is that his letters had hardly reached their hands before the plague broke out, although before that there had been no preliminary indications, and it swept through the city like a cloud covering the sky, causing the deaths of a great many of the inhabitants. Our priests, however, summoned out of danger by Philip's letter, returned thankfully to Rome.

---

[154] Cardinal Tarugi is the sworn witness to this, apart from the others. *The project of a foundation in Milan, sponsored by Mezzabarba, and originally requested by St Charles, was unsuccessful for many reasons, apart from the plague.*

X : THE YEAR OF CHRIST 1577 AND THE FIVE YEARS FOLLOWING

Philip is gravely ill
A.D. 1577; Gregory XIII year 5; Philip's age 62

115.   At the beginning of the year 77 of our century, Philip fell ill, with little or no hope of recovery. One night, when he found himself utterly unable to sleep, and all the bells of the city were ringing for Matins, he urgently asked for Communion to be given him.[155] When Francesco Maria Tarugi was told of this, he said it should not be given to him, for he feared that once he had received Holy Communion his violent tears and prayers would prevent him from sleeping at all, which would certainly be dangerous to his health. Philip got wind of this, and sent for Francesco Maria, to explain that the reason why he couldn't sleep was precisely his longing to receive the Body of Christ. He went on, that if he could once have his desire, he would receive the ability to sleep along with the Blessed Sacrament. And so it happened: once he had received, he immediately fell into a peaceful sleep, as he had foretold. And so it became the custom that whenever he was pressed by his disease he was nourished on the daily Bread of Heaven which alone fulfils all man's desires, and after receiving it, he would soon relax into a refreshing sleep. His longing for the Blessed Sacrament brought it about that, although he had not fully recovered from his long illness, he could renew his strength by celebrating Mass in church, which he did to the admiration of the congregation.

The Oratory is moved to the Vallicella
116.   Celebration of the Liturgy began in the New Church on 3rd February. It was Alessandro de' Medici, Archbishop of Florence, who celebrated the first Mass, with more pomp and circumstance, and a more elaborate performance by the choir, than had ever been

---

[155] Cardinal Tarugi gives evidence for this, on oath.

seen before. Pope Gregory, in order to increase the popular attendance, granted a generous Indulgence to all those who, having made a holy confession, were present at the Mass to receive the blessed Body of Christ, or who visited the church on that day. I remember seeing the church, decorated all around with hangings, thronged with a crowd of men and women, and filled with joyous music. In the afternoon Vespers was celebrated, with the same choir, and the same Archbishop presiding. Both morning and evening the church was continuously filled with people, and there were many visitors who came to the saving banquet of the Eucharist, after making a proper confession, on the occasion of such a generous grant of Indulgence. The eager appreciation of the people never died down, and their devout fervour never cooled, but rather grew from day to day, and is still outstanding today. In that same year, in April, the Fathers began to deliver their spiritual discourses at the Vallicella, abandoning the Oratory of the Florentines.

Others join us

The reputation of the Congregation spread, and the beneficial effect of the work they undertook grew steadily greater, so that many were spurred by the desire of serving God to the point of wanting to join our Fathers, and be instructed on prayer in their house. Many applied, but not all were admitted. Those who were enrolled in the number of our community in the year '77, after the Congregation had become established, were the following: first Pietro Perrachione, a priest; secondly myself, who am the author of this life, after joining the Fathers through the immense mercy of God, and becoming the servant and constant companion of our holy Father; and thirdly Agostino Manni of Canziano, a doctor of both Civil and Canon Law. The first joined the Congregation on the 23rd March, the second on the first of July, the third during October.[156]

---

[156] *Peracchione (1538–1608) was ordained in 1560, and so entered the Congregation as the second senior priest after St Philip; he was best known as a spiritual director. Gallonio himself (1557–1605) was to be Philip's constant attendant during the last years of his life. Manni (1548–1618) had a doctorate in jurisprudence from Perugia; he was the poet of the community.*

He delivers a dying woman from death

117. That year a woman called Ersilia Bucca became dangerously ill, and the doctors despaired of being able to save her.[157] She was bedridden, and virtually unconscious, till they feared death was imminent. In this situation, Ersilia's husband Giovan Francesco, who used to go to confession to Philip, begged him to visit her. When he arrived the woman was filled with such joy as she could never remember feeling before, and her joy overflowed when she saw Philip's smiling face and heard him say, 'Be of good cheer; it will not be long before you recover from this illness.' She felt better the moment he said that, and as the virulence of the disease passed, she got out of bed four days later, quite cured, which astounded her household.

A Prediction

At the end of that year '77, the Fathers decreed that Pompeo Paterio should be sent to Milan on some urgent business of the Congregation.[158] He was reluctant to go, considering himself quite unsuitable for the task, but finally agreed to submit his will to obedience, since Philip pressed him strongly to go. As he left Rome, Philip said to him, 'Be confident, Pompeo, put your hope in God's aid. Never question the commands of your superiors; everything will come out right for you, believe me.' The event proved how right he was: when Pompeo reached Milan and started to carry out his commission, he found great difficulty, and many influential opponents. He was threatened by powerful interests to abandon his project, but he kept Philip's promise in mind, and relied on his prayers, putting all his trust in them. Thus he overcame all the obstacles in his path of whatever kind, conducted his business more easily than he could believe possible, and brought the whole affair to a satisfactory conclusion before returning happily to Rome.

---

[157] I heard this from Giovan Francesco, who was there, as well as Ersilia herself who confirmed it on oath. *Giovan Francesco Bucca was a notary, who lived just opposite the Chiesa Nuova.*

[158] Pompeo Paterio himself tells the story, and swears to it. *Paterio frequently travelled on business for the Congregation, much of it concerned with sorting out the Mezzabarba legacy.*

He appears to a disciple who was experiencing temptation
A.D. 1578; Gregory XIII year 6; Philip's age 63

118. At the beginning of the year of Our Lord 1578, one of his disciples in virtue experienced Philip's assistance, when he was greatly disturbed because he thought he was in imminent danger of falling into sin.[159] Because Philip knew him to be a man of moral integrity, he asked him to look after a very attractive teenage boy, and to share his bedroom with him (sleeping in separate beds), because the lad was timid and afraid to be alone.[160] The disciple obeyed the holy Father's bidding, but was extremely anxious about doing so, knowing the snare the devil might set. While he was in anguish about the peril he was in, he suddenly saw the holy Father, unexpectedly one night, although he was a long way away in body, and seeing him he was amazingly relieved at having him present.[161] Philip sat down on the bed he was sleeping in, to increase the gladness he felt, and asked him how he felt. 'Badly, Father,' he replied, 'I am surrounded by temptations.' Then Philip touched his chest, and made the sign of the Cross from there down to his loins, telling him to be of good heart, because all the fires of temptation and all the anxiety of his soul were already gone. And saying that, he vanished from sight. The disciple remained there, after Philip had gone, filled with joy as if bathed in a great light. The vision was not fruitless: his later actions and behaviour showed how deep his virtue of chastity had become, and the greatest proof of that is that from then on he felt as safe with the teenager as if he were his brother or his son.

119. There was a certain young man who experienced something similar around the same time, because his thoughts were so distracted by impure imaginations, which became such an obsession that he could find no way to be rid of them; he got to the pitch that

---

[159] The priest to whom this happened told the entire story. *It was Germanico Fedeli, as he admits in the documents of the canonical process.*

[160] I know that from another source.

[161] A very similar story is told by the respected author Leontius in his life of St Simeon Salus, chapter 22; there is also something like it in Moschus, an equally famous author, in his *Spiritual Meadow*, chapter 3.

he was in constant peril of lapsing into sordid sins. Accordingly he begged for the help of our holy Father, considering that his best hope of help lay in him. Philip clasped him to his breast, and he became at once free from all anxieties about temptation. Nor was this the only benefit he gained, for he found himself so inspired with the fire of divine love that he was able to devote all his spare time to prayer.[162]

The number of companions increases

It was in that same year that our church was exempted from the jurisdiction of the Basilica of San Lorenzo in Damaso, from its titular cardinal and college of canons (what they call the Chapter), as you can see on the diploma dated on the first of September that year.

In the same year there joined the Congregation Flaminio Ricci of Fermo, doctor of both Civil and Canon Law, and Juvenal Ancina of Fossano, educated in Latin literature, who has abandoned his medical practice to devote himself entirely to theology. Juvenal was followed by his brother Giovan Matteo, a law student; then there was Bernardino Corona, a Roman, who next joined the Fathers, and Giovan Paolo Curiazio, and Ludovico Parigi of Florence.[163] In fact within a few years the number of fellows grew to about a hundred and thirty, although not all those who applied were admitted to the Congregation: I do not therefore propose to name each one of them.[164]

He delivers a woman from imminent death

A.D. 1579–80; Gregory XIII year 7–8; Philip's age 64–5

120. In the year 80 of the century, in early April, the noble lady Costanza de' Crescenzi again fell into a life-threatening fever, being

---

[162] *This was probably Tiberio Ricciardelli, later a canon of the basilica of Dodici Apostoli.*

[163] *Ricci (1545–1609) gave up a promising career as a lawyer in the service of Cardinal Caetani; he was Provost of the Roman Oratory in 1602 and 1605. Blessed Juvenal Ancina (1545–1604) after helping found the Naples Oratory, became Bishop of Saluzzo, where he was poisoned by a friar who resisted the reforms of Trent; his brother Matteo (1552–1638) remained at the Roman Oratory. Corona, Curiazio and Parigi all entered as lay brothers.*

[164] *I can't think of anything worth writing that happened in 1579. The Italian edition does include a story for that year, of the healing of Giovan Battista Boniperti.*

eight months pregnant.[165] She suffered greatly, and came out in spots or boils, dark in colour. The disease was so virulent that she was not far from death and she was given the holy Viaticum around midnight. After that the priest came to her to give her the last Anointing, but she began to consider how she might elude the advance of death. It occurred to her that the only possible remedy for her plight was that Philip should pray to God for her. Meanwhile the holy Father appeared as dawn approached, although no one had actually called him: he found the lady improving, and able to talk clearly. When she saw Philip, she said, 'I have had a bad night, full of fears and woes; I nearly died. I longed to see you, because I thought I could trust in you, and I was not wrong: when I began to implore God's help while thinking about you I soon began to improve, by the help of your prayers.'

Philip replied, 'While you were passing the night among all those terrors, I was never absent from you: be of good heart, you are not going to die now, you will be well soon enough.' She did not have to wait long: she felt better at once, and a few days later recovered her usual strength of mind and body, to the astonishment of all those who knew about her illness.

He is marked by the spirit of prophecy

121. There was a young man of very good family who felt himself called to fight the battles of the Lord, and decided to join our Congregation. Once he had joined, he started by behaving so well in all aspects that everyone thought very highly of him. It appeared that in his loyalty to our holy Father he had quite overcome all affection for his family, and hardly seemed even to think of them, but as it can sometimes happen, when he fell ill he was so terrified by the virulence of the disease, that, though still practising devotion, he conceived the idea of going back to his birthplace, for the sake of a change of air, to be more easily restored to health. He chose one of the Congregation to accompany him, who had himself been

---

[165] We have three sworn witnesses to this story, apart from Costanza herself. *She had already been healed by St Philip in 1574, see paragraph 106.*

recently ill, so that he too, as he averred, might benefit his health from a change of air.

The holy Father did not approve the young man's idea, presaging that it would be dangerous to his soul, but the other succeeded not so much in gaining as in extorting permission for his plan from Philip, who was exceedingly reluctant. On the day they were about to set off, he said to one of his disciples, 'Remember this: two of them will go away, but only one will return. The young one will be so taken by affection for his family that he will not come back to our house.' The priest who heard this was amazed, but Philip did not speak idly: the event turned out exactly as he had foretold. This happened in the year 80 of our century.[166]

Demons are driven away by hearing the name of Philip
A.D. 1581; Gregory XIII years 9–10; Philip's age 66–7

122. The next year, '81, a nobleman called Carlo Mazzei, who was a disciple of Philip and very old, became so ill that he was close to death.[167] On the night which was to unite him to Christ, he was diligently examining his conscience and preparing himself for a holy death, when the devil began to attack him savagely; the holy Father was a long way off at the time. The demon hurled many accusations against him, but the warrior of Christ simply replied, 'I appeal to Philip, I appeal to Philip.' By saying this he overcame the enemy, and drove him away, so that soon after the end of that night he peacefully rendered his soul to God. That was on the 14th of April.

He restores Michele Mercati to health, after the doctors had given up

It was in October of the same year that Michele Mercati, a very learned man, was severely ill and approaching death, but Philip restored him to his usual health.[168] He spoke to the sick man's

---

[166] Not only I but the whole Congregation knew about this; the priest to whom Philip had spoken repeated the story on oath.

[167] We have two sworn witnesses to this story.

[168] Orazio Ansaldi, who was present, affirmed this on oath. *Mercati (1541–93) was a doctor, noted also as a naturalist and the founder of palaeontology.*

father, Pietro, who was a skilled physician, and said to him, 'There is nothing to fear, this sickness will not kill him; he will recover his health and live for many years yet.' His prophecy was true: he had hardly spoken when Michele began to feel better, and he soon regained his strength, as if he had been summoned back from death. He recovered so well that he lived for another twelve years, and died in 1593 on the 29th of June.

New buildings acquired for the Fathers to live in
A.D. 1581–2; Gregory XIII years 10–11; Philip's age 67–8

123. Since new men kept joining the Congregation, the house was hardly large enough for us all, so another building was added to the house, through the generosity of Cardinal Pietro Donato Cesi.[169] He gave us twenty thousand crowns, to buy the adjacent houses and to construct the apse behind the high altar from its foundations. His brother Angelo, Bishop of Todi, followed the family tradition as well as his own great attachment to our Fathers, to the extent that he paid for the construction of the main front of the church, decorated with the finest workmanship in Travertine marble. He had already built a spacious and elegant chapel beside the apse of the high altar, on which he spent some five thousand crowns and more. The other apsidal chapel which remained to be built was adorned with precious marble and sacred ornaments at the expense of Alessandro Glorierio, clerk to the Apostolic Camera. Finally, after Philip's death, Cardinal Federico Borromeo, one of our greatest friends, spent four thousand crowns on the construction of the high altar.

124. I should also briefly note what happened to the Fathers when the buildings I have mentioned were being bought.[170] In 1581 they were thinking of buying the convent of nuns of St Elizabeth,

---

[169] *Cardinal Cesi (1521–86) was titular of S. Barbara and afterwards of S. Vitale; his brother Angelo Cesi, Bishop of Todi (1530–1606), was to complete the façade of the Chiesa Nuova in 1605.*

[170] I heard this from Cardinal Tarugi, also Father Pompeo has given sworn evidence for it.

which was adjacent to our house, after the nuns had been ordered to move somewhere else by Giacomo Savelli, the then Vicar of the city. This was because our property was so confined that it could not be extended except by buying that convent. However when Philip heard that the Fathers were considering this, he was so far from agreeing to their desires that he actively opposed them. 'First of all,' he said, 'you must pay off the debts you contracted in order to complete the essential work on the church, because it is wrong for you to take on a new obligation of five thousand crowns (that was the estimated price) when you are in debt already.' In fact Philip was in hopes that the convent would shortly come into their hands through the help of God and at the expense of others. Nevertheless the Fathers let themselves be guided by human prudence, and determined to bring the matter to a conclusion. All the interested parties had already met, in the presence of the judge (who was Mario Marzi) and the notary who was to write the names of the witnesses to the contract, and they had already reached the point of settling the price, when the judge suddenly declared that he was not satisfied with the guarantors of the stipulated money, and everyone had to depart without concluding the business. (The money had been requested simply as a sum, without naming anyone, as is normally done in cases like this.) When they told the holy Father about this, he began by thanking God, and then said, 'They (meaning our Fathers) will never get hold of that convent at their own expense as they imagine.'

He was proved right: scarcely five months later, Cardinal Pietro Donato Cesi bought it out of his own pocket, on the 30th June; such was his generosity of mind that he gave it freely to the Fathers in the following year, on the 15th of January. As well as the convent he also bought the house next door (that of the Arditti), and for no small price, on the 13th August the same year 1582, and he made it over to the Fathers on the 28th February 1583. These are the two houses that our community live in at present; as well as that there were two other houses bought for us by the same Cardinal Pietro Donato Cesi, who gave three thousand crowns for them, in order to build the apse of the high altar. That wasn't the end of his generosity to the Fathers, for he left us eight thousand crowns in his will to construct the apse, and although that sum was not sufficient for the entire work, a large proportion of the structure was paid for by him.

He raises a youth from death
A.D. 1583; Gregory XIII year 11; Philip's age 68

125. In the year of Christ 1493, Paolo Massimo died, aged fourteen, after a debilitating illness which weakened him progressively for nearly three months.[171] While he was dying, they sent for Philip, who was unable to come because he was celebrating Mass. When he had finished Mass he hastened to the dying boy, and found that Paolo had died half an hour before. His father Fabrizio had already closed his eyes, as is normal when someone has died, and the parish priest, Camillo, had solemnly commended his soul to the protection of God and the saints, after fortifying him with the sacraments of Christ; he had not left until he had witnessed that the dying boy had breathed his last. That was not all: they had already prepared hot water to wash the body in the usual way, and clothes to dress it in so that the corpse could be carried to church. One of the maids, called Francesca, who is still alive, was holding a pair of slippers in her hand to cover his nakedness.

Philip arrived in the midst of all this, and Fabrizio spoke to him, 'Oh, father,' he said, 'Paolo is dead, there is nothing more you can do.' Philip replied, 'Why did you not call me earlier?' But saying that, he went straight to the place where the dead boy lay. There he found the maid Francesca, bringing the clothes with which the boy's body was to be dressed, all ready to start. Philip came close, and asked for some holy water, with which he sprinkled the mouth and face of the dead boy; then he laid his hands on him and prayed. As he prayed, he stroked the boy, and continuing to pray and to touch him, he called aloud twice the name of the dead boy; thus in a strange way, Paolo was called back to life through Philip's prayers. He opened his eyes, and to the amazement of everyone who was present, replied to Philip in a clear voice. He then spoke with him

---

[171] The whole story was affirmed on oath by Fabrizio Massimo, a nobleman of Rome, his wife Violante, and Francesca Antoni of Castro-Civitella, who are the survivors of those who were present.

EI CHE DI MORTE GIA TRA LACCI STRETTO
E FREDDA SALMA DI REPENTE VIVE
E DI NUOVO MORRA DEL NERI A UN DETTO
A MORTE LEGGI E A VITA EGLI PRESCRIVE.

Paolo de Massimi risuscitato subito che S. Filippo lo chiama a nome, dopo aver seco lui parlato
circa mezz'ora, interrogato dal Santo se volentieri tornerebbe a morire, e rispondendo che si muore
la seconda volta, poiche Filippo gli disse: Muori che sii Benedetto, e prega Dio per me.

at length, for a quarter of an hour or more, though the bystanders could not hear what he said. After that, Philip asked him, 'Are you willing to die, or to continue longer in this life?' He replied that he wished to die, for he knew that he had a certain place set aside for him in heaven, to enjoy the splendour of God, the Best and Greatest, for ever. And so, in his longing for death, as if he were entering the land of the living, he breathed forth his spirit a second time, in the sight and in the embrace of the holy Father; this was on the 16th of March, in the year 1583 as I have said.[172]

Philip moves to the Vallicella

126. Although Philip was the instigator and director of everything his disciples did at the Vallicella, he could not be so easily induced to leave his home at the church of San Girolamo straight away. It was several years later that this was forced on him, through the agency of Cardinal Pietro Donato Cesi. Since he supported our Congregation with unusual affection, he used every means to bring Philip together with his followers. He went to see Pope Gregory, and arranged for him to give Philip an order to move to the Vallicella as soon as possible. Philip could not resist the Pope's command, for he believed that the will of God is clearly to be found in the orders of the Pope. But I do know for certain that Philip had intended never to leave San Girolamo, nor to escape from the crosses God had prepared for him there, and that he would not have lived at the Vallicella with his disciples had he not been compelled to do so by order of his superiors.

Accordingly, he set out from San Girolamo to the Vallicella, in the year 1583 since the birth of Christ, on the 22nd of November; then indeed our Congregation began to look like a single body,

---

[172] There are similar marvels which reputable authors have recorded to be done by the saints. See Evagrius and Palladius, in the lives of the Fathers, on Mutius; John Moschus, in the *Spiritual Meadow*, chapters 77, 78 and 93, particularly paragraph ii, beginning 'Abba Peter'; also the life of St Ebrulfus, chapter 4; and Eugippius' *Life of St Severinus, Apostle of Noricum, addressed to St Paschasius the Deacon*, chapter 36. We possess a good manuscript of this; the edition by Surius is faulty. Our author adds that part of the miracle is that, as long as Severinus was alive, no one knew about it except for those who were present.

head and members united and joined in a close union. Philip continued to give clear indications of his accustomed sanctity, for even though he was now living in our house, he hardly abandoned his former practice of solitude at all. He took his meals alone, and would allow no one to serve him at table. He celebrated Mass when he was summoned to do so. To inspire others with an example of obedience, he would leave everything and go at once to the proper place, as soon as he was called to offer the sacrifice. When he put on the sacred vestments, he did not ask for the more fancy vestments, as many of the other Fathers did, but for the old-fashioned ones. These points are not trivial, when you consider that he had total authority over the others, and would have been able to live exactly as he pleased, so to speak.

He would hear the confessions of all who came to him, and after finishing Mass would administer Holy Communion to those present. In addition he had a great desire for humiliation, and a love for others which was greater still; his careful vigilance in governing his sons was more than paternal, and it was wonderful how his presence delighted the eyes and minds of everyone. He was a man – and I think I have said this already – without guile, elegant in his manner, and agreeable like no one else, but his advice and his opinions were serious, and much admired by all.

127.   It was about the same time, I think, that a priest called Muzio lived outside the city; whenever he was in any danger, or suffering from any temptation, he would commend himself to Philip, and immediately feel himself delivered from that peril.[173] One day he came very close to slipping into the Tiber (being for once in Rome) which would certainly have endangered his life: he simply called on Philip, and at once got safely away.

He rebukes a great lady in a vision

There was a woman, whose name I shall purposely omit, who was so enraged against a certain relation of hers that she would listen to

---

[173] It was the same priest, Muzio Achillei, who told the story, on oath. *See also* paragraph 104.

no argument which might induce her to think of making peace.[174] She had continued this feud for a long time, and could not even bear to look on the man with civility, when one night, as she lay in bed, she felt her face being slapped. Then she seemed to hear the voice of the holy Father (she used to go to confession to him), saying, 'What a disgrace you are, keeping up this resentment! It is not fitting: now, set your anger aside, drive away hatred as you ought to, and reconcile yourself with that person as soon as you can.' The woman was dismayed by this, as well as astounded, for she knew that the holy Father was at that time a long way away from her in body. Struck with fear and awe, she burst into tears, and made peace with her relation as soon as she could. When day broke she went to Philip, and told him the whole amazing story exactly as it happened.

---

[174] It was she herself, to whom this happened, who gave sworn witness, and some of her servants corroborated her witness. *This was Costanza Crescenzi, whom Philip had already healed twice; see paragraphs 106 and 120.*

XI : THE YEAR 1584 AND THE FOUR FOLLOWING

He restores a sick man to his former health
A.D. 1584; Gregory XIII year 12; Philip's age 69–70

128.   In the year of Christ 1584, in June or July, it happened to a certain man of high birth (whose name I shall withhold) that an extremely painful ulcer broke out on his penis, so that he felt he was suffering continually from burning, and part of the glans had begun to turn black.[175] He summoned a doctor and showed him the affected part, but the doctor was horrified at the extent of the condition, and so scared the sick man that he fled to Philip in his terror. Before he had time to utter a word, Philip asked him to show him the affected part, saying this to demonstrate that he knew the whole matter through a revelation from God. The young man was embarrassed to do as he was told, and hesitated, until Philip insisted and he had to give in and show it him. Here is the miracle: as soon as Philip touched it, all the infection disappeared from the infected part. The young man waited a moment, in his astonishment, and then was convinced of the truth of the miracle; he turned to Philip and said, 'Let me run through all the streets of the city and tell them how you have been the cause of my healing, let me shout your praise!' Philip ordered him to be quiet, being a man totally opposed to his own praise, and told him to make sure he kept the whole matter secret. The young man observed Philip's request, and as long as he was alive kept the miracle secret, but as soon as Philip was dead, rather than incur the charge of ingratitude, he told the whole story to many of the Fathers of the Congregation and a lot of other important people, describing it under oath, with a great outburst of tears. He is still alive today, and comes regularly to receive the sacraments devoutly.

---

[175] It was the man who suffered this ulcer who told the story on oath. *His name was Francesco della Molara, a Roman patrician.*

Philip is molested by demons

129.   I think it was the same year that the devil appeared to Philip when he was in the church, under the form of a boy, to make fun of him.[176] Philip at once detected what it was that had come to mock him under another guise, and called it over, rebuked it and drove it out of the church. I will add at this point that when he was praying at the dead of night, lying in his bedroom where no one else was near him, people sometimes heard loud knockings and bangings, which no one need doubt were the work of the devil.[177] I have already described earlier how the devil used to attempt to terrify him when he was praying by night.

He delivers a dying boy from death
A.D. 1585; Gregory XIII year 13; Philip's age 70

130.   In the year 85 of this century, Giovan Francesco Anerio, who was fourteen years old, began to suffer from a dangerous fever; it was so virulent that the doctors gave up on him, and although he lingered on, they could see signs which left no doubt that death was imminent.[178] He lay unconscious for seventeen days, and his limbs felt as cold and rigid as those of a corpse; he was unaware of anything, and could take no food; he could not move at all, and could hardly be distinguished from a dead body, in fact the general opinion was that he had died, and many were astonished to see that the dying boy was able to continue breathing for days without receiving any nourishment. When Philip heard about it, he went straight to the patient, placed his hands on his forehead, and told those who were present to say the Our Father and the Hail Mary once for him. Then he knelt down and placed his hand on the boy's forehead and began to chide his mother, 'It's you who are killing him by starvation!' he said. Then he called to the bystanders, 'Bring me some Malmesey wine.' They brought him some, and he

---

[176] It was the same man as in the last story who tells this one, for he was present.

[177] One who heard the knocking gave evidence of it on oath.

[178] This happened in March or April, for Gregory XIII was still alive. Apart from Giovan Francesco himself, we have four eyewitnesses to this story, one of them being that powerful woman Giulia Orsini Rangoni. *Giovan Francesco (1562–1630)*

moistened the boy's lips with it, which benefited him greatly. He began to revive at once, and drank what was offered him; then he started to feel better, and after a few days got out of bed, safe and sound, giving thanks as best he could for the help the holy Father had given him.

The respect shown to Philip by Gregory XIII and by many cardinals of Holy Church

131. It was not only those who were at risk or were afflicted with disease who revered Philip greatly, but also some of the most important people including the popes themselves. Gregory XIII, a ruler of the highest integrity and wisdom, was devoted to him, and was always eager to listen to him; he often consulted him and accepted his help in different matters, and when he had listened to him he did many things. There were other popes later on who followed him with the same affection and reverence, as we shall recount in the proper place. As well as Pope Gregory XIII, the following cardinals revered Philip as a true friend of God: Charles Cardinal Borromeo, Archbishop of Milan; Guido Cardinal Ferrerio; Guglielmo Cardinal Sirleto, prefect of the Apostolic Library; Gabriele Cardinal Paleotti, the first Archbishop of Bologna; Frà Michele Bonelli, Cardinal of Alessandria; Antonio Cardinal Carafa; Giulio Antonio Santoro, Cardinal of Santa Severina; Alessandro de' Medici, Cardinal of Florence; Cardinal Nicolò Sfrondato, Bishop of Cremona, who later became Gregory XIV; Cardinal Agostino Valerio, Bishop of Verona; Cardinal Vincenzo Lauro, Bishop of Mondovì, and many others.[179]

Now let us turn to what Philip did under Sixtus V, the successor to Pope Gregory; he was declared Supreme Pontiff in 1585, on the 24th April, and reigned for five years, four months and three days.

---

was the son of the Maurizio Anerio who has been mentioned before; he too was a celebrated musician.

[179] *Of this distinguished list, St Charles Borromeo is the one best remembered today – even though he did have a strongly-worded disagreement with St Philip over the idea of an Oratory in Milan.*

A Prediction

A.D. 1585; Sixtus V year 1; Philip's age 70–1

132. In the year 85 of this century, a priest called Giovan Antonio Lucci, who was more than sixty years old, fell off the horse he was riding and struck the ground.[180] His life was seriously at risk, for his skull was fractured, so that the bones became visible, and an infection set in, till the doctors pronounced his life to be in grave danger. He was afraid of dying from that accident, and had Philip summoned. 'I am not ready to die, Father,' he said, 'since I have not yet made a will and signed it as I should like to.' Then Philip hugged the man and said, 'Cheer up, you will live to write your will in the way you want.' He was not speaking idly, for the patient immediately began to improve, and soon afterwards became quite well. He lived for many years more, and died in 1599, on the 28th of October.

He heals one suffering from a severe illness

In November of the same year, a well-born boy named Carlo Orsini, aged twelve, was stricken by a pain in his side accompanied by a high fever; the pain was especially severe in his left side.[181] The fever continued without any remission at all, the disease seemed to be fatal, and the doctors began to doubt they could save the boy's life. But in the meantime, one day when he was beginning to suffer greatly, Philip came towards evening, summoned by the boy's mother. He sent everyone outside and had the doors closed; then he began by asking the boy where the pain was, and then proceeded to ask whether he wanted to confess his sins. He said he would do so willingly. Philip then knelt down and heard his confession, keeping his hand on the part where the pain was. This was no empty gesture, for Carlo began to feel that the pain was diminishing as Philip touched him. As he left, Philip said, 'Do not be afraid, you are not going to die of this disease, you'll feel better

---

[180] The noble brothers Pietro Paolo and Giacomo Crescenzi gave sworn witness to this story. It happened in April or May. *This is the Padre Lucci who was in charge of the building of the Chiesa Nuova, and came under attack for so doing (paragraph 110).*

[181] Carlo himself, and his mother Livia Vestri, have given public evidence about this.

tomorrow.' And, amazingly, he had hardly left the house before the power of God suddenly freed the boy from all his pain; that night he slept well, though he had lain awake all the previous night; he slept peacefully through until dawn, and when he awoke he found that the disease had entirely disappeared and he was able to tell the astonished doctors that his former strength had returned. Carlo explained to them that when he was ill it seemed to him that Philip was drawing out all the pain through the hand with which he was touching the place that hurt.

Philip is ill again
A.D. 1586; Sixtus V year 1; Philip's age 71

133. In the year of salvation 1586, on the 16th of January, Philip was struck down by a sudden recurrence of his sickness, in a virulent and dangerous form. However he recovered from it rapidly, after being anointed with holy oil, despite expectations, and to the surprise of the doctors who called it a miracle.

The Congregation increases

The Fathers who lived in our house allowed themselves and their property to be controlled as Philip decided, and had no greater desire than to follow the divine will in all things. As a result, their reputation spread far and wide, and in various different places and regions they were sought for with the greatest eagerness. Hence from the Roman Oratory, as from a primal stock, many cuttings began to be transplanted to different cities of Italy, and rooted in fertile soil they began to spread their branches. Among these the most famous is the Oratory which was built at Naples through the efforts of Francesco Maria Tarugi. He was invited there in the year 86 of our century by the Archbishop, Annibale di Capua, and other leading men. When he arrived in Naples, he accepted lodgings at the hospital for the incurable, but soon afterwards with the help of the local citizens had a house and church built of great magnificence; it was Archbishop Annibale who laid the first stone for the foundations, in a splendid and well-attended ceremony. For the increasing benefit of souls, the Fathers of the house in Rome decreed that the following should follow Tarugi: Antonio Talpa, of San Severino; Francesco Bozio of Gubbio; Thomaso Galletti of

Nizza; and Michelangelo Tozzi, a lay brother. Later on three more priests went, Juvenal Ancina of Fossano; Pietro Pozzi of Palermo; and finally Flaminio Ricci of Fermo. Once these had begun to labour in raising up the seeds of the Word of God in the vineyard of the Lord, many others came to join our institute, particularly moved by the preaching and example of Tarugi, whose name was already well known. Soon it happened, through the favour of God, that more than sixty men had given their names to our Congregation to join in our spiritual ranks.

134. What can I say about the foundations of our institute in San Severino, in the Marches, and elsewhere, which have been established within the past few years to the great benefit of souls? Everyone agrees they were entirely due to the labours, example and authority of Philip alone. But I must advise the reader that our Fathers are determined not to take responsibility for the government of any houses outside the city, apart from Naples and San Severino, and those for good reasons. This was settled in the following decree: 'Let no one dissipate the Congregation under the pretext of increasing it; it is decreed that the Congregation should not accept any other locality, nor undertake the government of any other Congregation, save for those at Rome, Naples and San Severino, in order to avoid the confusion which an excessive number would cause, and in order that those joined to the Congregation in the bonds of charity should be brought closer together by their daily contact with each other, the character of each one be more easily recognised, and the face of each be so familiar as to be respected.' (Decree of the General Congregation)

Afterwards the Fathers, not wanting to appear to eliminate the establishment of new Oratories, added these words to the decree: 'Nevertheless, if they think fit, they may send some members to establish colleges of the same character in other towns, with the provision that they return home once this is achieved; these new foundations would not be subject to ours, neither would their clergy be members of the Congregation of the Oratory at Rome. Likewise they may receive visiting priests into their house as guests, so as to learn our customs, and after a suitable time be able to make their own foundation.' (Continuation of the Decree)

Despite all this, the Fathers were compelled by necessity to open a new Oratory at Lanciano, on the first of November in 1598. This is because the Congregation possesses an Abbey of St John (commonly called 'in Venere') near that city, which has the care of souls attached to it. Here also the Fathers have established a school for poor youths, with the intention of educating them in devotion and for all sorts of practical work. The abbey possesses ten towns, and the Fathers are lords of one of them, called Fossacieca.

Up to the present day, Oratories have been established in many other places, and more are being set up, on the Roman model.[182] That gives us cause to believe that the famous way of life established by Philip will shortly be propagated among all nations. A Congregation which was born to assist all nations should be of benefit to all, with no exceptions of place or climate. Oratories already established on the model of Rome, apart from Naples, San Severino and Lanciano, are these four: Lucca, Fermo, Palermo and Camerino. Those under construction at the moment are these six: Fano, Padua, Vicenza and Ferrara; the fifth is being set up in a town called Tournon, across the Mountains in the diocese of Geneva and Duchy of Chablis; the sixth is in the church of Notre-Dame des Graces in the diocese of Fréjus in Provence.

A Miracle

135. In November or December of that year [1586], Eugenia Mansueti was suffering from an infection of her nostrils for eighteen months; they not only swelled up enormously, but also pained her greatly as if with fire. None of the regular medical treatments and remedies appeared able to cure her of this complaint, but she applied to herself a linen band sprinkled with the blood of the holy man, and immediately was relieved of her distress, which never troubled her again afterwards.

---

[182] The Oratories for whose government we are responsible are these four: Rome, Naples, San Severino and Lanciano. *The principle of autonomy, by which every Oratory is a self-governing corporation answerable only to the Holy See, is one of the most fundamental characteristics of St Philip's Institute. It remains so today, despite occasional attempts to transform it into a centralised religious order. Most of the houses*

Philip is shown by God the most secret thoughts

It was in the same year, or at any rate the next, that a certain man of good family was gripped by an overwhelming desire to entrust Philip with some project he had in mind, which he had mentioned to no one. Either through timidity or embarrassment he kept deferring the matter from day to day, until one morning, at our house, Philip took him aside, and told him all about the problem he was thinking of, and resolved it, although he had heard nothing about it, and the man stood silent and amazed.[183]

A Prediction

A.D. 1587; Sixtus V year 2; Philip's age 72

In the year of Christ 1587, in March, a priest of our Congregation called Giovan Francesco Bernardi, from Piacenza, was taken dangerously ill. The sickness was so severe that he was soon given up for dead both by the doctors and his attendants. He had been anointed with the last Anointing when Philip visited him and whispered in his ear, 'Be of good courage, you will certainly not die of this disease.' His words did not fall in vain, for the patient began to feel better immediately, and on that same day when the doctors had predicted he would die, he made a good recovery, and soon afterwards regained his physical health entirely, against all hope.[184]

He sees into the secrets of souls

136. That same year (was it March or April?) there was a boy of respectable family (whose name shall remain hidden) who used to go to Philip frequently.[185] He used to go to confession to members of religious orders, and everyone was impressed by this, but he used to conceal certain sins in his confession, being embarrassed about them. Now while he was behaving like this, he went to see

---

listed by Gallonio have come and gone, but new foundations have continually been made throughout the world.

[183] This story was confirmed in public witness by the man to whom it occurred.

[184] The said Father Giovan Francesco confirmed this story, which was well known among us; Alessandro Alluminati who attended him in his illness also confirmed it.

Philip as usual: as soon as he saw him Philip burst into tears, and sobbed like a child being spanked by its mother, until he brought the boy to the same condition of weeping. Through his sobs and tears he managed to say these words, 'How comes it that you are not revealing all your sins to the priest who hears your confession? Confess to him, tell him the sins you have done, otherwise you are wasting his time.' The boy was taken aback at hearing this, given that what he was hearing from the Father was something he had mentioned to no living soul, and he trembled all over in shock and awe. He too began to cry like a child, and resolved at once to repent properly, and reveal his vice to the priest who heard his confessions. The following day he did precisely that, and made a confession of his whole life. Then he returned as usual to Philip, who looked at him, and although he knew nothing about his having gone to confession, he could tell what he had done by the changed expression on his face. He commended his action, and said he was a new person since the previous day. 'What is the meaning of this new bearing you have, this new expression? You seem to me quite different from yesterday: believe me, you have put on a new face.' This remarkable and unexpected insight so affected the boy that he was astonished again, and from then on he has regularly used the sacraments, from which he has drawn such spiritual strength that he has dedicated himself entirely to God, body and soul.

Philip is elected perpetual Provost of the Congregation

137. Now that Philip was living with his disciples, the Fathers finally decided that he, whom they held to be the father and founder of the Congregation, should also have the post of perpetual Provost General over the Congregation, with the function of presiding over the others with authority. All were surprisingly unanimous about this, after various opinions had been voiced, so on the 19th of June that year it was decreed, though he was unwilling and objected, shutting himself in his room. Philip fled from this task, for he was

---

[185] It was the boy himself who tells the story and swore to it. *It was actually Giacomo Crescenzi, one of the sons of Constanza.*

a man who longed for peace and a secluded life, adorned with the greatest humility.

The rule at that time was that a Provost General should hold office for three years, or at most six, after which he would have no further authority, and could not be re-elected. The Fathers revised this rule, so as not to restrict Philip. They therefore decreed and again confirmed that the authority of a Provost General, with the single exception of Philip, should be restricted to three years, with the possibility that at the end of that time the authority of a Provost could be extended for another three years, if it seemed good to the Congregation. However, after Philip's death, that rule was annulled in May of the year 96 of our century, by decree of the whole Congregation, and a new one established for the future, granting the Fathers the right to re-elect the Provost General not only once after his three years had expired, but again, a third time or more as long as they knew it would be advantageous to the Congregation.

138. I must not omit to mention that Philip was of the mind that he wanted the Congregation to preserve for ever that form of life and constitution with which it began. Therefore he desired everyone to be clear that it was his wish that those who joined the Congregation should be bound by neither vow nor oath, neither then nor in the future. If any were to be moved by a desire for a more perfect way of life and chose to embrace the Religious state, or to bind themselves by oaths or promises, they were perfectly free to attach themselves to whatsoever Religious community they preferred, but those who determined to live in the Congregation should not presume to change the pattern of life they began with. Their life should be bound only by the bonds of mutual charity, so that the good savour of Christ might be manifest to all, while they should still be careful to give the appearance of Religious through the example of their life and the preaching of the Word of God.

He also laid down rules which were well adapted to the vocation and spirit of our Congregation, and all willingly accepted them. Then in order to preserve the advantages of peace and concord within the house, he decreed that if any of them became disobedient, or caused offence to others by their example, they should be expelled from the Congregation as unsuitable for our way of life, if they could not be corrected. He also frequently admonished his disciples not to take delight in external matters, but in Christian virtue, and bade them strive with all their might to possess the virtues of humility, obedience, patience, charity, chastity, detachment from transitory things, gentleness and the rest. Their way of life was to be a golden mean between the freedom of secular life and the austerity of holy religious. Thus someone who dwelt in the laxity of this world, and felt he could not surrender himself to a Religious community because of the severity of their rule, could observe our way of life, and feel he had found a place of refuge, where he would be able to correct his vices, improve his virtues, and establish a devout and holy manner of life.

A Prediction

139. There was a widespread rumour in the city that a certain man of noble birth and adorned with Church dignities was about to be enrolled in the College of Cardinals, that very year, on the 18th December – I shall deliberately conceal his name.[186] As soon as Philip heard it, he said, 'That man will never attain the rank of Cardinal, neither this year nor in the future.' The event proved him right, for the man died at Rome without receiving any further dignities, in the pontificate of Clement VIII.

He corrects a priest who had been unknown to him

I think it was about the same time that a priest called Prospero Somai entered our church; he felt that he was being called by Philip, and presented himself when called.[187] Philip said to him, 'I called you here in order to warn you not to presume to associate with women, since you are a priest, and not to get into the habit of seeking their company. That is not appropriate for a priest, who should be concerned to cultivate chastity consistently.' When he heard this, Prospero was greatly astonished, particularly because he had not been acquainted with Philip, nor Philip with him.

---

[186] A priest who was the son of the sister of the man in question swore to this story.

[187] Prospero himself gave evidence for this story, on oath.

XII : THE YEAR 1588
AND THE NEXT TWO

He sees events in the future and at a distance
A.D. 1588; Sixtus V year 4; Philip's age 74

140. It was in the year 1588 that a noblewoman named Elena, daughter of Tamiria Ceoli, was expectant; she went into labour in September, but since the child did not appear, Philip visited her.[188] He took the woman by the hand and made her walk round her room; as she did so, he prayed the Lord for her. Then when he was about to leave, the woman begged him to agree to baptise the child when it was born. Philip refused, and gave a plausible excuse, but the woman was not satisfied with his reason, and begged him at least to send someone in his name to take his place. Then finally he told her that she would have no need of any man to baptise her child, and with that he left. Philip's words were not idle, for the following night the woman gave birth to a dead child.

In the same year, Giulio Savera of Modena was on his way to visit Philip when a letter was brought to him telling him that his mother had died on the 28th of August, although he had not even heard she was ill.[189] He read the letter, but told no one about its contents, continuing his journey in grief. When the holy Father saw him, he first put his own biretta on his head, and then looped his rosary about his neck, saying, 'Come on, come on, get over your tears, your mother's death was such that you can believe the best about her.' And yet the matter was unknown to all except Giulio; he heard Philip's words with great consolation, as well as astonishment.

He restores a sick woman to health

141. That year too, Vittoria Varesi, a Roman, was suffering a flux from her head, what they call catarrh; this spread to her right hand,

---

[188] As sworn witness to this story we have the noble lady Tamiria.
[189] It was Giulio who told the whole story under oath. *He later became a laybrother of the Congregation, first in Naples and afterwards in Rome.*

causing a chilling pain, and so it infected the whole arm as far as her thumb, resulting in a great swelling.[190] She used all medical means in vain, and continued to deteriorate daily. Finally it occurred to her to call on Philip, and she was the more driven to do this because she realised that the disease was eating away her strength, and the sinews of her right hand were contracting so that she could use it for nothing, and could hardly bend it or straighten it. She went to Philip therefore, full of confidence, during the holy season of Advent, and told him about her complaint: he took hold of the affected limb, which was bandaged up, and prayed for her healing; as he prayed he stroked the hand he was holding, and pressed it strongly. Finally he finished his prayer, and said, 'Go away, Vittoria, do not be afraid, you will recover your usual health.'

She went away happily when she heard this, and returned to her home. As she went, she began to ponder thus, 'Should I not honour Philip as a holy man, a friend of God? Shouldn't I put all my hope of recovery in him alone? Enough of human remedies! Away with the medicine!' Thinking this, she unbandaged her bad hand, and threw the bandages into the fire. From then on she felt so much better that she washed the affected arm in cold water (to the horror of the doctor) and used it for whatever she wanted, till she made a complete recovery, in a short time, with no further medical aid.

A Prediction
A.D. 1589; Sixtus V year 5; Philip's age 74

142. In the year 1599, both Elena Cibo and her husband Domenico Mazzei were seriously ill at the same time, and Elena's mother Tamiria thought that they were both dying.[191] Philip said to her, 'Put your fears aside; only one of the two of them will die.' He was proved right, for it was only Domenico, Elena's husband, who died, on the 17th of June.

---

[190] Vittoria herself gave witness to this on oath, and her servants confirmed it.
[191] It was the above-mentioned Tamiria who told this story, under oath.

He delivers the dying from the jaws of death

That same year, a girl of noble birth named Laura Morona, aged twelve, was taken by a grave illness, which progressed to the extent that no one had any hope that the girl would survive.[192] The doctors gave up on her, and she lay in bed, quite unconscious; she could not hear, she could not speak, even though the parish priest had anointed her with holy oil. As her parents saw her scarcely breathing, with no hope of recovery, they grieved over her as if she were already dead. Everything was arranged for the funeral and burial, and they had given orders for a grave to be dug. Then Philip turned up; when he arrived he blew on the face of the girl, then he slapped her, then taking her hair in his hand he swung her head by it, calling out loudly to her, and ordering her to call on the name of Jesus. Upon this, the dying girl opened her eyes, spoke the holy name of Jesus, and began to feel better; she was soon pronounced out of danger, the fever left her sooner than anyone could hope for, and she eventually recovered her health as before.

143.   That same year, on the 20th of December, a lay-brother of our Congregation called Giovan Battista Guerra, from Modena, was decorating our church with long hangings when he fell down from a very high place.[193] He fell so far and struck the ground so heavily that his skull was seriously fractured. In falling, his head hit the marble, and the shock would surely have been fatal. When they found him he could say nothing, and heard nothing of their cries; they took him up for dead, and carried him into the nearest room, expecting him to die. He lay there some hours, unconscious, and several of the Fathers were saying the prayers for a holy death to assist his passing, as they supposed. Meanwhile they sent word

---

[192] Apart from Laura herself, there are three sworn witnesses to this *including her parents Girolamo and Giulia Moroni, who also said that they had dedicated the shroud they had bought for their daughter to Our Lady of Trastevere.*

[193] We know nine eyewitnesses who swore to this occurrence, including our doctor, Angelo Vittorio, who considers the outcome miraculous. *Guerra came from a family of artists, and his brothers were well known as painters and workers in intaglio. He entered the Congregation in 1583, with particular responsibility for the fabric of the church.*

of Giovan Battista's fall to Philip; he sent everybody away, and told them to pray earnestly to God for him, as if to say he was unwilling for him to die then. They also summoned the doctors, who found the patient virtually dead, with a fractured skull, and observed blood seeping from his wound. They pronounced that the situation was very critical, and that the injuries were probably fatal. Angelo Vittorio, the fathers' doctor, agrees with this diagnosis. In fact all the doctors were in complete agreement that the situation was critical, but there was considerable disagreement among them on how to proceed. One of them, called Giovanni, was of the opinion that the wound should be scraped with a scalpel and opened up, to uncover the bone and discover the nature of the fracture. Others, on the contrary, including Giuseppe Zerla, a very famous practitioner, thought that this should by no means be attempted.[194]

They had already got the instruments ready to section and trepan him, but since the most experienced doctors disagreed on the procedure to follow in treating his injuries, they did not treat the patient at all apart from simply anointing him with turpentine, and giving him oil of almonds to drink. While they were doing this, Angelo Vittorio came to Philip and told him the injuries were certainly fatal. He smiled and said, 'I would rather he didn't die until he has finished decorating the Church', but then speaking seriously, he added, 'I will ask the Lord for his recovery, for I know he will undoubtedly recover from his injuries.' So it happened: Giovan Battista made a remarkable recovery, and no infection set in after his injuries, although the doctors had expected it. Moreover, he felt no pain, even though no treatment had been given him except what I have described. Though there were still some doctors who said that surgery was necessary, the patient did recover his former health, contrary to what everyone expected.

---

[194] *Angelo Vittorio was chief physician to Gregory XIII, and an old friend of St Philip. Zerla was another old friend, who was eventually buried in the Chiesa Nuova.*

He acquires the bodies of the holy martyrs Papias and Maurus, Roman soldiers, through the agency of Cardinal Agostino Cusano
A.D. 1590; Sixtus V year 5; Philip's age 75

144. Our church had by now reached its present dimensions, but was devoid of any relics of saints. Accordingly, Cardinal Agostino Cusano, who held Philip always closer to his heart than all others, decided to enrich it with such a great treasure.[195] He thought this over, and decided to do all in his power to have the relics of the holy martyrs Papias and Maurus transferred to our church, with papal permission, from the diaconal church of Sant'Adriano of which he was the titular at that time.

The occasion for this was as follows: they had decided to restore the high altar of that church, which was very ancient, and to redecorate it. When they began this, the workmen who were destroying the ancient altar discovered several bodies of distinguished martyrs, namely the virgin Flavia Domitilla, her eunuchs Nereus and Achilleus, Marius and his wife Martha, and finally Papias and Maurus, officers in the Roman army, buried in three separate compartments, with the original inscriptions. At Philip's desire and request, Cardinal Agostino asked Pope Sixtus V for permission to transfer the sacred bodies of Saints Papias and Maurus from the diaconal church of Sant'Adriano into our new church of Our Lady and St Gregory in the Vallicella. This was granted, by the Pope's generous command.

On the 11th of February, 1599, the receptacle in which the bones of the holy martyrs were contained was unsealed and opened, and a small portion of the saints' bones extracted, as the Pope wished, to be retained in the church of Sant'Adriano as a witness and reminder of their long repose there. The receptacle was then closed and sealed up, and placed within a wooden chest, tied up with red silk cord. The coffin was then lifted out of its resting place onto a bier, and placed in front of the high altar in front of a large congregation. Germanico Fedeli, who was Prefect of Ceremonies, gave the signal, and the procession began to move, from the church

---

[195] *Cardinal Cusano (d. 1598) was of noble Milanese origin; he lived near the Chiesa Nuova in the present Palazzo Sora, and left 200 scudi a year to the Congregation.*

of Sant'Adriano towards the Arch of Severus, then to the Capitol, thence to the Piazza Altieri, along the Strada Pontificia to Monte Giordano, and so finally it came to rest in our church.

145.   It was quite a sight to see. The holy relics, glittering with gold, were carried along on an open bier, under a silk canopy, attended devoutly by the priests of our Congregation, with the choir singing a delightful harmony. In front of them went the tokens of the blessed martyrs, then members of the households of holy men, then a large number of clergy and laity who used to attend our church and Oratory regularly, all of them carrying lighted torches in their hands. Two silver thuribles were carried, and a great many wax candles; the Swiss Guards surrounded the sacred bier, to restrain the crowds. So they bore the bodies of those holy martyrs with solemn pomp and devout service, and they were welcomed at the bottom of the steps of the church by the following cardinals:

> Alfonso Cardinal Gesualdo, Bishop of Porto.
>
> Gabriele Cardinal Paleotti, Bishop of Albano.
>
> Domenico Cardinal Pinelli,
> of the title of San Lorenzo in Panisperna.
>
> Ippolito Cardinal Aldobrandini, Major Penitentiary,
> who is now Bishop of the Catholic Church
> under the name of Clement VIII.
>
> Girolamo Cardinal della Rovere,
> of the title of San Pietro in Vincoli.
>
> Scipio Cardinal Gonzaga,
> of the title of Santa Maria del Popolo.
>
> Mariano Pierbenedetti, Cardinal of Camerino,
> of the title of Santi Marcellini e Pietro.
>
> Federico Cardinal Borromeo, deacon of Sant'Agata.
>
> Agostino Cardinal Cusano, deacon of Sant'Adriano,
> who handed over the bodies of the holy martyrs with
> some well-chosen words, at the command of Pope Sixtus V,

to our holy patriarch Philip Neri of Florence,
founder and originator of our Congregation.

Guido Cardinal Pepoli, deacon of SS. Cosma e Damiano.

All of these showed their reverence to the coffin as it was placed on a wooden platform set up in the middle of the church, and covered with a cloth of gold. Then there arrived Nicolò Sfrondato, Cardinal of Cremona of the title of Santa Cecilia, who afterwards became Gregory XIV.

After four days the bodies and heads of the holy martyrs were removed from the nave and taken into the sanctuary, where they rested until the consecration and dedication of the church itself and of the high altar, which had been completed with great splendour. This dedication took place last year, in 1599, celebrated with solemn and splendid ritual by Alessandro de' Medici, Cardinal Priest of the Holy Roman Church, and Archbishop of Florence. You may read about the final translation of the relics of the holy martyrs in a long and detailed account by Giacomo Buzio, canon of the Lateran Basilica, and His Eminence Cardinal Girolamo Rusticucci, Vicar Notary, who were both present.

A nun appears to Philip

146. One day Philip took the opportunity to speak about Caterina de' Ricci, that famous holy nun of the Order of St Dominic, whose life has been written in three volumes by Serafico Razzi of the same Order.[196] He began with these words, 'While she was alive, Caterina appeared to me', and then went on to describe her appearance, her manner of speech, her height and complexion, in great detail. Now who could deny that was a miracle, for Philip had never left Rome, and Caterina had never left her community in Prato? The occasion on which he spoke like this was the actual day she died, on the 4th of February that year.

---

[196] We have five sworn witnesses to this story. *St Caterina de' Ricci (1522–90) was a member of the Dominican community in Prato; she was deeply devoted to the memory of Savonarola, and concerned for reform in the Church, as well as being an ecstatic visionary. She was not canonised until 1747.*

He sees the secret thoughts of the soul

Ettore Modio of Calabria came to Rome in February of the same year, where he began to confess his sins to Philip, but he was accustomed to keep silent about the violent temptations to impurity which constantly assailed him, as well as about his own negligence in taking steps to avoid them.[197] Philip discerned the young man's habit, and the peril his soul was in because of it, and took the opportunity when he was confessing his actual sins to ask, 'Why do you not accuse yourself of those thoughts of lust and impurity that you have, not to mention your negligence in driving them away? Tell all your sins, if you want God to be pleased with you.' Ettore was astonished at this, but immediately admitted with deep compunction that he had failed in these matters, and assured Philip that he was resolved henceforth to live with greater vigilance.

He restores the sick to health

That same year (was it March or April?) a priest of our Congregation called Prometeo Pellegrini began to suffer from such a dire dysentery that he felt as if his insides were falling out.[198] He was confined to his room, and suffered terribly, as his pains increased. Philip therefore went to see him, and in a jocular manner took hold of the patient's hand, pretending to be concerned about some business of the community; then he made the sign of the cross with it over the sick man's chest, which filled him with hope.[199] Philip remarked that there was no need to be concerned, and promptly left. Within a quarter of an hour, Prometeo realised that all his pain had disappeared, and told us about it.

147. That same year the noblewoman Livia Vestri suffered from a severe dizziness in her head, for more than four months; she took

---

[197] Ettore himself told this story, and swears to it. *He was a nephew of Giovan Battista Modio, previously mentioned.*

[198] Father Prometeo himself tells this story and swears to it. *He came from Poggio Catino, entered the community in 1589 as a laybrother, and was ordained priest in 1593. He died in 1631.*

[199] This is what St Romuald used to do when working miracles, as St Peter Damian tells us in his life.

an infusion of what they call *Legnosacro*, but it did her no good at all, and she was very liable to fall.[200] One day, after she had received the sacraments in our church, she was setting out for home, but as the vertigo seized on her, she was unable to walk, since whatever she looked at seemed to be swimming around her. Father Angelo Velli noticed this, and advised her to go to Philip. She obeyed him, and told the holy man what was happening; he laid his hand on her head, and told her to forget her anxiety. And amazingly, at once, after a single touch by Philip, she felt herself quite free from the complaint, and after that she did not suffer even the slightest recurrence of the problem.

He restores health to one despaired of

In August of the same year, a Roman named Bartolomeo Fugini was so ill that they despaired of his recovery; the doctors had given him up. He had been anointed with holy oil, and was on the point of death, partly through the virulence of the fever, and partly through the severe pains he felt in his head.[201] When our Philip heard of this (it was three hours after sunset), he turned to those who were with him, and said to the sick man, 'May the Lord bring you a sure assistance.' He prayed for him that night, and found him in the morning, not only free of the fever but also delivered from the pain that had affected him so badly, though the night before he had been considered all but dead. He is still alive, a reliable witness to the way his health was restored at the holy Father's intercession.

That is enough of such stories. We must turn now to matters which happened under the same Pope, but the date of which I have not been able to establish.

Secret thoughts revealed to Philip by God

148. There was a certain woman, of very good family, who conceived the idea of doing some great business for God; she kept the

---

[200] Livia herself gave evidence publicly to this story. *She was the mother of Carlo Orsini, whose cure is related in paragraph 132.*

[201] There are two eyewitnesses, apart from Bartolomeo himself, who confirmed this on oath.

idea secret, and told no one about it.²⁰² She was unsure about what to do, and was reluctant to explain what she was thinking to Philip, so that she was anxious about the decision. But one day she came to Philip, intending to make her confession, but before she had uttered a word, he told the astonished woman all about what was in her mind, as God had revealed it to him.

Some more people cured by invoking him

The general opinion about Philip's holiness was such that some would call on his help in his absence, as if he were actually present.²⁰³ Patrizio Patrizi was suffering one night from a severe stomach ache, and thought of the holy Father, imploring his aid. He was not disappointed: his pain disappeared entirely, and he jumped out of bed in the morning quite fit and well.²⁰⁴

An honest woman called Maria Paganelli was afflicted with the same disease: she applied to the suffering part a strip of cloth stained with Philip's blood and serum, and was instantly cured.²⁰⁵ On another occasion she was suffering from a severe headache, but recovered her health at once at Philip's touch.

He gladdens the sorrowful, and marvellously assists those struggling with temptation

149. Philip seemed to have been born for the relief of the sick and the consolation of those in distress, for that was his special concern. We will give another couple of examples. A woman who was of

---

²⁰² The woman herself and her sons have given sworn witness to this. *Yet again, this was Costanza Crescenzi.*

²⁰³ The saints were invoked even during their lifetime. See St Mark's life of Porphyry of Gaza, Surius on Auxentius, Theodoret on Philotheus, Cyril on John the Silent, Bandomina on Radegund, Theosteristus on Nicetas, Peter Damian on Romuald: and you can find the same thing in many other lives.

²⁰⁴ Father Germanico Fedeli heard the story the following day from Patrizio, and has given evidence on oath.

²⁰⁵ She it was who tells the story under oath. Many miracles have been worked through the clothing or such like of living saints, as their Lives recount. See Theodoret on Philotheus, Cyril on John the Silent, Metaphrastes on Cyrus and John, Bede on Cuthbert and finally Gottfried on St Bernard, book 4, chapter 1.

good birth, but very devout, was suffering from a deep depression; after enduring this for six months, her confessor advised her to go to Philip.[206] She told him about the anxious state of her mind; he looked at her, and gently touched her, filling her with hope. 'Go home,' he said, 'you will have no further trouble.' He had hardly said this when the woman was suddenly relieved of all her depression, not only for the present moment, but forever after, which surely could not have happened without a miracle.

There was someone who was troubled with scruples while saying the Divine Office, to the extent that he had all but given up hope.[207] He had tried many means to overcome this difficulty, before eventually applying to Philip. He listened to the case, and then shut the door of his room after sending the man away and promising to pray to God for him. The other went home, and started to recite his Office, when he discovered he was completely free from the trial the devil had imposed on him. And there were many others, who were troubled by great anxiety, who went home happily after simply talking to Philip.

---

[206] She has given sworn evidence to what happened to her. *Livia Vestri again.*
[207] It is Federico Cardinal Borromeo who gives evidence of this on oath.

XIII : WHAT HE DID UNDER POPES GREGORY XIV AND INNOCENT IX, IN 1590 AND 1591

The favour showed to Philip by Gregory XIV
A.D. 1590; Gregory XIV year 1; Philip's age 76

150. Now we can turn to what Philip did under Pope Gregory XIV (having nothing to say about Urban VII whose pontificate was so short).[208] It was Pope Gregory who gave the holy Father permission to celebrate Mass in a private chapel adjacent to his room. There it was that, in his longing for ever closer union to God, after saying the words 'Lord I am not worthy...', he would ask those who were present, including the server, to go out, remaining on his own in the chapel. Alone, and without witnesses, he would often not consume the sacred Eucharist, nor drink the Precious Blood, before he had passed two hours, more or less, in contemplation of the Blessed Sacrament, with deep feelings of devotion and much shedding of tears. Once he had received the Body and Blood of Christ, he would admit the server, and complete the ceremony. After Mass was over, he often seemed so abstracted from his senses that you would think him more dead than alive. The same pope dispensed Philip from reciting the Divine Office, because he was so often ill or abstracted, and allowed him to say the Rosary instead; he did therefore recite the Rosary when he was ill and the doctors specifically forbade him to say the Office and canonical Hours, but when he was well he would never take advantage of this dispensation but regularly recited the Divine Office in its present form.

---

[208] Gregory XIV was elected on 7th December 1590, and reigned for ten months and ten days.

A Prediction

151. In the year of Christ 1591, there was a prominent lady who fell into a serious illness in her old age.[209] One of her relatives began to fear she was going to make the Fathers of the Congregation the heir to her property. Philip used to visit the sick woman every day, out of charity (having been used to hear her confessions). He was not interested in her money, as her relative thought, concerned only for her salvation. The relative became more anxious and suspicious, believing that Philip was more avid for property than souls, and this obsession deprived the man of all calm and rest, either by day or night. He decided to deter the holy Father's visits with threats, and, having failed in that, determined to prevent him having any access to the house, let alone the patient. His schemes came to nothing, for God's servants may be humble enough on their own behalf, but amazingly obstinate in pursuit of the business of God. Philip therefore remained determined to continue his practice, and was so strong-willed that he ignored the dangers that threatened him: every day he would visit the sick woman, once or twice or even more often. Despite her attendants he got into her room, with no protection against the fury of men other than his confidence in God. One day, when he was setting out to see her as usual, some of his disciples warned him that he was running into certain peril. 'I am going to see that woman,' he said, 'for the sake of her soul. And I am not going to abandon that duty even if they do kill me.' When they heard that, they again begged him not to continue with his purpose, saying he should adapt himself to the occasion and yield to necessity. He replied, 'I have already told you, I am not going to stop visiting that woman. I am not in the least afraid of being killed because of that. On the other hand, I would like you to be aware that the patient, although in danger of death now, will recover from her sickness, but her relation, who is in such good health, will die quite soon.' And as he had predicted, so it came to pass.

---

[209] There were four priests who gave evidence about this matter on oath, and it was widely known. *It was Lavinia della Rovere Orsini, and the pugnacious nephew was Giulio Cesare Colonna.*

He delivers Manzoli from death

152. At the beginning of June that year, a Florentine named Giovanni Manzoli, who was one of Philip's oldest disciples, fell into a serious and dangerous disease.[210] As the illness grew steadily worse, he came to his last extremity, the doctors gave up on him, and no hope remained of recovery. He was anointed with holy oil one evening, and sent word to his nephew Giovan Battista to ask Philip to send a priest at once to assist him at his death. After requesting that, he entrusted himself wholeheartedly to the holy Father as if he were actually present, with great confidence, because he remembered that Philip had predicted that Giovanni would survive him. Need we be surprised that as long as he could draw breath he would not give up hope of life? While he was in this frame of mind the doctors visited him; they took his pulse and in other ways determined that death was imminent. Concluding that he could not possibly live another hour, they advised his family to begin to make preparations for the funeral.

Meanwhile the priest whom Philip had sent arrived (it was Mattia Maffei), who in his earnest prayers commended the dying soul, fortified by the sacraments of the Church, to the protection of God and His saints. The hour had scarcely passed during which the doctors had predicted he would die (their names were Girolamo, Cordelio and Vito), when the patient's eyes seemed to become fixed on the wall adjacent to his bed; when those present saw this they began to lament his death, and lit the customary candle. Looking at each other, they muttered, 'Look, he is dying, look, his spirit has gone forth.' Since the death was slow and peaceful, and Manzoli had lost consciousness, knowing no one and hearing nothing, Mattia went home. He went to Philip and reported that Manzoli was in extremity. But when Philip heard this, he spent the rest of the night in prayer, and his prayers were heard: during the night the patient began to feel better, he relaxed into a refreshing sleep, and slept for two hours. When he awoke he called out aloud to his attendants, and asked for some food, having recovered his strength of mind

---

[210] Apart from Manzoli himself, there are two other witnesses from among those present who have given evidence on oath.

and body. In the meantime, at daybreak, the little brothers of the Company of Mercy arrived at Manzoli's house, believing him to be dead. They asked to have the body to wash it, but were struck with amazement when they heard that so far from being dead he was not even in danger, for that night his life had been spared. They refused to believe what they had heard until they could see for themselves that he was better, and heard him clearly able to speak.

153. I ought to add the following story. Early in the morning Philip sent the same priest, Mattia Maffei, to visit Manzoli. As he set out, Monte Zazzara arrived to tell him about Manzoli's death, and began to say, 'O Father, I have lost a dear friend today. Giovanni Manzoli died last night. I am sure of this, because the Company of Mercy have been summoned for the funeral.' But he had hardly said this before Philip interrupted, saying, 'Manzoli is not dead, nor is he going to die from this illness.' Meanwhile Mattia returned, and when the holy Father asked him how Giovanni Manzoli was, replied 'He's dead.' Philip answered, 'You are not telling the truth, he is alive: hurry off and go back to him, don't delay, don't stand around!' Mattia was still reluctant to do as he had been told, saying that he had already been assured by Manzoli's servants that he was dead, but Philip was even more insistent, and forced him to do as he commanded.

Mattia then left, though as he went, he was thinking, 'What is the use of going back here? There is no point in returning to Manzoli's house, I will only hear again what I have already heard: Giovanni is dead.' But while thinking thus, he arrived at the house and went into the room where he found the dying man not only alive but in good spirits, talking clearly and aware of those around him; at this he was astonished, he returned to Philip, told him what he had seen, and passed on Manzoli's greetings.

Now to return to the main story, the doctors came back to Manzoli when his servants summoned them, although at first they were reluctant to do so, believing him to be dead. However, they took his pulse, and at once realised to their amazement that he was clearly on a good way to recovery. 'A miracle,' they said, 'a miracle', as they observed Manzoli improving from moment to moment. He did not remain long in this condition, for shortly afterwards his strength steadily increased until he was quite well again. He lived on until the year 97 of our century, and died more than two years after our holy Father.

Niccolò Gigli, who was dying, is comforted by Philip to a marvellous extent

154. Niccolò Gigli, a priest of our Congregation, and a man of many outstanding virtues, although with no self-conceit, became gravely ill, and the disease appeared to be so dangerous that he was close to death. Philip visited him regularly, for his singular virtue made him dear to him, and he encouraged him in his struggle against the assaults of the devil. It happened on one occasion that, as he approached his end, he began to be attacked by the Enemy in various ways, which on this occasion came to our notice. Philip was celebrating Mass in his private chapel, and the Fathers were having dinner, when we heard a noise above the ceiling of the refectory. The place where Niccolò lay was quite close, as was the chapel where Philip was offering the saving sacrifice to the divine majesty. Now when the noise began, some of the fathers thought it was thunder, while others heard what sounded like large and heavy stones being violently dragged across the vaulted ceiling of the refectory. In fact not everyone could hear the noise, but of the priests, Pietro Consolini and Prometeo Pellegrini heard it. While the noise was going on, Philip was praying earnestly for the sick man, and then summoned his servers. Consolini was the first to arrive, and he said to him, 'Go to Niccolò at once, I want to know what is happening to him straight away.' Consolini rushed off, and found the dying priest with his hands joined, his face calm and joyful, saying, 'Let us give thanks to the Lord our God: he came, he went, he is conquered.' He kept repeating these words, from which it could be deduced that he had been struggling against the devil, whose appearance he could not avoid, and had been miraculously helped by Philip, through whose aid he had been delivered from the rage and threats of the devil.

When our holy Father arrived, Niccolò said, 'Oh, Father, my Father, how could it have happened that I never knew you until now? Now that I am dying, now I begin to realise what sort of a man you are.'

Since Niccolò Gigli was a man who lived in our Congregation for many years, with notable integrity, I will take the opportunity to say a few other things worth recording about him. He was given to devotion more than others, to the extent that once he had been called by God he retained nothing of his former life, save to 'forget thy people and thy father's house' [Ps 44:11]. He was so oblivious to his relations that he never even thought of them at all. As a result, when letters came to him in Rome from France, he would not read them, in fact he would throw the bundle of letters tied together into the fire. He was diligent in prayer, and more apt to obedience than anyone, exceeding all in his lack of concern for himself. He was very assiduous in hearing confessions, outstanding for his love of God and his charity towards others, while considering himself beneath contempt. For a long time he directed the convent of St Frances of Rome with mildness and without arguments. He foresaw the day he would die before he took to his bed, and spoke about it; as he neared death he was strengthened by the sacraments of the Church, and spent his last day giving every sign of holiness. He died, as I have said, in 1591, on the 14th of June.

He predicts the future

155. On the 22nd of July, Father Desiderio Consalvi, of the Order of St Dominic, fell into a severe illness; this was followed by a dangerous fever, to which succeeded a delirium.[211] He lay ill in bed, overcome by his suffering, and without hope of recovery, if you were to believe the doctors. While he was approaching his end, Philip was called out to Father Francesco Bencini, who was also seriously ill, though not to the extent that the doctors despaired of him. But Philip at once said, 'He will not recover from this illness', and then on visiting Father Desiderio he repeated, 'Bencini will die of his present illness.'

To continue: he had hardly reached Desiderio's room when the patient came to his senses, and was so delighted at seeing Philip with him that he thought he was already cured. He was not wrong

---

[211] Apart from Father Desiderio, and his doctor Giovanni Comparotti, two other eyewitnesses have given public testimony to the whole story.

in this opinion: Philip laid his hands on him, and said, 'Be confident, you will be well very soon.' It did not take long; the patient realised that he had been delivered from his delirium and lethargy, and that the remaining fever was passing off. Thus he was called back to life from the midst of death, and his friends began to call him 'Lazarus Revived' instead of Desiderio: even now a few people still call him by that nickname. The doctor, Giovanni Comparotti, who was tending both patients, saw the result of Philip's prophecy, and began to revere him more and more as a friend of God. He confirmed that Father Desiderio had been restored to health when the holy man prayed for him, and added that he was most impressed that Father Bencini had died, although the doctors had not at all given up hope for him, whereas Father Consalvi who was considered by all as good as dead had made a full recovery from his disease, against all medical opinion.

He assists a dying woman, working marvels with her in her last agony

156. In August of the same year, there was a noblewoman who was brought to the last stages of illness, and suffered so greatly that every symptom indicated that death was imminent.[212] Philip was very fond of her, and came to visit her. He prayed for her for a short time asking God's mercy, and then went on to visit someone else who was ill. As he went he kept saying to himself, 'What a woman! How she needs help! The situation demands that we should do something to help her.' When he got as far as the Piazza della Rotonda, he said to those of us who were with him, 'Let's go back to that dying woman', for God had revealed to him that he should go back to her, as she was struggling against the devil. He found her in much the same condition as before, and you might think she was quite strong enough to continue to live at least for another day. But to help her, Philip asked those who were sitting around her bed to go out, and then he blew on her face once or

---

[212] Not to mention other witnesses, the sworn evidence was given by the noble ladies Beatrice Caetani and Giulia Rangoni, both of whom were present at the event. *The woman was Porzia Orsini of Anguillara.*

twice. Then he prayed to God for her, and briefly spoke to her about God to comfort her, ending with these words, 'In the name of God, I bid you, holy soul, to depart from this body.' And after he had said that, the woman expired at once, to the surprise of all those present, who at first did not believe it had happened.

He delivers a dying woman from death

In the same year, I think in October, a Roman woman, Vittoria Varesi, suffered a great pain in her left shoulder, which caused her so much suffering that she could scarcely breathe, nor could she rest at night or even lie down.[213] She thought of the blessed Philip in her distress, and went to him for help, asking him earnestly to cure the illness she suffered. She was not disappointed: Philip immediately struck the affected part with his fist, saying 'Go away, you will soon recover from this affliction.' Amazingly, Vittoria felt better at once; she had only just reached her home (which was close to our house) before she realised that she had been restored to her usual state of health.

The love which Gregory XIV had for Philip

157. Here I must tell you how much Gregory XIV loved Philip, both as Cardinal and as Pope; he was very fond of him, and took great delight in his company. He always welcomed him with a smiling cheerful face, and hugged him affectionately, nor would he allow him to stand in his presence, or talk about anything until he sat down and put his biretta on. One day the Pope was rushing to embrace him as usual, and I was there; he burst out into these words, 'Oh how fortunate you are! You have far surpassed us in holiness, Father, even if we outrank you in rank and power, being, as we are, the Vicar of Christ on earth!' There were some very high-ranking cardinals of the Holy Roman Church present, who under that pontificate used to pay great attention to Philip, and were also delighted with his company: these were Gabriele,

---

[213] Vittoria herself tells the whole story, on oath, and the servants have confirmed the matter.

Cardinal Paleotti, Frà Michele Bonelli of Alessandria, Giulio Antonio Santoro, Alessandro de' Medici, Agostino Valier, and Vincenzo Lauro, and in addition there was Ippolito Cardinal Aldobrandini, the Major Penitentiary, who is today responsible for governing the Church with such a reputation for holiness and wisdom, distinguished under the name of Clement VIII. Then there was Girolamo della Rovere, Archbishop of Turin, Scipio Gonzaga, Federico Borromeo, Giovan Francesco Morosino, Agostino Cusano, Guido Pepoli, Paolo Camillo Sfrondato, Ottavio Paravicini, and some others. Indeed, Philip was always held in great esteem and respect by the popes, the senior cardinals and the principal laymen, but he was never elated by these honours, for he made no account of transitory things, thinking always of eternal honours and eternal glory, for which he longed so much.

So much for what Philip did under Gregory XIV. Now we must turn to what he did under Innocent IX, who was elected Pope on the 29th of October 1591, and reigned for two months.

He sees the secret thoughts of a man, by the help of God
A.D. 1591; Innocent IX year 1; Philip's age 77

158. Towards the end of 1591, someone called Matteo Guerra came to Rome, a man who was greatly devoted to God, and he was received as a guest in our house.[214] He went to confession to Philip, for he had heard of his great reputation for sanctity. But this is what happened: one evening there were some leading noblemen visiting the holy Father, and he, being familiar with them, was chatting to them in his usual light-hearted and affable manner, joining in occasionally in their gentle laughter. Our guest found this in some way offensive, and said to himself, 'If this man were really as holy as they say, he would conduct himself in a very different manner, and what others call politeness he would call sin.' When

---

[214] He himself told the story, on oath. You can find something similar in the life of Saint Saba, and St Gregory Nazianzen's 46th Letter, to Amphilochus. *Guerra (1535–1601) was an uneducated peasant who founded a religious community in Siena, modelled on the Oratory. He was a frequent visitor to the Roman Oratory and devoted to St Philip.*

it was light he went to see the holy man, and embarked on confessing his sins, but of what he had been thinking the night before he said nothing. Philip looked at him, and warned him not to omit to mention any sin, while making his confession, however trivial it might appear. After this, he went on, 'It was you who found me an occasion of offence last night', and he told him everything in detail. Guerra was astonished when he heard this, and completed his confession by uncovering his thoughts, and begging forgiveness for them.

Visions

Here I must add another remarkable thing about the Father, finding no better place to insert it. Almost always, when the Roman See was bereft of its pastor, Philip could be heard, sometimes in his sleep, sometimes awake, saying out loud the name of him who was about to be chosen Supreme Pontiff, which he used to reveal to a few people.[215]

Now, after the two months' pontificate of Innocent IX, we come to Clement VIII, now gloriously reigning, who succeeded him on the 30th January, in the year of our salvation 1592.

Here our Author ends his second book.

---

[215] Not to mention others, Cardinal Tarugi tells us this, and swears to it.

BOOK III

XIV : THE YEAR OF CHRIST 1592 AND THE TWO SUBSEQUENT YEARS

He predicts many things by God's agency
A.D. 1592; Clement VIII year 1; Philip's age 77

159. Pietro Filippo Lazzarello had been granted an ecclesiastical benefice by Innocent IX, but because the Pope died suddenly, he was unable to obtain his apostolic letters of appointment.[216] Clement VIII took the place of the deceased pontiff, and Pietro Filippo did all he could to expedite the matter, but a certain powerful nobleman had got hold of the Letter of Supplication (as it is called) with the aim of transferring the position to someone else. As a result, Pietro Filippo in desperation conceived the idea of murdering that nobleman with his crossbow, and had accordingly ceased to celebrate Mass and recite the Divine Office. While he was so minded, he happened to come into our church one Sunday morning, and knelt down there, not far from our Philip. He felt some inner force driving him to approach him, so, without knowing what he was doing or what he wanted, he fell at Philip's feet, saying not a word, uttering not a sound, you would have thought he was dumb. The holy Father took him gently by the left ear and said, 'You are burdened with debts, aren't you?' He replied, 'Yes, Father'. 'Be of good heart', continued Philip, 'within a fortnight you will be free from your anxiety.' When Pietro Filippo heard this he was overjoyed, and went away happily, full of confidence; within the stated time he was delivered from his difficulties, despite all expectations, and the letters were made out granting him the ecclesiastical benefice he had hoped for.

The same year, Girolamo Pamphili, a man of the highest rank and Auditor of the Rota, was seriously ill, to the extent that he began

---

[216] It was Pietro Filippo himself who told us this, on oath. *Lazzarello later founded an 'Accademia dei Conferenti della Florida' in the church he had thus obtained, and made it available to the Oratorian community in San Severino.*

to decline and the doctors were in despair.[217] Philip visited him at the end of April, and embraced the man kindly, telling him to put away all his fears, and promising him that the disease would soon go. His promise was kept, for not long afterwards he got out of bed, safe and sound. I must not forget to mention here that it was frequently noticed how sick people about whom the doctors had given up hope recovered their usual health after Philip had assured them that they would survive that disease; on the other hand, there were those of whom the doctors had no bad expectations, who paid the debt of nature after Philip had predicted that they were about to die.

160. There was a nine-year-old girl called Caterina Ruiz, whose nose was affected by unpleasant scabs, what is called the 'mulberry disease', which gave rise to the suspicion that it was plague, for she had recently visited a house where some people suffering from that had lived.[218] They treated the girl with medicines, but to no avail, for although the scabs did occasionally disappear, new ones of the same type continually appeared in her nose. She had suffered under this complaint for a whole year, without the doctors being able to cure her, until her mother brought her to Philip in April or May of this year. When he saw the girl, he stroked her nose gently with his hand, and said, 'My dear, you will never have any more trouble with this sort of affliction.' Caterina began to feel better immediately, and soon afterwards recovered her usual good health, nor did she ever afterwards suffer from that disease.

In the same year, in August, Vittoria Cibo came to Philip to cleanse her soul in the sacrament of confession.[219] He asked her afterwards, 'When did you last see your sister?' She said, 'Just now.' He replied, 'Go and see her often, because she will die fairly

---

[217] Both Girolamo and his cousin have given sworn witness to this story. *Girolamo Pamphili (1544–1610) was a penitent of St Philip's from childhood. He was eventually created Cardinal on 25 June 1604.*

[218] Apart from Caterina herself we have three other eyewitnesses who have given evidence of this.

[219] This was confirmed in public witness by a noblewoman called Tamiria. *Actually, according to Bacci, the nun sister was called Vincenza.*

soon.' This sister was a virgin consecrated to God, given the name Vittoria like her sister when she left this world to join the community of Saint Frances of Rome. At that time she was in excellent health, living peacefully and happily, being aged twenty-one. But she was suddenly stricken with disease and died within a month, on the 19th of September to be precise.

161. That same year, on the 23rd of September, four youths were entrusted to the care of the Fathers, all brothers, and Jewish by religion. They were very obstinate in clinging to their Hebrew traditions and superstitions. When Philip saw how stubborn they were, he predicted that they would soon give their names to Christ, and it came to pass in this manner.[220] One day, an hour after sundown, when they were more determined than ever before to remain in their Jewish superstition, they affirmed that they wanted to live and die in their ancestral ancient religion, and refused to listen to anything that they were told about Christ. Philip was not only undaunted by their pride and obstinacy, but felt himself more and more eager to bring them to Christ. He encouraged them, therefore, to pray to God that He would show them the truth, and added that he would offer his Mass the following day for their conversion, confident that his entreaty would be heard. The next morning, therefore, although they remained of the same mind, and were determined to keep to the Jewish Law, they found themselves suddenly and unexpectedly driven by the power of God towards the Christian faith – at the very moment that Philip was offering Mass. They told the priest, Pietro Consolini, that they wanted to become Christians. Later, after they had been properly instructed in the faith, they were baptised by His Holiness Pope Clement VIII in the Lateran Basilica, and changed their names; the eldest took the name Alexander, the next Augustine, the third Hippolytus, and the youngest Clement.

---

[220] There are many sworn witnesses to this matter. *Their original names were Reuben, Judah, Solomon and Abraham Corcos; their uncle had already become a Christian and taken the name Ugo Boncompagni: it was he who introduced them to Philip.*

He predicts the imminent death of two people
He reads a woman's thoughts

162. A noble Roman named Virgilio Crescenzi began to feel ill in November of this year, but the sickness at first seemed so trivial that the doctors did not think there was any danger of death.[221] Philip was asked to pray to God for him, and said quite plainly that the patient was going to die from that disease. They pressed him again to dispel the disease by his prayers, but he answered, 'We must obey the will of God in all things: God wishes him to die of this illness, so we must conform ourselves to His will.' To our surprise, the sick man did indeed die of that same illness a few days later.

I should insert something here about his wife Costanza.[222] Philip was with her, for he used often to visit her, and she began to reflect, 'My husband has died, and he was not old at all, but here is this man in extreme old age (she meant Philip) and he is still alive, still enjoying life.' Philip was aware of what she was thinking, and said to her, 'Your husband is dead, though he was so young, and here am I, an old man still clinging to life: isn't that so? Why are you so silent?' She was so astonished to hear him say this that she was unable to speak.

It was in the same year and month that Philip observed that Patrizio Patrizi was suffering from a mild illness, and warned him to fortify himself with the sacraments of the Church, acknowledging that he was mortal.[223] Both Patrizi and his household thought this was excessive, for no one had the least suspicion that the disease was terminal, and he began to think he could defer following Philip's advice until later. However, the holy Father insisted, and the sick man finally accepted the advice given him; he was fortified with the sacraments of holy Church, and so passed away from human affairs.

---

[221] Three witnesses have sworn to this story.

[222] It is she herself who tells this story, and swears to it. *She has already featured several times in this history.*

[223] Two witnesses have given sworn evidence for this.

Though falling into serious illness, he recovers through God's aid

163. It was in November that year that Philip fell into a continual fever, which never let up; it was severe and dangerous, troubling him acutely for forty full days. As the disease grew daily worse, everyone thought death was not far off; but beyond all hope, he was suddenly restored to full health. The doctors considered this was miraculous, taking his age into consideration, and have said so publicly on oath.

Something remarkable happened to Girolamo Cordella, one of those who tended him in this illness.[224] One evening he found Philip in a very bad state, and said, 'Philip is now in such a perilous condition that he must be considered in danger of death.' He came back the next morning, and asked anxiously how he was. Philip had heard nothing of what Cordella had said, but called him apart and told him, 'Cordella, this disease I have is not as fatal as you imagine; I shall get up again from it.'

While he was suffering from that same illness, there was a number of boys whose confessions he was accustomed to hear, and he refused to allow them to go to anyone else for confession, for many good reasons. 'Wait a little,' he told them, 'do not worry, I myself will hear you confess your sins at the feast of the birth of Our Lord Jesus Christ'. It happened as he had predicted; he shortly afterwards recovered completely from his illness, to the surprise of the doctors who had expected Philip to depart this life before then. He heard the boys' confessions, and those of many others.

It was noticeable how often the holy Father was restored to health after dangerous illnesses, which in the opinion of the most experienced doctors had brought him into peril of his life; although human remedies had been of no use, or had not even been tried, it was God's power that saved him. This is something the doctors who looked after him have confirmed on oath. It was noticed also how Philip could be restored to full bodily health after a dangerous illness so quickly that the doctors who thought him close to death

---

[224] There are sworn eyewitnesses to this story.

in the evening found him the following morning completely rid of his affliction.[225] I should add that the best doctors also considered it miraculous that when Philip was already advanced in age he was able to sustain life with so very little nourishment, whether he were in sickness or good health; some of them have confirmed this on oath as a divine miracle.

He reads the thoughts of a friend

164. At the end of the year, Claudio Neri, a Roman citizen and doctor of both civil and canon law, famous throughout the city, was being tormented by an evil spirit with such acute scruples of conscience that he did not dare receive Holy Communion because of them.[226] In his distress he determined to consult Philip, intending to follow his advice; he went to see him and had a long conversation, but while telling him all sorts of other things, he failed to mention what he had come to ask about. Philip was aware of the whole business through a revelation from God, and so began to question him whether he had anything on his mind that he wanted to disclose. Claudio said not, at first, but Philip pressed him again. He denied it again, and made to depart, but the holy Father would not let him. In order to make him talk, he described the problem that was vexing him as a fictitious case. 'I have a friend,' he began, 'who was troubled with a scruple like this (specifying the point that troubled Claudio) and since he was unable to find any peace, he decided to consult me.' He went on to describe how he had relieved his friend's anxieties, and as if he were being absent–minded, he sometimes said 'my friend' and sometimes 'Claudio'. It was as if Claudio has described the whole problem to him already. The latter was astonished by what Philip told him, amazed to realise that the holy Father knew perfectly well what no mortal man other than himself could possibly have guessed. He returned home, and never stopped talking to his family and friends about what he had experienced of the holiness of that blessed man.

---

[225] There are several witnesses who have sworn to this.
[226] Claudio himself, his wife and children, have all recounted this story on oath.

THE YEAR OF CHRIST 1592 AND THE TWO SUBSEQUENT YEARS

The Devil attacks Philip
A.D. 1593; Clement VIII year 2; Philip's age 78

165. In the year of Christ's birth 1593, Philip was praying earnestly one day, and the devil who is always eager to prevent anyone from praying, spattered his clothing with filth, for Philip was one whom he could not endure.[227]

In June of that year, Antonia Carracia, the wife of Antonio Pasquini, gave birth, and was suddenly stricken with a pain in her right side.[228] As the pain increased, her servants put her to bed; it increased much more, and she began to be racked with a violent fever. Suffering from this fever and these pains, she was reduced to the condition that she could not move herself in any direction. She lay thus afflicted for a fortnight, and no medical treatment was of any use. Antonio decided it was time to apply to Philip for help. He told him, 'Go away, your wife will be all right', and after saying that sent him away. However, the disease appeared to be getting worse moment by moment, and her stomach rejected everything she tried to eat, till the sick woman was unable to sleep at all, neither by night nor day. Antonio went to Philip again, and begged him repeatedly to agree to help his wife in her distress, for she was so racked by fever that she was on the point of death. Philip answered, 'Your wife will not die of this present illness; what's more, she will recover her health and strength as before. Go home: I will follow you there.' When he reached her, Philip asked her what was wrong with her and where the pain was. On learning that, he touched the painful area, and she was at once filled with such joy at his touch that she hardly knew where she was for delight. Philip became aware of what God had done through him, and withdrew, comforting the woman with these words as he left, 'Be glad: you have nothing to fear.' He had hardly gone away before she began to turn herself from side to side, without needing help as she had before. This appeared to be putting her health at risk, but as she did it her former strength was revived, and she realised that she

---

[227] Those who were present have sworn to this. *Something very similar happened to the Curé d'Ars.*

[228] Antonia herself and her husband have told us the whole story on oath.

was quite rid of her fever and all the pain. Joyfully, she called her husband, and to his astonishment showed him that she was cured.

He voluntarily resigns the office of Provost General

166. Philip always longed for a quiet life, and in his humility found it a great burden to govern others; following the example of St Francis, the patriarch of friars, he determined to resign the office of Provost General. Once he had made up his mind, he summoned those Fathers who normally took part in decisions, and told them what was on his mind. He begged them to pay no attention to their own preferences but to consider the good of the entire Congregation, for all should submit their will to the common cause. Without delay they must choose a Provost General who could preside over the others, someone stronger than him both in mind and body. 'I am old, my Fathers,' he told them, 'and worn out; I do not think I can conduct your business properly, and I don't think it fair for me to have to carry this burden any longer. I entreat you, therefore, again and again: choose someone to succeed me in my old age, set me free from that office, deliver me from responsibilities so that I can prepare myself for death.'

He realised that every argument he used to influence the wishes of the Fathers to do what he wanted served only to encourage them to resist following his advice; accordingly he began to petition Cardinals Agostino Cusano and Federico Borromeo to intercede for him with the Fathers so that they might permit him to resign the Provostship. Once they understood this, they were glad to undertake that commission for him. On the 30th of June, therefore, the cardinals called together the Fathers who had the right to cast a vote, and explained to them that Philip really wanted them in earnest to allow him to resign the office of Provost, because of his advanced age. Then, they said, let the Congregation choose as Provost Cesare Baronio, one of the first of his disciples, for they assured them that the Holy Father the Pope would be pleased with that choice, being in agreement with the whole idea, and thinking Baronio should be declared Provost General. When he heard this, Baronio began to speak, 'I object to this very strongly, and I cannot talk of this project of our Father without grief. However, since he himself is so eager to lay down his burden, and their Eminences the

Cardinals have begged us in his name, let the will of the Most High be done, let the Congregation cease to resist his wishes.'

167. Since Philip remained of the same mind, the Fathers agreed to elect a new Provost. As each gave his opinion, and each placed his vote in the ballot, Baronio, although he had already spoken, added, before the rest of the priests had given their vote, 'I can't endure the prospect of being elected Provost General.' He refused the task, as something beyond his powers, and said he would never accept it, unless the method of election laid down in the constitutions of the Congregation was observed. The priests must be free to vote for whomsoever they pleased. With all his heart he entreated the cardinals who were present, as well as Philip himself, assuring them that if the Pope knew about our constitutions, he would not be at all displeased. He said all this, and much more to the same effect, and the priests who were present agreed with his opinion, deciding the matter should be referred to God in prayer. They decided to write to the Fathers at the house in Naples to tell them about the election of a new Provost and to ask their opinion, and having done all that, the meeting was adjourned.

After thinking everything over in depth, much fervent prayer, and many Masses offered for the intention, the Fathers were summoned by the bell to meet again in one place, on the 23rd of July, being the day consecrated to the commemoration of Blessed Apollinarius, Bishop and Martyr. Philip remained of the same mind, so they began the process of electing a new Provost. Each Father placed his vote in the urn, the votes were duly taken out, and declared, and Baronio was returned Provost, with no dissenting vote other than Baronio's own. All were pleased with this, for we considered him very worthy to succeed our holy Father. He governed the entire Congregation to everyone's satisfaction for three years, performing the duties of his office with great ability and skill, despite the great responsibilities which distracted him. Once the three years had passed, when we would normally proceed to a new election, the Fathers were in as full agreement to confirm him in the office as they had previously been to elect him, but this had hardly happened before he was co-opted as a member of the College of Cardinals, along with Francesco Maria Tarugi, Archbishop of Avignon, by our Holy Father Pope Clement VIII, as we have already mentioned. With Baronio created Cardinal, Angelo Velli became the second successor of Philip, by unanimous consent, in the year of the redemption of the world 1596, in June.

He hears the voices of the angels

168. Philip was so holy that he could enjoy the singing and the music of the Angels.[229] When Elena Massimi died, at the age of thirteen, he heard them singing very beautifully. Elena was a girl who was wonderfully in love with God, and modelled her life in every aspect on her confessor's advice. She would weep profusely over the death of Christ, with great feelings of devotion, and three times a week would sustain her soul on the blessed Bread of Angels. When she received Communion she could be seen to be bathed in tears; she was regular in her prayer, she loved the Cross, ignoring herself, and used to long to be able to suffer for the glory of Christ. When she died she received holy Viaticum, which was administered by Baronio, who observed that she was totally suffused by the precious Blood of Christ. She foresaw and predicted the day of her death (the holy Father told me that himself), and after she died, her body was brought to our church, placed in its coffin there, and committed to burial. She died on the 9th of September, in the year of Christ 1593.

The Blessed Virgin shows herself to Philip when he was on the point of death
A.D. 1594; Clement VIII year 3; Philip's age 79

169. In 1594, during May, Philip recovered from a continuous fever which had troubled him for about twenty-five days, but almost at once was afflicted with a serious kidney complaint. The pain was so sharp and prolonged that it gave him no respite. He suffered like that for ten to twelve hours, and he was unable to pass water, so that not only the doctors but also his community were sure that he could not recover, and that he would certainly

---

[229] Cardinal Cesare Baronio tells us that on oath, as does another priest who was then present. *Elena was the daughter of Francesco Massimi and his second wife Violante.*

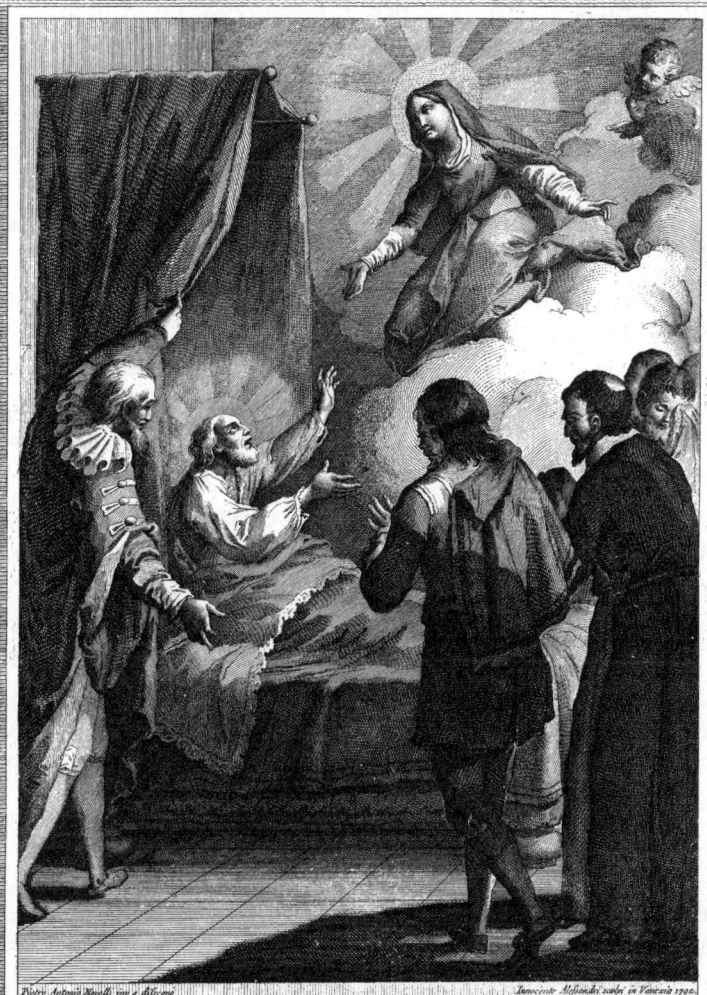

MENTRE DEL BUON FILIPPO IL FRAL LANGUIA,
RAPITO IN DIO RISANA IN UN ISTANTE,
POICHE DAL CIEL A LUI SCENDE MARIA.
CHI DI PARI FAVOR FIA CHE SI VANTE?

die within the next few hours.²³⁰ In this dangerous condition he became so weak that we thought he was more dead than alive, but it suddenly came about, by God's power, that he was restored to his usual health, in the presence of his physicians Angelo Vittorio and Ridolfo Silvestri, who saw it happen, making the miracle even more certain. Apart from the doctors we have mentioned, there were present with the holy Father: Alessandro Alluminati, Francesco Zazzara, and the author of this biography. I will tell you the whole story as it happened:

Philip was scarcely able to move at all, so drained of strength was he, and scarcely able to speak audibly, until, three hours before sunset, he began to shout in a loud voice, which everyone could hear: 'Anyone who wants something other than God is a fool! Anyone who loves something other than God is a total wreck!' He said this once or twice, and then, as if he had suddenly recovered his lost energy, he began to sit quite upright, although no one was supporting him, and everyone around him was in tears together. He seemed to be embracing someone, that no one else could see, and called out very clearly, despite his frequent intermittent sobs, 'Oh Virgin, how dear to me you are! You have come to see me, to cure me of my pain! O Virgin, how beautiful you are, how elegant, how noble! How can I be worthy of your visit? No, no I am not fit for such a favour; there is nothing in me which could bring you to love me; I am quite unfit to be able to see you! What have I done to deserve this, holy Virgin, most renowned, that you should bring yourself to come and visit the least of your servants?'

170. Then he moved his hands, while still bathed in tears, as if he were hugging the Blessed Virgin in his arms, and he began to call out in these words: 'O most holy Mother of God! Summit of all creation, most beautiful of all!' Now while he was saying this, his entire body was lifted up, by the space of about a cubit or even more, with no assistance from anyone, to our astonishment. We heard

---

[230] The whole of this story was confirmed by the public testimony of Cardinal Cusano, who believed that Philip really had seen a vision, as well as by Cardinal Baronio, and fourteen other witnesses.

him say, 'O most holy Virgin, O sweet Mother of God, what have I done to deserve a visit from you? I fling myself into your arms, Blessed Virgin, for you have come to me today; what can prevent me from doing that?' The holy man continued for a long time in this state of ecstasy, and kept on calling to the Mother of God, in a familiar manner, by name. Then he became quiet, and seemed to lose control of his senses. He finally came to himself, and said to us who were there, 'Did you see her, the blessed Mother of God? Did you see that she was here and has totally cured my illness?' He then hid himself under his top sheet, and began to cry like a child. When he had recovered from that, he begged the doctors not to tell anyone what had happened, or what they had observed while they were present. I must not forget to add what was even more remarkable, that at the very moment when the Blessed Virgin appeared before him, he immediately recovered all his usual health.

When he discovered a little later that it had become public knowledge that the Mother of God had appeared to him, being a man who hated to have a reputation, he did everything he could to have the matter glossed over, if he could not conceal it altogether, imitating the saints in this.[231] It was all in vain: there were too many reliable witnesses who had heard from his own lips that he had really seen a vision; those who have come to know Philip's humility, and are familiar with the lives of the saints, can never be surprised at what he was capable of.

He predicts the imminent death of a nobleman who was then in good health

171. At the beginning of August that year, they were talking about Alessandro Crescenzi in Philip's presence, when he said, 'Sandro is an excellent person, but he is going to die soon.' A few days later, the man died (it was the 16th of August) which proved the truth of Philip's prediction.[232]

---

[231] The saints went to great lengths to conceal their miracles and visions from others. See Theodoret, life of Philotheus, chapter 3; and the lives of Saints Theodore the Siceot, Audoen, Odilo, Bishop Annon, and Bishop Godefrid.

[232] We have two sworn witnesses to this.

Marco Antonio Corteselli appears to Philip after his death

Marco Antonio Corteselli was one of the earliest of Philip's disciples; immediately after his spirit had departed he came to the holy Father in his sleep, and remained with him for the space of two hours, before rising into heaven, shining with the light of the blest, as Philip looked on. He died in October of this year.[233]

That was not the last of Philip's visions of this sort: he was once speaking to his dear friend Cardinal Federico Borromeo and a few other trustworthy men, whose virtues he saw to be in some peril, and he took the opportunity to tell them that he had often seen the souls of his own disciples as well as many others ascending into the blessed realms of heaven and shining with the most brilliant light.[234]

---

[233] Several people tell this story and swear to it.

[234] Cardinal Baronio tells us this on oath, allowing the others to remain anonymous.

XV : THE LAST YEAR OF PHILIP'S LIFE, AND HIS HOLY DEATH

Barsum, Archdeacon of Alexandria in Egypt, is restored to health

172. Barsum, the Archdeacon of Alexandria, came to Rome in the year 94 of our century, in order to reconcile to Rome the Church of Alexandria, which desired to be cleansed of heresy.[235] During October, while this business was in progress, he fell seriously ill. The disease caused him to spit black blood, which in the opinion of the doctors came from ruptured capillary veins, in the neighbourhood of the lungs or liver. He was also greatly troubled by fever, a constant cough, and difficulty in breathing. The coughing brought up blood, and kept him awake all night and all day, so that he was unable to sleep, the worst of his symptoms, for days and nights on end.

Cordella was very doubtful if he would survive, and Girolamo Vecchietti, who also attended him, took the case to Philip. He found him vested for Mass, and with his chalice already in his hand, and asked him to remember the Archdeacon of Alexandria who was gravely ill. Philip promised that he would pray for him, and, O wonder, at the moment he began to offer the divine sacrifice, the sick man fell into a soothing sleep. They discovered this afterwards by comparing the times: it was just as the holy Father was celebrating Mass that the Archdeacon fell asleep after being awake so long. He slept for several hours, and as soon as he awoke began to feel better. Philip had by this time completed Mass, and remarked, 'Barsum will recover from his present illness.' Then he called for Vecchietti, and said, 'Have the Archdeacon moved to Cardinal Federico Borromeo's house at once; he is to remain there

---

[235] Apart from the Archdeacon, there are two other eyewitnesses who have confirmed this publicly. *Gregory XIII and Clement VIII made enormous efforts to bring about the reconciliation of the 'Monophysite' Christians of Egypt, though as always the result was that some entered into full communion with the Church while others remained outside. Vecchietti made a visit to Egypt to further the process.*

until he is quite recovered.' Vecchietti was unsure what to do when he heard this, for he dared not move a man so seriously ill, considering it extremely dangerous, and he thought he could not obey Philip's command without first asking permission of his superiors. Accordingly, in his perplexity, he tried to make excuses, but the holy Father insisted even more, ordering him to obey, until he gave in, as if the order had come from heaven. Trusting in Philip's prayers and his help, he had the sick man moved on a bier.

I should not omit to mention that Philip persuaded Vecchietti to bring the sick man to himself, before going on to the house of Cardinal Federico Borromeo. This he did, for the sake of curing him, and it was not in vain. Philip embraced the man, and he was restored to health. He broke out into a copious sweat, at once felt himself restored to health, and was cured of the spitting of blood (except for what had already gathered in his lungs, which he did afterwards expel). After that, Philip ordered him to be carried to Cardinal Borromeo's house, but as he left he begged the holy Father to beseech God for his recovery, putting all his hope in him. Philip agreed, bidding him to hope for every joy and expect a full recovery. He was not wrong, for a few days later the patient completely recovered from his illness.

He predicts the death of Girolamo Cordelio, the doctor
A.D. 1595; Clement VIII year 4; Philip's age 80

173. In the year of Christ 1595, during February, I was with Philip as I usually was, and somebody came to tell us that one of the servants of Cordella's wife wanted to see me at the door, to pass on her greetings and speak to me. While I went down to the woman, Philip suddenly broke out into these exclamations (as I heard afterwards from those who were there), 'O Cordella! Cordella! He is surely now going to die, I know for certain he is dying, look, now it is time for him to die!' The people with him were amazed when they heard Philip talking to himself like that, since no one had told him what the woman wanted, or even that Cordella had been ill. In fact no one was aware of it, for it was only that day that he had begun to feel ill in the slightest.

When Philip was informed of Cordella's recent illness, he again began to say, 'Cordella is dying: he will not recover from this illness.

His last day of life is upon him, he will go very soon.' Some of those with him said, 'If we cannot now be of any assistance to his body in its peril, Father, at least his soul surely can be helped.' He replied, 'Indeed it can: I am very willing to apply myself totally to that end, to assist his soul, while ignoring the condition of his body.' He was not deceived: Cordella died of that disease a few days later.[236]

The sequel is no less extraordinary. Early one morning I went to see Philip, along with Pietro Consolini. I went into his room (and since I was responsible for it, no one from outside could have got in), and he began to talk, 'Look, Cordella gave up his spirit last night, at such an hour' (and he was specific about the time). We were wondering how he could have learnt this, but made a note of the time and sent out at once to those who would know, to find that everything was exactly as the holy Father had foreseen.

He liberates His Holiness from the pains of gout

That year Pope Clement VIII was afflicted with great pains of the gout, during Eastertide. When Philip heard this he went to see him, but when he went to embrace him as usual, and to take him by the hand, the Pope cried out, 'Stop, Father, please don't come any closer, my hand is hurting me very much.' Philip replied, 'I am not worried if you are ill, because that gives you a chance of a little rest, but I am concerned if you are in pain.' He seized him by the hand, and then let him go, and at once the pain entirely left him.[237]

Philip is ill again

174. In that same year 1595, on the 30th of March, Philip was taken by a very severe fever, which began to be alarming. It was so severe that when Cardinal Agostino Valerio came to see him, he was unable to speak a word to him. The fever afflicted him throughout the whole of April, but because he was particularly eager to celebrate Mass on the feast of the holy Apostles Philip and

---

[236] I heard that from sworn witnesses.
[237] I heard this from Cardinals Cusano, Borromeo, Tarugi and Baronio, who told me they had heard it from the Pope himself, though I had also heard others speak of it while Philip was alive.

James (whose proper day is the first of May), he implored the aid of those great Apostles on the day before their feast, and his prayers were answered. He got out of bed, celebrated Mass, gave the Body of Christ to those present, and did all that with such agility that those who had been aware of his physical weakness were astonished. They considered that it was the Lord who had provided strength to Philip's heavenly soul, and in this they were right.[238]

For the next three days he refrained from offering Mass, not so much because he wanted to pander to his physical weakness, but out of obedience to his physicians. In place of the Sacrifice, he received Holy Communion each day, with great love and devotion, not to be deprived of the benefit of that divine good on those days. After the three days he felt better, and the doctors agreed he could begin to offer Mass again, which he did up to the 12th May. On that day he was unexpectedly attacked by a new illness: first thing in the morning he suddenly vomited a great quantity of blood – I was there – and then lay back on his bed; he looked as if he were dying, hardly able to breathe, and very pale in the face. I called the doctors, and they took his pulse, examined the symptoms, and said that it was all over with him. We were afraid that he was going to die at once, so he was quickly anointed with holy oil by Cesare Baronio, while Cardinal Federico Borromeo was there and looking on. After the anointing, Philip began to open his eyes a little, as his breath returned to him. When Cardinal Federico noticed this he turned to Alessandro Alluminati, who was the holy man's usual medical attendant, and asked him to check his pulse and say whether he would be strong enough to receive the holy Viaticum of Christ. They ascertained that he was, and so Cardinal Federico himself brought him the most precious Body of Christ. Cardinal Agostino Cusano, the rest of the Fathers and Brothers of the Congregation, and a great many others were present, and we were all in tears at the thought of our great loss.

175. Then happened something worthy of remembrance. Borromeo had hardly entered Philip's bedroom, carrying the sacred

---

[238] We have several sworn eyewitnesses to this.

Body of Christ in his hands, when, although Philip was unable to move at all, he began to cry out, his voice choked with tears, and astonished us all. 'See,' he cried, 'see my love, my love! Here He is, in whom is my delight, He alone is my darling! Bring Him to me, bring me my love, bring Him to me at once!' He uttered these words with so great a strength of spirit that those who were present were moved to tears as well as wonder.

When Cardinal Federico said 'Lord, I am not worthy...' in the usual manner, Philip repeated the words very clearly, although he was still in floods of tears through his desire and longing for Christ. 'I have never been worthy,' he said, 'that I should feed on Thy body.' Then he received Viaticum, and said, 'I have received my physician under my roof'.

On the same day, in the evening, he vomited blood again, three or four times: it was very red, and copious. After vomiting he began to cough, and he very nearly suffocated as a result of the flow of blood. We were all amazed at how patient he was while he suffered so much, for his spirit was not crushed by his great affliction, but seemed to be strengthened and renewed.

The principal medical treatment he received was cupping: a little burning tow was dropped into the cups, the mouths of which were then applied to his body, and held on until they adhered. After a day or two had gone by, Philip said to the doctors as they arrived in the morning, 'Go away. I have a much more effective remedy than you can offer. First thing this morning I sent someone to distribute donations to various religious communities, asking them to say Mass for me. And immediately my vomit of blood stopped, the pain around my heart and lungs ceased entirely. I feel much better, and I have recovered the strength I lost.' The doctors then examined him, felt his pulse, and compared the spittle he had previously produced with what he produced now; they had to admit from the difference they observed that he had been restored to his previous health, and they were astounded at such a miracle. From that day until his death he enjoyed excellent health. For several days he remained in good spirits, celebrated Mass every day, and heard the confessions of his subjects. He seemed so strong that the Fathers were given just reason to consider that he could continue to live for several years. This however did not happen, for God was to call him suddenly to receive his reward.

He predicts his own death

176. When Francesco Zazzara was eighteen, about three years before Philip's death, Philip had told him that he was not going to die before telling him what state of life God intended for him.[239] The young man often reminded the holy Father about this, and he would reply, 'Don't worry, I am always praying to God for you, and before I die I will tell you what he has revealed to me about you. You have placed yourself and your prospects in my hands; I will not let you down.' Now surprisingly, although from that day until the beginning of the year '95 Philip was often ill, and often in danger of death, in the opinion of the physicians, he never spoke a word about the subject to Francesco. However, after he had recovered from his vomit of blood, he immediately expounded to him what manner of life he should follow – this was on the 17th of May, eight days before the death of the holy man.

To give you another example: once he had returned to his previous condition after the vomit of blood, he was visited by Nero, son of Agostino de' Neri.[240] He was congratulating Philip on recovering his health, but Philip said to him, 'I may have survived the disease of the moment, and feel well now, but my sons will not rejoice for long. The end of the conflict is near, and I shall die in such a manner that when it happens hardly anyone will know, they won't believe it when they hear it, and to begin with it will be just a rumour.' His prophecy was amply fulfilled.

Also, when he was still suffering from that attack, he said to Germanico Fedeli who was looking after him very well, 'You have given me enough attention, you have worked for me long enough,

---

[239] Francesco himself tells this story and swears to it. *Zazzara joined the Congregation in September 1595, and was ordained in 1601. After the death of Gallonio, he continued the process of Philip's canonisation.*

[240] It was the same noble Neri who has recounted this story, on oath. *Neri liked to think he was related to Philip, and took a leading part in enshrining his memory; he paid for the decoration of the chapel where the saint is buried, and bequeathed his family coat of arms (the blue shield with three gold stars) to the Congregation of the Oratory.*

the end of your task is at hand.' Then he took him by the hand and said, 'What things you are going to see in the next few days!' In these words he indicated that his death was imminent, and it was only a few days later that he escaped from the bonds of flesh, as if from a prison house, full of joy.[241]

177. Now here is something just as remarkable in my opinion. A little afterwards, the same Father Germanico was about to travel to a village called Carbognano, but refused to leave the city until he had been assured by Philip that he would find him alive and well when he returned to Rome. Philip listened to him, and then asked him by which date he intended to return. He answered, 'At the latest, the vigil of the day when we keep the annual feast of the most Blessed Sacrament.' Philip was silent for a moment, as if thinking what to reply, and then uttered the words, 'Go, and come back'. Now in the night before the day which is the vigil of the Feast of Corpus Christi, Germanico had a dream. He thought he was in Rome, in the holy Father's bedroom, and saw him lying ill in bed. He heard him say, 'Germanico, the end of my life has come', and Germanico answered, 'Father, that must not happen; you have been more seriously ill than this before.' Philip replied, 'No, this is my last hour: see to it that they say Mass for me.' He was asleep; it was a dream. When he woke up he took it as a warning, set out, and started home at once. It was a day's journey, and he found it very long, so eager was he to see the holy Father. When he reached Rome, he found Philip sitting on his bed, but well, and in good health. Philip said to him, 'So you have come back?' and Germanico replied, 'I have, although I very nearly put off my return until another day, since the people there asked me.' Philip replied, 'You did well to come back on the day you said you would. Had you delayed your return, you would have regretted it.' He did not say this without good reason, for it was on the following day that the holy man fled this world for heaven, contrary to everyone's expectation. Now let us turn to another matter.

---

[241] He himself told us this story as well, on oath.

178. At the beginning of April 1595, Philip had asked the same Germanico Fedeli to write a letter on his behalf to Flaminio Ricci, a priest of our Congregation, who was staying in Naples.[242] In this he wrote that he should return to Rome at once, because he wanted to see him before he died, for he could foresee that it would not be long before he folded up his tent. Flaminio wrote back and made some excuse, asking permission to remain until September, which the holy old man refused, writing again to the same purpose, and begged Flaminio for his sake to make no delay but to return to Rome as soon as had read the letter. Yet again, because Archbishop Annibale di Capua had asked him to do so, Flaminio delayed his return, so that Philip wrote one last time calling him back to Rome because he longed to see him. Flaminio still would not obey our holy Father's bidding, for some new business had come up, and a few days later Philip died.

About the same time – no, it was the day before he died – he seems to have told Pietro Consolini quite openly that he was about to die.[243] They were chatting together when Philip asked him to say Mass for him. Consolini replied that he would be glad to do so, adding that he knew that there was really no need to pray particularly for his health, since Philip was so well. 'No,' said Philip, 'I mean I want you to say a Mass for the dead.' What he meant by these words was made abundantly clear the following day by his death.

Another wonderful thing that happened that month was that on the 15th of May (which that year was the second day of Pentecost, celebrating the outpouring of the Holy Spirit on the Apostles) Philip called Gian Battista Guerra to him. I was celebrating Mass at the time, and had asked him to take my place in attendance on the holy Father.[244] Philip asked him what day of the month it was, and he replied that it was the fifteenth. 'Then in ten days' time,' continued the old man, 'I shall die; that will be the twenty-fifth.'

---

[242] Germanico Fedeli himself was the sworn witness to this story, which our community knew well enough.

[243] Consolini himself affirms this on oath.

[244] Gian Battista himself has confirmed this on oath.

The outcome proved that his prophecy was true, for it was effectively that day that he died, although after midnight.

His holy death

179. For three days before he died, Philip was bathed in divine light and joy more than ever before, as if he knew that he had been summoned to the wedding feast of the Lamb. Each day he celebrated Mass with an unbelievable delight and gladness. On the 25th of May, which was that year the feast of Corpus Christi, and his last day, he celebrated the liturgy with such joy that he seemed to be singing. At the beginning of the sacrifice he looked towards the vineyards near the church of Sant'Onofrio, as if he could see something which escaped our eyes. Whatever it was he saw, he never spoke of it, and none of us knew it. He spent most of that day hearing confessions, and he gave Holy Communion to many of his disciples with his own hands. All through those three days he appeared to be in such robust health that he never went back to bed after getting up in the morning until his usual hour of going to bed at night. On that day which was to be his last, Angelo Vittorio was with him, and said, 'I am not coming to visit you as your doctor, Father, just as a friend.' When he left the room he remarked to me and the others, 'Philip is so fit that I expect to find him as well as he is now in ten years' time.'

That very day Philip knew that his death was imminent, for God had revealed it to him, and he showed his joy in his face. He greeted his visitors in a friendly manner, and listened attentively to the lives of the saints which Francesco Zazzara was reading. He was always delighted with that sort of reading. They were reading the life of St Bernadine of Siena, when Cardinal Agostino Cusano came to see him, accompanied by Girolamo Pamphili, the Auditor of the Rota. A little later Spinello Benci arrived, a man of great integrity, and the first bishop of Montepulciano. They all recited the Divine Office with Philip, and stayed with him until the day darkened towards evening; as night fell they all went home.

180. An hour after nightfall, the holy man took his usual frugal meal. After supper he was as well as before, and gave no indication of having even the slightest indisposition, let alone being in any danger of death. Moreover, he was so happy that you couldn't imagine anything less likely than that he would die within the next few hours.

Once he was in bed, he knew well enough that his last hour had come, and began to say to us who were standing by him, 'So, we shall die eventually.' Then he asked again what time it was, and finding that it was three hours after sunset, he began to murmur, as if talking to himself, 'Three hours, then if you add two onto that, it makes five, if you add three, it makes six.' He turned to us and said, 'Off to bed with you.' As he said that he was so vigorous that from his words and gestures it was very clear that he was exceedingly happy, as if he were already enjoying the delights of heaven. We did not suspect there was any danger, and so went away to bed.

At midnight I had hardly gone to sleep when I was woken up, and I heard Philip walking about. Then I was frightened, and got out of bed at once and rushed off without bothering to dress fully – I just pulled on my cassock over my trunks and went straight to him, to find him sitting on his bed. His throat was so full of blood or phlegm that I was afraid that he would choke, with good reason. When I saw him I asked him what was the matter. He said right out, 'This is my last hour, I am beginning to die.' I was the only one there with him and on my own was unable to do anything for him, so I dashed off to find Alessandro Alluminati. He followed me back at once. Then while we waited for the doctors, since the sickness had come on him so strongly, we tried putting cupping glasses to him, without the irons, and then attempted to massage him. We began with his arms and legs, leaving out his chest; then we put tourniquets on his thighs, arms and shins, to stem the flow of blood, and tried all sorts of remedies without doing him any good at all. Philip did not refuse any of our attempts, and after a quarter of an hour or so the phlegm stopped accumulating in his throat, there was no haemorrhage, and his throat became clear so that he could speak quickly and easily. You would think all danger of death had passed.

181. All this took very little time. Then he turned to us and said, 'Unless you have some other treatments to hand, stay here, for

DOLENTI FIGLI DEL BUON PADRE AL LETTO
CORONA FAN ANZI CHE A DIO SEN VADA.
SEMBRA CH' EI DORMA E PIU NON SPIRA IL PETTO
SI MUOR IL GIUSTO, E L' PECCATOR NON BADA.

I am beginning to wrestle with death.' He fell silent after that, to be quiet in himself. Now the closer he approached to death, the more clearly he showed us that he had no fear of it. As if challenging death to a fight, he raised himself up into a sitting position from the bed he had been lying on, and as long as he continued to breathe he remained in the posture which he then assumed.

All the Fathers gathered around Philip in his last hour, finding him so unexpectedly close to death, although they had shortly before left him alive and well. They all began to cry like children, for grief, for no one could be unmoved at the departure of such a great man. Who could look on while Philip died and restrain his tears, Philip, who had always loved helping others, with no concern for himself? The Fathers were inconsolable in lamenting their common Father, while Cesare Baronio commended his soul to God and His saints in the usual manner, his prayers interrupted by sobs. When he had finished, the doctor warned him that Philip was on the point of death, so he turned to him and began to call out, 'Oh, Father, my Father, why cannot you say one word to us? Speak to us, I beg you, as a Father to your sons whom you have begotten in Christ with so much labour; that would console your sons in their grief, or diminish it at least! If, Father, you were to give your blessing to your sons, that would comfort us in our sorrow!'

Philip heard this, raised his eyes to heaven, and prayed for a moment for his sons. After praying he looked at us, as if to strengthen us with his blessing, and then without any tremor of his limbs at all, without any sign of distress, gaining strength in death itself from which all others flee, he peacefully breathed out his soul. It was the 25th of May, which that year was the solemnity of Corpus Christi, after midnight, so that his prophecy was fulfilled in the event; it was in the year of Our Lord 1595.

XVI : ON WHAT HAPPENED AFTER HIS DEATH, AND ON HIS BURIAL

He appears to many after his death
A.D. 1595; Clement VIII year 4

182. At the very moment that Philip expired, he was seen by many.[245] There was a certain virgin who was noted for the piety of her life, to whom he appeared in a dream as soon as he died; this woman engaged him in a long conversation about some trivial point, till he said, 'Let me continue on my journey, you have delayed me quite long enough, and so have they (meaning his disciples).' And saying that, he was lifted up and disappeared. At the same hour, indeed at the same instant, another virgin, consecrated to God, saw the holy Father while she was asleep.[246] He was dressed in white clothing, glowing with celestial light, with two youths on either side of him; he said to her, 'As you can see, I am being carried up to heaven to receive the reward of my labours: you must therefore do all you can to persevere until death in the way of life you have undertaken. If you do that, you will come to share in my joy, and you have nothing to fear, for I will pray to the Lord for you continually.' And having said that, he vanished from her sight. The virgin awoke from her sleep, in joy and wonder, and pondered in vain what that vision could mean. She spent the rest of the night unable to sleep, thinking deeply about the matter until dawn, when someone came to tell her that Philip had died at the time that she had been given her vision. Now the woman understood what was the meaning of that apparition of the night. She rejoiced, and from then on became more and more convinced that Philip was already enrolled among the blest, as one of the holiest of men.

---

[245] We have two sworn witnesses to this. *The sworn virgin was M. Maddelena Orsini (1539–1605), the foundress of the Dominican convent on Montecavallo.*

[246] Apart from the nun herself, there are two priests who have sworn to this on oath. *This nun was Ortensia Anelli, from S. Cecilia in Trastevere.*

There was a devout nobleman, whose name I shall omit out of respect for his modesty:[247] he lived in one of the cities of Italy, about a hundred miles from Rome, and he too saw the holy Father quite clearly at the exact moment that Philip departed from this life; he is unsure whether he was awake or asleep at first. Philip said to him, 'Peace to you, my brother, I am now on my way to a better place.' He had hardly said that when the nobleman woke up entirely, now quite certain that he was not sleeping, and still he seemed to see Philip, whose face looked so joyful, and who was repeating the words, 'Now I am going to a better place, now I am arriving at a place of joy', and after these words he vanished from his sight.

His body is brought into the church

183. In the meantime, Philip's body was washed and clothed in priestly vestments in the usual manner, and it was carried down to the church on the shoulders of the Fathers, about an hour after midnight. All the members of the Congregation followed the bier, and those who were not actually carrying him held lighted candles around the body. They sang Psalms alternately as they went: it was a sight to reduce everyone to tears.

As soon as the news of Philip's death became public, a huge crowd of all sorts of people began to gather to see the body. Those who came could not have enough of sating their eyes, their souls, on the blissful face of the holy man. And so they came to venerate our holy Father as he lay on his bier; the greatest of the cardinals of the Holy Roman Church, archbishops, bishops, monsignors of every rank, monks and friars, princes, and a vast throng of great ladies. We did not see anyone come who failed to venerate the sacred body of that blessed old man. As they clustered around the bier, they feasted their eyes on the wonderful appearance of Philip which they wished to remember, and many there were who burst into copious tears and frequent sobs at the death of such a man, grieving bitterly at the loss of such a father. There was no one so unmoved that they held back from kissing his beloved hand with

---

[247] He himself has given public testimony about the whole matter, on oath. *This was Matteo Guerra, then living in Siena.*

ECCO IL FRAL DI FILIPPO IL POPOL FOLTO
A LA BARA D'INTORNO UMIL SI SERRA.
FUGGE L'INFERMITÀ GLI SPLENDE IL VOLTO.
QUANTO È NEL CIEL CHI TANTO È GRANDE IN TERRA.

(1) Al Corpo di S. Filippo esposto nella Chiesa della Vallicella succedono molti miracoli.

every sign of affection, and touching his sacred remains with hands or rosaries. You could see the sacred body completely covered in roses and other flowers, but they were continually being taken away by the crowd and carried home out of love for him; the Fathers could not get enough roses to deck him, for the number of those who came to take them away to cure their diseases. It was marvellous how everyone competed to be able to take even a scrap of his clothing, to retain a relic of that great man of God for themselves, and the Fathers were quite unable to watch him with enough vigilance to stop things being taken away, as we discovered afterwards.

184. When night came the doors of the church were closed, about three hours after sunset, and the body was opened, in order to examine it as well as to prepare it for burial. The Fathers invited the following to be present at the autopsy: Doctors Angelo Vittorio and Giuseppe Zerla, their assistants Marc'Antonio Belli and Alessandro Alluminati, and then of our own community Germanico Fedeli, Giulio Savera and Giovan Battista Guerra, and from outside, Francesco Zazzara, Spinello Benci and some others.[248] I myself was not present at the autopsy – not that I would not have been able to endure watching the spectacle, but because I happened to feel rather unwell just as they began to cut into him.

During the autopsy something remarkable happened, which I take as a sign that God confirmed the truth of his virginity. The surgeons had gathered around the body to take out the entrails, and many of the Fathers were watching. To make it easier to dissect him, they undressed the body, and then, amazingly, although his body was bloodless and devoid of life, his hands were moved by supernatural power to cover those parts of his body which in life would have been unseemly to expose.[249] This happened more than once, every time it was necessary to move the body, and when Angelo Vittorio noticed it he called out aloud, so everyone could hear him, 'What wonderful purity the man possessed! What

---

[248] Zazzara had not at that time been aggregated to the Congregation.

[249] All seven of those who were present and saw it have given evidence on oath about the occurrence.

exemplary chastity! Look, see how the man is covering up his privates even though he is dead!' The same thing had happened when they washed his body, as the Fathers who were present observed.

185. When they opened the upper part of his chest, they found to their astonishment that two of the so-called floating ribs on the left side were broken – these were the fourth and fifth. The fracture was visible at the front of his chest, where the ribs should have joined onto the cartilage; both ribs were raised up, as everyone agreed, by the thickness of a fist or even more. Who could fail to acknowledge that this was God's way of ensuring that his heart was not damaged when it palpitated? He had not previously suffered any fall, blow or other violence which could have caused the fracture, neither did it cause him any pain in the slightest, nor did any inflammation arise from it. Contrary to all medical experience, he lived with this fracture of the ribs for more than fifty years without feeling any pain from it. It was originated by the force of divine love, and the excessive ardour of his heart which affected him particularly during contemplation. The doctors debated this for a long time, and pondered over it, eventually coming to an agreed opinion, which they wrote down and affirmed on oath, that this fracture of the ribs had happened to our holy Father through divine intervention.[250] They suggested several reasons for this: firstly, it was so that he should not immediately be killed by the overwhelming force of divine heat during times of contemplation; secondly, so that when his heart expanded under the most ardent heat of love, it would find sufficient space; thirdly, so that his lungs could more easily dilate more than usual; and lastly, so that the lungs could take advantage of the greater space available to bring more air to the heart, so that there would be sufficient breath to keep it cool.

186. When they opened his chest they found no damage to his praecordia.[251] When they examined his heart they found it was

---

[250] The doctors present were Antonio Porto, Andrea Cesalpino, Angelo Vittorio and Giuseppe Zerla.

[251] Doctors Vittorio and Zerla, who observed this, gave evidence on oath, to pass

large and muscular, more than normal. Andrea Cesalpino and Antonio Porto considered that this was due to the excessive heat derived from the fervour of his spirit, and they publicly ratified this on oath. The pulmonary arteries, whose function is to carry blood to the lungs, so that it can be aerated, and thus return to the left ventricle of the heart in order to nourish and cool it (I learnt all this from the doctors and others who were present), was twice as large as usual, because Philip needed to use them more often than most for bringing fresh air and breath into his heart, so that he could endure those excessive heats of heavenly fire which customarily assailed him, without damage to his health, not to mention danger to his life.

Having examined the heart, and cut into the tissue, they found no fluid in the pericardium (which surrounds the heart like a wrapper) according to the distinguished doctors Angelo Vittorio and Giuseppe Zerla, who recorded their evidence on oath, giving it as their opinion that it had been dried up by the fervour of his contemplation.[252] In the ventricles (there are two of these on each side of the heart, like ears), no blood was found, as Zerla testified. Once they had finished the inspection of the chest, they removed the intestines and left the body empty, with no unpleasant odour. The parts removed (heart, lungs, liver, spleen and bowels) were placed in an earthenware bowl and deposited in the burial place reserved for the Fathers, covered with earth. The body was destined to be exposed in the church on the following day for all to see, to satisfy the people. The crowd that gathered on the next day far exceeded the numbers that had come the day before, for the news of the holy Father's death had spread more widely, so that a greater throng assembled, of people of all sorts.

---

over the other witnesses. *Most of the first-class relics of St Philip are tiny fragments of this praecordial tissue, removed on this occasion. It is noteworthy that they were already aware to some extent of the circulation of the blood, five years before William Harvey came to Italy to study medicine.*

[252] These two doctors have explained their evidence, under oath.

ON WHAT HAPPENED AFTER HIS DEATH AND ON HIS BURIAL

The sick are healed by contact with his body

187. While the body of our holy Father lay on its bier, people were talking everywhere about his extraordinary deeds, predictions and miracles, among those who had themselves witnessed and experienced them, or had learnt of them from reliable witnesses. As they were so talking, new wonders were being added to those already known.

Agostino de Magistris, a Roman, had been suffering for nearly seven years from ulcers on his neck, which no medical skill could cure.[253] There were two ulcers on his neck, of which the one on the left side had risen to the point that it affected his mouth; from this much matter used to flow, mingled blood and pus, which sickened those who saw it oozing out. When Agostino heard that a holy man who was famous for miracles had died in our house, he came straight to our church, got close to the bier and fell on his knees. He venerated the sacred body, then rose from his prayer and kissed the dead hand, assuring himself that he was bound to be cured by touching it. His devotion was not unrewarded, for as he touched the hand of the blessed man to his neck, where the infection lay, he was immediately cured.

His younger sister Margarita had been suffering from the same complaint for six years altogether, and was brought to the church by her mother.[254] However, they were caught up in such a crowd that they were hardly able to get through to the holy body, until the mother picked up her daughter and forced her way through to reach the bier. She applied the hand of the dead man to one of the affected parts, but was unable to reach the other part, because Philip's chalice was in the way, as well as the crowd, and a noblewoman was also pushing in. She found that the whole infection had departed from the side that had been touched, while the other side, which Philip's hand had not reached, was not cured.

Their father, Alessandro, who was over sixty years old, had suffered for two months from a discharge from his head, flowing into his eyes. In the evening he could not even bear the sight of lighted

---

[253] Six sworn eyewitnesses have recounted the whole story.
[254] There are six sworn eyewitnesses who gave public testimony to this as well.

torches.[255] He was afraid that the continuous flow of liquid would cause him to lose his sight, and so came to see Philip's body, and put his hand to his eyes. As he did so, he began to feel better at once, and soon afterwards recovered from his complaint entirely, with no further medical attention.

188. Epifania Colichia of Recanati, who was fifty-five years old, had suffered from severe difficulty in breathing for about seven months. When she was worst affected, she could not draw breath at all, or speak a word, or breathe without making a noise; she could not sleep at night, or even lie down on her bed. She was compelled to support her head high in bed, because she could not breathe except when she was upright, and walking about and going upstairs were exceedingly difficult for her. She had heard of Philip's sanctity and his miracles, and came to our church as best she could. She fell on her knees before the bier and begged the blessed Philip with all her heart, praying with many tears that he would restore her to her usual health. Then after praying a while, she took some of the roses which lay on the holy body, and applied them to her stomach, with total confidence. She perceived at once that her health had returned.

Artemisia Cheli had a hard and permanent tumour growing on the wrist of her left hand, the sort that doctors call a ganglion or node.[256] The tumour had begun when she was small, and grew gradually until it reached the size of a walnut or slightly more, and became egg-shaped. When she heard of the death of Philip, she came at once to venerate his body, and touched her hand to his relics – only the unaffected part, being shy of the people who crowded around. Then she took some roses from the bier, and tried to get rid of her tumour by rubbing it with them. She did this in simple faith, and with the intention that the blessed Philip should pray for the healing of her body, and the ears of God be open to his intercession. The affliction disappeared shortly afterwards, with no further medical attention.

---

[255] There are only four sworn witnesses to this story.
[256] Cardinal Baronio, who was her confessor, told the whole story on oath, not to mention other witnesses.

ON WHAT HAPPENED AFTER HIS DEATH AND ON HIS BURIAL

A girl called Maria Giustiniana, of very good family, had scabies or pustules on her head.[257] The disease proceeded to cover her head, and medicine was of no avail. When her mother heard of the death of our blessed Father, she brought her daughter to see the body, where she prayed to God that he would restore her to her former health through the merits of Philip. Then she surreptitiously cut some hairs from his head, and carried them off home like a great treasure, rejoicing as if her daughter's health was already secure. When they got home, she lightly rubbed the girl's head with Philip's hairs, saying as she did so, 'I beg you, holy Philip, to grant my daughter the health I expect of you, for the sake of those meditations in which you passed so much time for the benefit of Christ's faithful.' Her devotion was not unrewarded: the girl began to be better from that moment, and after three days found that her head was free of the infection, except that on her forehead there remained just one ulcer about the size of the gold coin that we call a farthing, and pus or blood continued to ooze from it. The mother applied the same remedy a second time (ignoring all human remedies), and soon afterwards that ulcer disappeared as well.

His body is laid to rest

189. After three days had passed, the Fathers decided to enclose the body in a wooden coffin, and bury it in the common burying place near the high altar. When Cardinal Federico Borromeo heard of this, he took it very badly, for he was devoted to the memory of blessed Philip. He thought it was not fitting for such a great man to be buried in that place, for God had distinguished him through miracles and virtue, and all posterity would come to know of the outstanding holiness of his life and death. Accordingly, he began to put pressure on the Fathers to have him buried elsewhere, with greater honour befitting his greatness. They conferred with Cardinal Alessandro de' Medici, and he was deposited for the moment in a higher place. The event proved that this was the will of God more than of man, for the place of burial chosen for him was one which, as it turned out, he himself had predicted a few days before

---

[257] There are sworn eyewitnesses to this fact.

his death, albeit in an obscure manner.²⁵⁸ At the command of the same Cardinal Alessandro, they constructed a new wooden coffin, so that Philip's body might be more decently laid to rest: in this he was laid, dressed in priestly vestments, while his sons grieved over him. It seemed remarkable to many of us that although his body had been bereft of its soul for three days, it retained the same appearance as before; you would think he was only just dead, or even still alive. His cold limbs had not stiffened in death, which is what we observe usually happens to dead bodies, but could be flexed in all directions as if he were alive. His flesh seemed as soft to the touch as that of a child.

Finally, the workmen constructed an arch over the recess where the body lay. The place of burial where Philip was first buried began to be treated with great veneration by everyone, as it still is today. You could see little models of gold, silver or wax attached to his grave, and votive tablets, the sure sign of the miracles that were there worked.

A sweet odour emitted from his tomb

190. There was a woman who came from a high-ranking family, but was more endowed with devotion than wealth, and was one of those who regularly came to our church. Soon after the death of Philip she came to pray at his tomb, and she noticed there a sweet and pleasant odour. She found this wonderfully refreshing, and wondered where it came from; there were no flowers there, and nothing else that could produce such a scent. Eventually she discovered to her astonishment that it came from Philip's body, although it had not been anointed with any perfumes, nor embalmed.²⁵⁹ The scent smelt like the perfume of roses, violets and similar flowers. The woman who told us this (her name was Giulia Orsini, a woman whose longing was for heaven), seemed to be a

---

[258] *According to the evidence of G.B. Guerra, Philip had made some remark that he would not rest long in the place prepared for him 'under the altar on the Epistle side' but would end up back 'in the room where I am standing', which was effectively where he lies now.*

[259] There are several weighty authors who have recorded how the bodies and tombs of the saints often emit a wonderfully sweet scent. Compare St Jerome's

new St Paula because she was so totally dedicated in charity for the poor, receiving them into her care even at the risk of her own health. She made such spiritual progress that everyone admired her. When she was called home by her Bridegroom, she died on the last day of September, 1598. This brief account of her is as much as I can put in this history, nothing like enough to satisfy me.

To conclude: what could this odour of sweetness indicate other than that this was a body that had shunned every sort of corruption and filth while it was alive?

life of Hilarion; Angrad on St Ansbert, the bishop; Iso on St Othmar; Egilhard on St Burchard, the bishop; Hildegard on St Disibod, bishop; Osbert on St Dunstan; Theodoric on St Dominic; Pope John XXII in the Bull of Canonisation of St Thomas Aquinas; and John Brugman on St Lidwig. You can find the same thing in the lives of many other saints, *notably St Pius of Pietrelcina.*

XVII : VARIOUS MIRACULOUS GRACES, GRANTED TO HIS FOLLOWERS AFTER THE BURIAL OF THE SAINT

191. I must not omit to tell you how, three days after the death of Philip, a certain man of high degree was grieving, inconsolably, in Philip's room, but barely a quarter of an hour had passed before he felt himself bathed in immense joy. His mighty grief transformed into the greatest happiness, he left the place gladly and with a light heart. That man was troubled by great anxieties, and was unable to come to any conclusion over some business or other which demanded serious deliberation, so he went to Philip's grave and pressed his heart against it. He was not disappointed: he began to feel the same inner heat and strength that he used to receive from embracing our holy Father while he was alive, till a great sweat broke out all over his body. That was not all: he was quickly relieved of all his anxiety, and the business turned out in the manner for which he had hoped. There were strangers too who were affected by unwonted joy and delight simply from visiting Philip's grave, and burst into tears of devotion, not of grief.

He heals Claudio Neri when he was suffering in his feet and kidneys

192. Shortly after the death of the blessed man, Claudio Neri was suffering from a severe pain in his right side, caused in some way by his kidneys, and this had been going on for two months.[260] The pain affected him continually, and he was so ill and so miserable that if it became necessary for any reason to move him, the pain forced him to scream aloud, as some way of making it more bearable. As the disease developed, new pains appeared without lessening the old, for Neri began to suffer greatly in his left knee. He endured

---

[260] Claudio, and his wife and children, have given evidence about the whole affair.

this new pain for three or four hours, afraid that if it increased it would stop him sleeping, like a previous attack which he had suffered a few days before in the joints of his left hand. Giving up hope in human aid, he turned to God, for the two severe sources of pain compelled him. Accordingly he applied to the affected parts Philip's linen nightcap, and a bag containing some of his hair, and immediately he was cured of all his pain.

On the following day, Neri told all the friends who visited him about the miracle, in gratitude for the benefit he had received. There were some who told him that it could have occurred entirely naturally, or just by chance, so God permitted it to happen that on the following day he was affected by a new pain, this time in his right knee, quite as acute as the former ones. In order to make it clear that the previous pain had been relieved by the intervention of God, and by no human aid, Neri resolved to resist this new pain manfully, and to bear it until the evening. He refused to apply the relics of blessed Philip to the affected part, knowing by experience that pains of this type increase as the day declines towards evening, and become more acute. As night fell, the pain and its accompanying fear increased much, and became so great that he could scarcely bear it. Anticipating that he would once again be unable to sleep, he decided to apply the same remedy to his disease, and as he did so the pain and the swelling disappeared at once. These two miracles brought double joy to Neri and his family. and the holiness of Philip became more widely known.

He delivers Frà Simone the Capuchin from a complaint of his arms

193. Frà Simone, a Capuchin, had been suffering for ten months with a complaint affecting his arms, that originated from catching cold.[261] He was reduced to such a pitiable condition that he could not put his hands behind his back, neither could he lift them up. When he was celebrating Mass, it was only with great difficulty that he could elevate the Sacred Host, and he could not put on the

---

[261] There are four eyewitnesses who have sworn to this story. *Frà Simone was the brother of Monte Zazzara, one of Gallonio's own penitents.*

VARIOUS MIRACULOUS GRACES GRANTED AFTER THE BURIAL

priestly vestments before Mass unless he had someone to help him. He also suffered severe pain, which troubled him continually, being especially acute in his left arm, which was the worse affected. The movement of this arm was so restricted that he could not raise it enough to scratch his head. He tried medical treatments, but none of them did him any good.

The affliction was getting worse, when his superiors ordered him to go to Rome, in June of 1595. There he heard about the death of Philip and what had happened afterwards, and of his miracles. He put great trust in the favour of so blest a man, and asked his brother Monte Zazzara, who was one of Philip's disciples, to see if any of the holy man's garments survived, and if he would be good enough to get him some to apply to his withered arms. Monte was moved by his story, and brought him some of Philip's hairs, and a scrap of cloth soaked in his blood, which Frà Simone gratefully accepted. He left Rome without using any medicine for his condition, and came to the town of Campagnano, where he decided one day to apply for the help of the blessed Philip and give up all human treatment, for it was doing him no good at all.

To carry out his purpose more effectively, he decided that the following day he would make a general confession of his sins, and then celebrate Mass, praying to God with the single intention that He would restore his health through the merits of his servant Philip. He came back the next day and celebrated Mass in his room; then he took some of Philip's hairs, chopped them into tiny particles and mixed them with water. He prostrated himself on the floor, where he recited the Our Father and Hail Mary before an image of Christ, then made the Sign of the Cross with the cup, and besought the holy Father earnestly to drive away his pain; to this prayer he added a vow that if Philip procured him his health, he would always keep the vigil of his feast as a day of fasting. On finishing his prayers, he took the cup into his hands, full of confidence; he brought it to his mouth, he drank it, and was cured.[262] He could

---

[262] There are weighty authors who tell us of miracles worked through drinking potions in this manner. See Gregory of Tours, *On the Glory of the Martyrs*, book I, chapter 31, and book II, chapter 5. Also his *On the Miracles of St Martin*, book II,

move both arms very easily, put them behind his back, bend them, and stretch them. He felt that his right arm was perfectly normal, whereas the left was still slightly restricted in its movements: he could move it wherever he wanted and bend it in any direction, but as he did so he felt for a moment a mild degree of pain.[263] After applying the same remedy a second time, he soon afterwards got rid of that pain too. Frà Simone was delighted at the favour he had received, and gave thanks, to God first, then to blessed Philip, telling his friends all about it and repeatedly extolling the praises of the blessed man for the help he had received. The miracle became widely known, and was mentioned in many sermons. This was the occasion that began the cult of Philip, which increased daily as new miracles were reported, as it shall increase forever: 'Thus shall he be honoured, whom the king hath a mind to honour' (Esther 6:9).

He restores Marc'Antonio Maffa to health when he was dangerously ill

194.   Marc'Antonio Maffa was a man whose life was well known and much loved because of his integrity and practical skills.[264] On the 5th of August that same year 1595, he began to suffer great pains in his loins, deriving from kidney stones. At night the pain increased so much that he was brought to the pitch that he could not sleep at all – no, not so much as a wink. No remedies did him any good, and the usual treatment by emetics or heating which are applied to those suffering from this complaint were of no benefit and did not help at all. Exhausted by the intensity of his pain, his strength drained, he went to bed after midnight, having tried all medical skill in vain, and begged the help of blessed Philip, in whom alone he placed all his hope of recovery. With no delay, as

---

chapters 1, 39, 51 and 52, and book III, chapters 12 and 43, and book IV, chapters 9, 28, 37 and 42. You could also consult Stephen's *Life of St Moduald, Bishop of Trèves*, chapters 11 and 12.

[263] It often happens that the sick are not totally cured: see Gregory of Tours, *On the Miracles of St Martin*, book II, chapter 45, and the *Life of St Ludger*, book II, chapter 27. Also see Rutilius Benzonus, *On the Jubilee Year*, book I, chapter 49. In fact anyone can easily find similar stories for himself in the best authors.

[264] He himself has given public testimony to confirm the whole story.

he applied himself to his prayers, he fell at once into a light and soothing sleep; he slept for an hour and when he awoke the stone, which was larger than a bean, had been expelled. It was slightly larger than another one that he had voided previously. Maffa was impressed at so swift an outcome, and his admiration was the greater because when he had previously suffered from a kidney stone, despite the fact that it was smaller than this present one, it had caused him excruciating pain for two days after it had emerged from his kidney and descended into the bladder; it had made his urine hot and acrid, and the bladder inflamed, until at last after two or three days it emerged.

195. The same person, in the same week, on the 6th of August, drank a cup of cold water, fasting, after Mass; after drinking it he was stricken first with shivering, and then a pestilential fever began to affect him, causing great drowsiness (what the Greeks call 'lethargy'). The sickness began at the new moon. What particularly indicated the danger in which he lay was that he did not find the slightest relief either from an enema, or stomach massage, or any other method of relieving the drowsiness which oppressed him, or the headaches he suffered. The doctors advised him to allow a vein to be opened to let blood, but even that did him no good, and the doctors began to doubt of his recovery, although the patient was normally not dry but full of humours.

When night fell, Maffa fled to Philip for aid, and saw him soon enough, in a dream. He seemed to be in a house which was on fire, and saw men there who were doing everything they could to damage it and destroy it. While this demolition was going on, there were two others with him, who were trying to persuade him to take refuge in flight, they themselves being very strong, but they were suddenly overwhelmed by a falling wall. Maffa was terrified by this, and thought he was about to die. He was so disturbed in his mind that he did not know what to do next, but while he suffered all this pain and grief, Philip appeared next to him, and rebuked the youths who were demolishing the house, crying out, 'Save Maffa! Save Maffa!' repeating the words twice. His plea was answered, for at once Maffa found himself delivered safely from all danger, and the truth of the vision was proved by what happened later.

The fever left him the very next day, and the weakness which usually follows a fever for some days was altogether relieved so that he felt all his former strength had returned. Healthy and strong, he left his bed. The doctors, well aware of the danger Maffa had been in, confirmed that he had recovered by a miracle.

196. In gratitude for the benefits he had received, Maffa returned to the grave of our Holy Father to give thanks. When he had thanked God and blessed Philip, he was the first to have a painted tablet attached to the tomb. It bears this inscription:

> To Jesus Christ, King! Marc'Antonio Maffa, priest of Salerno, placed this to blessed Philip who delivered him on the 7th August 1595. When I was attacked by a raging fever, I had a dream in which I was trapped in a house, which was being consumed by fire, with no means of escape. Two men who seemed to be with me counselled me to flee, but were killed by a collapsing wall. When I was terrified and expected to die, I saw and heard blessed Philip repeatedly calling out to those who were destroying the house in these words, 'Save the priest!' The fever left me the next day which I believe to be due to his merits and prayers, in testimony of which I here affix this tablet in the name of the Father and the Son and the Holy Ghost, and to the honour of the same blessed Philip. Amen.

He heals the sick

197. Ridolfo Silvestri was a highly skilled physician, who was suddenly taken with severe stomach pains and other symptoms, on the 11th of August.[265] He found no solace in his medicines, and determined to seek for aid from another source. He remembered the holy Father in his peril (for his survival was in doubt), and confidently implored his assistance. As soon as he had done so he began to feel better, and fell into a soothing sleep. After sleeping

---

[265] Ridolfo himself gave evidence about this matter.

VARIOUS MIRACULOUS GRACES GRANTED AFTER THE BURIAL

for an hour and a half, he got up and found himself quite free from pain. Then he went to reverence the holy Father's tomb, and had a votive tablet affixed there to certify the miracle to posterity, with this inscription:

> As I felt myself dying, under various acute symptoms, I implored the aid of blessed Philip, and a soothing sleep took hold of me; at once I was cured.

That same year, Girolamo Pamphili, the Auditor of the Rota, fell ill.[266] This was followed by a severe headache, so that the patient was all but out of his mind. He placed blessed Philip's nightcap on his head, and through the intervention of God the complaint disappeared altogether.

He delivers a youth from danger of sin

198. Here is another less trivial miracle. At the beginning of August that same year, a youth called Stefano happened to be passing the house of a woman of ill repute. She called to him, and he went in, where she invited him to sin. He was so distraught by anxiety that he didn't know which way to turn, knowing that it would be vile to assent, dangerous to refuse. He was close to falling when blessed Philip came to his aid. He had some of his hairs and a scrap of his clothing in a pouch around his neck, and he felt it striking against his breast, pressing on his heart. Then he heard Philip's voice, 'Look what you are doing: get away from here or you are lost'.[267] Such a clear indication of his Father's concern spurred him to make his escape and elude the woman's clutches. Believing that this was due to Philip's charity, the boy had a votive tablet fixed to the tomb, which you may see there, a reminder of the peril he had escaped, and a monument to a great miracle.

---

[266] Girolamo Pamphili himself has given sworn testimony on this.

[267] The boy to whom this happened gave testimony on oath about it. *The boy's name was Stefano Calcinardi, the girl was called Lucia, and came from Bologna.*

He expels a fever

199. In early September of the same year, a prominent lady called Isabella Priorata was taken by a light fever one night, of that type of fever which is recurrent; the fever would be followed by a severe headache, such as she had never experienced before, which grew to such a pitch that she was nearly delirious.[268] When her servants noticed that she was getting worse, they decided to try a different remedy. Three hours after nightfall, therefore, they surreptitiously applied to her head a small reliquary capsule containing a scrap of cloth soaked in the holy Father's blood. The ruse succeeded, for the sick woman at once received healing. She fell peacefully asleep, and when they awoke her in the morning she found that all her illness had disappeared. She gave thanks to God and also to blessed Philip, rejoicing that she had received such a favour.

That same year and month, Eugenia Mansueti was confined to bed with fever.[269] She was tormented by the high temperature, and asked them to bring her some water. When they brought it, she dipped a piece of the blessed man's clothing into it, drank it, and the fever left her.

He delivers Drusilla after she had fallen headlong from a high place

200. At the end of September that year, Drusilla Porcacci had washed her clothes and was hanging them out to dry in the sun, when she accidentally fell from a very high place, and was severely injured.[270] The balcony from which she fell was about twenty-six yards up, and she fell onto a pavement made up of bricks set on edge, though it was so old that a lot of it was worn out and crumbling. They tell us that her head was bruised and fractured, and her right eye so damaged that everyone considered she would certainly

---

[268] There are four witnesses who have confirmed this on oath.

[269] She herself and two eyewitnesses have given sworn evidence about this. *She was a servant of the Crescenzi, and did Philip's laundry, pilfering the occasional item until she had a basket full of his clothing.*

[270] Six eyewitnesses, including the surgeon who attended her, have given sworn witness to this.

VARIOUS MIRACULOUS GRACES GRANTED AFTER THE BURIAL

lose it, that is if she recovered at all, which no one thought likely. The eye was right out of its socket, and her nose was badly crushed. She was also bleeding profusely from the mouth, and they were unable to stop it. Her jaws were severely bruised, and her lower lip cut through. In the course of her fall she received two actual wounds, that in the lip which we have mentioned, and the other in her left hand, in the palm. Also her teeth should not be forgotten: they were so distorted by the fall that she was in danger of losing them too. Such was the wretched state that the woman was in after missing her foothold and falling straight down. Her friends and family picked her up, thinking she was dead, and carried her to her room, laying the broken body on her own bed. Barely half alive, her injuries left her unable to hear, to see or to speak, and the neighbourhood were already beginning to talk about her death, as if the fall had killed her.

201. At the time this happened, her husband, Antonio Fantini of Faventino, was away from home. Someone nervously brought him the news, and he ran at once to the tomb of blessed Philip. There he fell on his knees and raised his hands and eyes to heaven; swimming in tears, he begged the blessed Father's aid, promising in his prayer that he would bring a painted tablet to the tomb to remind posterity about the miracle, if he would save her, whom no human skill could save. He ended his prayer and came home, to find his dear wife close to death.

In the meantime they had called in a doctor, whose name is Antonio de Franchis. He examined the woman, and declared that it was all over with her. Since he had no hope that she would recover, he made no attempt to cleanse her wounds, necessary though it might be, because it would only cause her greater pain. All he did was to put some white of egg on her cut lip, no medication on her hand, and a plaster of the type they call *albo lene* on her eye. This was all the treatment he gave the woman, since he believed her to be as good as dead; but I believe it was through the prompting of the Lord, so that the glory of his servant Philip might be made plain.

Her husband made a point of visiting the tomb of the holy man every day, in his concern for his wife, and there he begged Philip's aid, with abundance of tears. His trust was not misplaced, for one day as he was praying, Philip suddenly appeared to his dying wife. She was at once filled with extraordinary delight when he came, and reverently implored his aid. He took up a clean towel, which was there for her use, and put it to her mouth, then he gently inserted it into her throat, and drew it out covered with blood and pus. While doing this he said, 'Do not be afraid, this trouble is not going to finish you.' With no delay her head and face were immediately freed from all their injuries. Her husband then arrived to visit his wife, and the holy Father vanished at once. The woman was upset at this, because she had been hoping that all her suffering would have disappeared, had he not vanished, and she burst into tears. Antonio asked her what she was crying about. She answered, 'May God forgive you! If you had not turned up, blessed Philip would have taken away all my pain, but the moment you began to come into my room, he went away to heaven.' She told him about her vision, and showed him the miracle. In the meantime the doctor arrived, who observed that her cut lip had been healed through no medical means, and admitted that it must be classed as a miracle.

202. The woman's left knee then swelled up, so that a greater miracle might occur, until it reached the size of a large loaf. The surgeon wanted to open it with a lance, but she was terrified of this, and asked him to defer the operation until the following day. That night she begged and implored blessed Philip as earnestly as she could to help her. As she lay awake in prayer, he appeared to her again, shining with the light of heaven. He removed the plaster which had been applied to the affected part, and restored her knee to its usual size.[271] When Drusilla observed that her knee was cured, she called for her husband, telling him to come and see

---

[271] That saints have medically tended the sick, I can cite, among other authors, George's *Life of St Theodore the Siceot*. You will find similar stories about working cures in the best authors, such as the anonymous book *On the Miracles of St Stephen* circulated under the name of Evodius, book I, chapter 11, and book II, chapter 2. Also Gregory of Tours, *On the Miracles of St Martin*, book II, chapters 31 and 41.

another great and marvellous miracle. She gave the greatest thanks to God and blessed Philip. When the doctor arrived next morning with the intention of opening the swelling so that the corrupt matter could come out, she said to him, 'Cut away, slash it open as much as you like: there is nothing wrong with my knee!' When he heard this, he began by examining the affected part closely, and felt it with his hand; finding by sight and touch that it really was cured, he declared, with admiration, that a new miracle had been added to the old.

Drusilla was now so eager to get out of bed, that she again entreated blessed Philip to help her. She was not disappointed: he appeared to her one more time, while she was awake, and she says that he was so beautiful that you could not imagine anything more delightful. He stretched out his hand and touched her limbs, beginning with her head and shoulders, and after doing that, vanished from her eyes. As day broke, Drusilla gratefully rose from her bed, and tears of joy sprang from her eyes, as she would not stop giving thanks to the blessed Father. Her injuries lasted in all less than ten days.

He heals the virgin Fiammetta when her feet were crushed

203. A lady called Fiammetta Nannoni, aged 55, was travelling when she was knocked down by some vehicle, and found that she was unable to get up, for one of her feet had been crushed by the wheels of the vehicle.[272] The foot swelled up, and the swelling then began to cause her great pain. Being unable to stand up, she was placed on a stretcher, and doctors were called in, who tried to salve the suffering part with various forms of treatment. It was all in vain, for not only did the affected foot cause her considerable pain, but it was badly damaged, and the nerves severed. She bore the suffering for nearly eleven months, until October of this year, when she felt herself prompted by God, if she wanted to get well, to vow a votive tablet to blessed Philip, and to offer her prayers to him and

---

[272] Cardinal Baronio, who used to hear the confessions of the injured woman, has told the whole story on oath, as have certain others. *She was either a tertiary or a laywoman resident in the Augustinian convent of S. Lorenzo in Lucina.*

the Virgin Mother of God. She made her vow, and at once recovered the use of her limbs as before, so that she was able to walk. She had a silver foot hung up at the blessed man's tomb, as a sign of so great a miracle.

He recalls a dying infant to life

204. In the same year, towards the end of October, Caterina Lotti of Milan was already eight months pregnant, when she fell into a severe sickness, a very acute pleurisy. The effect of the illness on the woman was to throw her into premature labour, with the result that after suffering the pains of childbirth too soon, she was delivered of a dead child, or at least the infant gave every indication of being dead. The midwife who was attending the patient was very experienced, for she had assisted at births for thirty-five years, and she applied all the remedies she knew to the child, but all in vain.[273] Nothing she could do was any good, for no medical treatment can recall the dead to life, and so the midwife realised that the only hope of a cure was to abandon human aid and rely on that of God. She called on the most holy Mother of God, and made a vow. When her prayers were not heard, the thought of blessed Philip occurred to her, and she began at once to address him thus, 'O blessed Philip! I beg you, ask the holy Mother of God to raise this child from the dead, so that he may be washed in Baptism, and not perish eternally.'[274] Then she applied some of the blessed man's hairs, and at once the dead child returned to life. He was baptised immediately, and named Giovan Pietro. He lived for twenty-one days, and was then carried off by some illness, leaving this world for heaven. The mother, Caterina, had already died, five days after giving birth.

---

[273] There are five witnesses to this.

[274] The anonymous author of the *Miracles of St Stephen* tells something similar (book I, chapter 15), as does St Augustine, in the Sermons *de Diversis* 32 and 33. See also St Antoninus' *History*, part 3, title 23, chapter 7, para. 14; and finally Pope John XXII in the Apostolic Letters of Canonisation of St Louis, Bishop of Toulouse.

VARIOUS MIRACULOUS GRACES GRANTED AFTER THE BURIAL

He delivers a nun from an incurable illness

205.   That same year there was a very pious old nun (whose name I shall conceal, since she insists on this), over forty-five years old, and a malignant cancer appeared in one of her breasts. It started no larger than a walnut, but grew every day, and became harder, causing her great discomfort, until she was in continuous pain, always conscious of the hard lump. Although she was suffering like this, she wouldn't think of having the condition treated, and bore with it for six months. The pain increased daily, and she knew that the tumour was growing and spreading, but she was too shy to show the affected part to any doctor, and imagined that everyone would shun her because the disease was so embarrassing. Hence she kept putting off telling anyone about it. Eventually, as the growth was causing really severe constant pain in her breast, not knowing what else to do, she revealed the whole matter to the priest who heard her confession. He understood, and told the nun at once to show the affected part to the doctor, if she had any concern for her health. However, he might as well have been talking to the wind, and could not induce her to expose the tumour to a doctor, she being so shy.[275] Then he remembered that he had with him some linen soaked in the blood of blessed Philip, and gave it to the patient for her treatment. That was successful: the nun accepted the gift, and applied it to the affected part, and no sooner had she done so than she began to feel better.

The following night, when she had just gone to sleep, Philip appeared to her in heavenly glory, and as she lay there touched the affected part with his hand, then gently stroked it, and so cured it at once. As he stroked her, he said, 'Do not be afraid, this disease is nothing.' (Those are the exact words he often used to have in his mouth while he was alive.) Then he advised her to be diligent in her prayers, and vanished from her sight. The outcome shows that the vision was not false, for when the nun awoke she found that her breast was quite cured, and got out of bed very happy. She had a painted tablet fixed to his tomb in witness to the miracle.

---

[275] St Gregory of Nyssa tells a similar story in his life of St Macrina. *The shy nun's name was Ortensia Anelli, from S. Cecilia in Trastevere.*

He heals a nobleman from the illness that gripped him

206. Claudio Rangone, who is the present Bishop of Piacenza, was suffering from a recurrent fever that year, which had gripped him for more than two months, until he was not far from danger of death. When Giulia Orsini came to hear of this – she was a devout lady, closely related to the patient – she sent him a scrap of linen soaked in the holy man's blood, with the instruction that as soon as he received it he was to apply it to his neck. Her trust was rewarded, because as he did this the fever entirely disappeared. This happened in December: normally fevers of this kind either finish off the sick person, or else last for a long time, and never come to an end except in spring or autumn.

XVIII : MIRACLES PERFORMED IN THE YEAR AFTER HIS DEATH, AND THE THREE FOLLOWING

He dispels diseases of various sorts
A.D. 1596; Clement VIII year 4

207. In the year of salvation 1596, in January, Settimia dei Neri, aged eighteen, was sitting by the fire with her sisters Olimpia and Faustina, about three hours after nightfall. It chanced that as Olimpia was picking up the bellows, the iron tube attached to them, which was glowing hot, hit Settimia in the left eye, and not only damaged it severely but even burnt it. That was not all: very soon a cyst appeared in the eye, giving clear indications that it had been burnt, and this caused intolerable pain, leading to spasms. The girl was unable to close the injured eye, and her sight was so damaged by the burning that she was unable to see those around her. Racked with pain, she trembled all over. Her mother Clelia Bonardi, in an attempt to relieve her daughter's suffering, applied some rose water mixed with white of egg to the injury, but with no effect: in fact that treatment might have caused the eye to burst.

Having tried all remedies in vain, they turned to another source of healing.[276] In tears, the mother knelt down and begged the aid of blessed Philip for her daughter; to her prayers she added a vow that if Settimia recovered the sight of her lost eye, she would bring a votive image of silver to Philip's tomb, in witness to the miracle. When her prayer was not granted, the daughter herself took refuge in the holy man, though she was all but overcome by the pain. From her heart, in the midst of her suffering, she begged him, saying, 'Blessed Philip, if it is not your will to cure me of this injury, at least make the pain go away.' She had been suffering now for three hours. When she had finished her prayer, she touched her

---

[276] Settimia herself, her mother, brothers and sisters have given sworn evidence for this.

injured eye with the nightcap which Philip used to wear, repeating the same words. Her hope and her prayer were not in vain: the pain ceased at once, the cyst disappeared, and the eye was completely cured. The girl soon fell peacefully asleep and slept until dawn, and when she woke in the morning she could see the sky, for her eyes were healed.

208. In the same year and month, Evangelista Mariotto was prostrated by a severe fever, which allowed him no sleep, nor even any rest in bed.[277] He lay there for several days under this illness, and his suffering increased beyond all bounds, until one night about four hours after sunset, he asked for the sacraments of the Church to fortify him, not so much fearing death as expecting it. One of those with him, who pitied him, suggested that he should commend himself to blessed Philip, to console him. They brought him a scrap of the holy man's clothing, which he accepted with great devotion. Dividing it in two, he hung one part around his neck, and chopped the other part up small, mixed it with water, and drank it. Once he had drunk the potion, the pain ceased altogether, and any food he took was not rejected as before; from that moment the patient was quite cured, through the intervention of God.

It was about the same time that a nun, consecrated to God, named Giulia, was suffering great pain in her sides and bowels.[278] The illness was so acute that she was in constant pain, both day and night. On the doctors' advice, she tried several remedies for her illness, but since they did not bring about the slightest alleviation, one of the sisters suggested that she should try the same remedy as Evangelista had, and when she did so, she found herself very soon restored to health.

---

[277] Apart from Evangelista himself, there are others who have told the story on oath. *He was a canon of S. Angelo in Viterbo; the relic was brough to him by Lorenzo Massimi, canon of Viterbo Cathedral.*

[278] She swore to the whole story, and was not the only witness. She lives in Viterbo, in the convent of Our Lady.

MIRACLES PERFORMED IN THE YEARS AFTER HIS DEATH

209. In February of the same year, Pietro Pozzo, a priest of our Congregation, was in Palermo, when it happened that one of the servants of the Fathers in our house at Palermo fell into a recurrent fever, which was fiery and likely to be mortal.[279] Every day he was seized by a fit of shivering, at the same time of day for about an hour, and his whole body shook. Because of this he used to be wrapped up in much clothing; his legs and feet, indeed his whole body had to be covered for the sake of keeping him warm. When the shivering passed off, it was followed by the burning fever which affected him so strongly that his chest was afire with heat, accompanied by intolerable thirst. No remedies they tried seemed to be of any use, and everyone began to fear for his life. But one day, Pietro was sitting by him while he was complaining that he was feeling much worse than usual, and it occurred to him to think of the holy Father. Struck by the thought, he took some of Philip's hair which he had with him, to use as a cure for the disease, and as soon as he did so, the sick man recovered with no further medical attention.

210. In March that year, Antonio Parma had an apostema on his heart which caused him great pain.[280] The pain was more than he had ever suffered before, and denied him any rest at all by day or night. The doctors were unable to see the apostema: when ulcers are obvious, they can easily be cured, but when they are concealed, no treatment can affect them. The condition worsened day by day, unknown to the doctors, and there was no suitable medicine to help; the patient was all but overcome by his suffering, and undoubtedly hastening to his death. As the illness worsened and he came into extreme peril of his life, he was aided by some hairs of blessed Philip, for he had heard of his power to heal so many others. The disease, which had yielded to no previous treatment, began to pass off; he felt better, was able to sleep, and so was cured. However, before two days had passed, he felt another attack of the

---

[279] The same Father Pietro Pozzo tells the story, on oath. *He was received into the Roman congregation in 1581, and founded the Oratory in Palermo in 1593.*

[280] Apart from Antonio himself, there are two other eyewitnesses who have given evidence publicly about this story.

pain, which was most severe: this only lasted a quarter of an hour, until the apostema burst, though neither he nor the doctors were aware of it, and no medical treatment had been applied. As soon as that had happened, he became completely free from his disease.[281]

211.   In April of that year, a woman from Corneto called Gora was afflicted by a quartan fever which had lasted thirty-two months.[282] She was unable to move except from her bed to the fireside, from the fireside to her bed. They applied to her a reliquary containing some hairs of blessed Philip, and she began to feel better at the beginning of the shivering which usually preceded the fever; before the end of the day both the shivering and the fever had quite ceased. However, many days later she was travelling during a particularly heavy rainstorm, and the fever came on her again, but when she used the same remedy, she immediately felt better. Hour by hour, moment by moment, her strength increased until she was soon perfectly well.

In May that year, Cardinal Agostino Cusano sent a gift of a brocade covering of great value, to adorn the holy man's tomb.

212.   Ottavio Rositano, from Naples, had been suffering from dysentery for two months by early June of that year, with a ceaseless haemorrhage which no medical treatment could stop.[283] The dysentery was accompanied by a continual and pestilential fever, tormenting the man both day and night. He showed every indication that he would certainly die. But while he was hourly awaiting death, he was advised by a friend to implore the aid of blessed Philip. He did as he was advised, and added to his prayer a resolve to join Philip's Institute if he recovered. Then he drank some water which had been in contact with his relics, and immediately found healing for his disease. He began to speak clearly, and on the

---

[281] Compare St Gregory of Tours, *On the Miracles of St Martin*, book I, chapter 32, book II, chapter 60, and book IV, chapter 2.

[282] We heard this from sworn eyewitnesses. Compare the references to Gregory of Tours already given.

[283] There are six eyewitnesses who have given sworn evidence about this.

following day, to the astonishment of his doctors, the haemorrhage ceased, and the fever left him. He was soon afterwards completely well again, enjoying his usual health. He now lives in Naples, a member of our Congregation there.

Two months later, the same man suffered an intolerable pain which invaded both his arms. It derived from the two tendons around the arms, and the illness was so severe that the patient could not rest for a moment. He used the same remedy and at once the pain ceased entirely, so that he was able to sleep. In token of the benefit he had received, he sent a silver votive image to the holy man's tomb in Rome.

213. In early October that year, Caterina, the brilliant daughter of Giuseppe Castiglione, who was nine years old, was gripped by a burning fever which put her in peril of her life.[284] The fever was accompanied by continuous diarrhoea, rheum and constant catarrh. She also found all food so repugnant that she was quite unable to eat. One day, although they had given up hope of her survival, she told them that, as she slept, the holy Mother of God had come to her, accompanied only by Philip (she and her parents had already applied to him for aid). The Mother of God had told her not to trust in medicine, nor to be afraid, for she herself would bring her help, and by the intercession of blessed Philip would drive away her sickness. Certainly her family and their servants could see for themselves evidence of her recovery: the girl became better, was able to eat again, and day by day improved, to the great relief of those who loved her. Shortly she recovered her usual health.

In late December that same year, Alessandro Foligni began to suffer from his bowels (a complaint which he frequently suffered to a severe extent), and implored the aid of blessed Philip as soon as the illness began. All the pain and discomfort disappeared at once.

---

[284] We have two sworn eyewitnesses to this.

He cures more sick people
A.D. 1597; Clement VIII year 5–6

214. At the beginning of the year 1597, a priest named Giovan Battista Felice, aged seventy-five, was suffering from terrible toothache.[285] He was in so much pain that it could rank among the greatest of tortures. It grew continually worse, but he applied a handkerchief of the blessed Father to his gums and teeth, and the pain and suffering disappeared at once.

In the same year, in early March, a nobleman called Marc'Antonio of the de Sanctis family was in danger of death from a pestilential fever. The doctors despaired of his recovery, but one night he tied round his neck a bag containing some of blessed Philip's hairs, and began to feel better at once. That very night his life was secured, and after four days he was totally healed. With sincere gratitude to God and blessed Philip, he had a silver votive plaque of considerable weight sent from Naples to Rome for Philip's tomb, in fulfilment of his vow.

On the 31st of March that year, Marcello Lorenzi, who is now bishop of Strongoli, was suddenly seized by severe pains in the groin, so severe that he was sure he would not be long for this life, unless God were to save him.[286] The pain had racked him for about four hours before one of his servants reminded him of blessed Philip, saying, 'Commend yourself to blessed Philip; implore that holy man to help you, he will surely come to you and help you.' He did as he was advised, and called on Philip. To be brief, immediately on invoking his name he found all his pain gone, he fell asleep, and when he woke up soon afterwards (having slept for about a quarter of an hour), a large stone emerged, as big as a pine nut. He claims that it was through his prayer to Philip that he was delivered from imminent danger.

---

[285] The priest himself has told the story and swears to it.
[286] There are two eyewitnesses besides Marcello himself who have told the story on oath.

MIRACLES PERFORMED IN THE YEARS AFTER HIS DEATH

215. In May that year, a physician of good family named Fabio Apicella, a citizen of Naples, suffered from pains in his feet and in his groin.[287] The pain was so acute that it deprived him of sleep entirely. Spurning human means, which could do his illness no good, he applied some hair of the blessed Philip to the affected part, and not in vain. The stone immediately descended to his bladder, the pain vanished entirely, and without impeding his urine, the stone emerged: it too was as large as a pine nut. Astonished by this, he affirmed in public testimony that he had been cured through no human agency, but by the power of God at the intercession of the holy man. On another occasion he was suffering from the same pain one night, but using the same remedy he was cured at once.

At the end of May that year, a hanging lamp was given to adorn Philip's tomb, wrought of pure silver; it was the votive gift of a prominent lady whose name I shall pass over in silence, since she wishes it kept secret.[288]

216. In July of that year a little boy called Giuseppe Sermei, four years old, was suffering from a burning fever and in serious pain for several days. The disease was so serious that everyone thought he was in danger of death. Three days passed, during which he ate nothing but three yolks of egg, and the disease grew worse and worse. The signs of imminent death appeared: he had a cold sweat on his brow, his whole body grew limp, his arms and legs drooped, his eyes closed, his breath laboured, all heat departed from his body. The extent of the disease is indicated by the fact that the child could neither see nor speak. When his mother realised this, she took a scrap of cloth soaked in Philip's blood, and laid it on her dying child. With no delay the boy opened his eyes at once. He called out aloud for his mother, then he got out of bed healthy and strong, asked for some food, dressed himself and walked unaided around the house. His mother and father, and everyone there, were amazed, and cried for joy.[289]

---

[287] Apart from Fabio himself, two other witnesses have sworn to this story.
[288] *But we know it was Costanza Crescenzi again.*
[289] There are three sworn eyewitnesses.

In August that year, Ortensia de Lelli was suffering from a recurrent fever, which steadily increased, with severe stomach pains. When she realised that her medical treatment was not even relieving the fever, let alone curing it, she decided to use some hairs of the blessed Father as a remedy. She applied them to herself, and at once began to feel less pain. It did not end there, for the fever ceased completely that very day.[290] She sent someone to Rome (she lived outside the city), to attach a votive tablet to the tomb of the holy Father as evidence of the miracle.

Arcangela Ancaiani is restored to health
A.D. 1598–9; Clement VIII year 7–8

217. A nun, consecrated to God at Spoleto in the convent of St Catherine, called Arcangela Ancaiani, had suffered for five years from a recurrent and dangerous fever.[291] It had been a daily recurrence, every day at the same hour, but for the last two years it had become continuous, steadily increasing, and no medical treatment was of any avail. She was advised in a letter from Maria Maddelena Orsini, a very distinguished lady, to implore the aid of Philip. When she did so, she was at once delivered from her illness, to the astonishment of the doctors. That happened on the 14th of August, 1598.

The Maria Maddelena I have mentioned was the same one that Lallio Anguillara had married, that famous man who was lord of the town of Cerio. When Lallio died she decided to embrace the religious life, eager to serve Christ, rather than remain any longer in the world. She picked on the order of St Dominic, and consecrated herself to the greatest of kings. It was during the reign of Pope Gregory XIII that she began to lead the religious life, in a convent which she had built in Rome, on the Quirinal. But that is enough about her: let us return to Philip.

218. In July 1599, the same nun, Arcangela, had an inflammation of both the upper and lower lids of her left eye, which swelled up

---

[290] We have sworn eyewitnesses to this story.

[291] There are eight sworn eyewitnesses, one of whom is the doctor who was tending the patient.

MIRACLES PERFORMED IN THE YEARS AFTER HIS DEATH

and stuck together.[292] This complaint led on to the inflammation attacking the left eye itself, which became red and bloodshot. The doctor was called, and applied some treatment for the condition, but with no success, for the eye grew steadily worse. The sick nun realised from various indications that she ought to seek aid from blessed Philip, and in hope of recovery she prayed to him one evening that he would bring her healing through the power and mercy of God. Then she touched her bad eye with his picture, and went to bed. She fell asleep, but when she awoke she realised at once that she had been cured; the inflammation was quite gone. When the doctors and others saw it in the morning, they were astounded. Since then Arcangela has not ceased to give thanks to the best of her ability to Philip, from whom she is delighted to have received such a benefit.[293]

219. There have been many others who have received similar benefits, in many places, who have recovered after severe illnesses of which there was little hope of recovery, but we cannot go through all the miracles of that blessed man one by one. I shall therefore pass over in silence more than eighty miracles. Among these, ignoring the others, we have ten people who were dying, one deaf woman (Teodosia Lucatella of Faventino), and a young man whom Philip had tried to help towards desiring and attaining virtue while he was alive: because he had not listened to him, Philip scared him by sending him a miraculous vision of a terrible monster.[294] In the same year, Alfonso Visconti, Bishop of Cervia, who was soon afterwards made a member of the College of Cardinals, gave a donation to Philip of a scarlet garment of brushed silk, from the spoils of Sinan Pasha, captain of the Turkish fleet: it is a marvellous piece of Phrygian work, beautifully embroidered with flowers in gold and silver.

---

[292] To this too we have the same eight witnesses, including the doctor.

[293] There are sworn eyewitnesses to that as well.

[294] A prominent man has confirmed that whole story by public witness. The great Simeon Salus did something similar, as you may find in his life by Leontius, chapters 31 and 33.

XIX : A SUMMARY OF THE VIRTUES OF BLESSED PHILIP

220. In the foregoing chapters I have spoken as occasion demanded about some of Philip's virtues: now I must say a little about the rest. Let us begin with humility – I will select just a few points to tell you about, rather then tire the reader with too long an account, for many marvellous things are told about Philip's humility.

Humility

He made a particular point of humility; he loved it always, and embraced it, being constant in his practice of it. He used to say that it was through humility that virtues are retained, whereas once humility is lost all virtue is destroyed and comes to nothing. For this reason he would commend it to others as the head, source and guardian of all other virtues.

Of himself and of his achievements he had so little opinion that he would consider himself the very least of mortals, and nothing annoyed him more than hearing himself praised or called a saint. If they did so, he would reply, 'May God make me what you call me! But alas, there are innumerable country girls and peasants who will find more glory in the sight of God than Philip!' He claimed for himself neither power nor piety, but when he found himself fêted by crowds of people, and flourishing in men's admiration, he would say he was plunged into depression to think he responded so little to the opinion people had of his holiness. That was the reason why so often, in grief and anguish of mind, he broke out into words like these, which showed his true humility: 'I have never done anything worthy of the life of heaven. I know myself to be of all men the least pleasing to God; all others should be an example to me of virtue and devotion.' When he was ill, he used to say, 'If my life is prolonged, I will try to reform myself for a better end.' He could never stop wondering why God's power should use his efforts to convert so many souls, although nothing he did was of any virtue, as he used to say.

221. He never boasted at all of being the founder of the Congregation, although he was so. 'Do not imagine,' he used to say, 'that it is any credit to me that I founded this society, and have called back many from miserable error to the true path of salvation: no, it is more a proof of my own insignificance before the power of God, for it is He who has used the worthless efforts of the least of his servants to achieve what has been done. It was never my intention to found a Congregation.'

Towards the end of his life, when they asked him to pray to the Lord in the words of St Martin, 'If I be necessary to your people, I do not refuse the labour', he replied at once, 'Far be it from me to pray like that! I am not the sort of person who can be trusted to be of any use for the salvation of anyone.' He used to say to Baronio, his confessor, that it caused him great sorrow that people thought so much of him, adding that he had often begged the Lord not to work miracles through him, and that anything of the sort that did happen might be credited not to himself but to the faith of those on whom the miracles were wrought.

222. It was from the fountain of humility that there flowed that disdain of himself which marked his whole life so wonderfully. He always did all he could to avoid honours and dignities, for he knew that honour does the soul no good and brings no happiness. For himself he sought nothing but poverty, and a low opinion of himself, detachment from all things, and a secluded life. He did admirable things, but hated to be admired. That is clearly shown in that when he had done some great thing, he would conceal his wisdom under the guise of foolishness. To escape the attention of men, he followed the advice of St Paul, 'He who would be wise, let him become a fool' [1 Cor 3:18].

What a truly divine man he was! Like St Ephraem the Syrian, he desired more to be good than to seem to be so; this was the intention for which he strove with all his might. He delighted in using simple language, with no interest in fine composition or courtly phrases. He preferred people to treat him in the old-fashioned way without dissimulation. He was greatly embarrassed if anyone of any class, even the lowest, stood up in his presence, or took his hat off, or attempted to kiss his hands. I could tell you much that is worth reading and remembering, but for the sake of brevity I shall omit most of it. In short, his constant aim, his purpose in mind, was to conceal his holiness as much as he could, both from his friends outside and those who lived with him, by mingling jokes with his serious teaching.

Love of Poverty

223. Both as layman and priest he regularly cultivated poverty. While he lived in Florence he bore with great constancy the serious losses his family sustained through a sudden fire. When he arrived in Rome, he never asked for anything from his family or anyone else, growing accustomed to poverty as he earned his bread. The desire he had for poverty is demonstrated by the fact that, as a teenager, he repudiated his uncle's inheritance, and at the end of his life he constantly prayed God to bring him to such a pitch of poverty that if he were in need of a silver coin he might find no one to give it. This, however, he never achieved, but he did not lose the merit in God's eyes which such a condition would have brought.

Constancy in Prayer

224. He also had a great longing for prayer, so that had it been possible he would never have ceased praying. Whatever spare time he had, he dedicated to prayer, and whether he was standing or sitting, walking around or doing anything at home or outside, he was so attached to prayer that he seemed to have dedicated to spirituality not only his body and heart, but even his work and time. The degree of prayer which he attained was such that it seemed to be the work of God rather than of himself. When he wished for union with God in contemplation, he was so pierced by God's love that he was forced to lie down on his bed as if he were ill and weak. He would turn his face to heaven, singing psalms with both spirit and mind. When he kindled a fire of meditation, as we have already heard, he would tremble all over, and become heated with the force of that heavenly flame. His body became very feeble (if that is the right word to use of the debility brought upon him by the love of God), but it was because of his love of God and of heaven rather than through any physical infirmity. He was readily able to spend much of the night in prayer, or even stay awake all night

through. He always tried to find himself a place that was distant and high above ordinary business, to be a more suitable place for contemplation.

The Gift of Tears

225. His tears flowed so readily that almost every time he prayed he would burst out weeping. When he meditated on the life and death of Our Lord Jesus Christ, he was so grief-stricken that he could not bear it. He wept copiously over the sins of others as if they had been his own. He could hardly listen to anyone talking about the Passion and death of Christ without tears starting from his eyes. In fact, he wept so often and so copiously that those who saw the extent of his tears considered it a miracle that he did not lose the sight of his eyes.

But let us finish this chapter with an example. It was while Gregory XIV was Pope, and Philip was seriously ill: he found himself unable to bring to his mouth the cup of chicken broth he was holding in his hand, because the thought of the death of Our Lord Jesus Christ suddenly came into his mind, and he cried out, in floods of tears, 'Oh my Christ, O my Lord! You are on the cross, and I, your servant, am in my bed. You had no one to care for you, stripped of all consolation, hanging on the cross – I am lying in my own bed surrounded by so many of my sons, whose only concern is for my good, who are looking after me alone!' And after saying that, he was unable to restrain his sobs, and the tears which flowed so copiously from his eyes.

Gentleness

226. His manner was so gentle that he was incapable of anger. When it was necessary to correct his disciples or anyone else, he did so with the greatest tact and tenderness. To be brief, he brought himself to such a degree of mildness that he had vanquished and restrained every impulse towards anger, keeping it entirely under his control. If he gave an order, it seemed more like a request than a command; he asked for nothing with severity, but usually requested like this: 'Please do this', or 'I would love you to do this', or 'I could do it for you if you find it difficult', or 'I would like to give you this task – what do you think?'

He used to look at his friends, both those in the community and those outside, with so joyful a countenance, that it was easy to tell from that alone how charitable he was towards everyone, how gentle. It was that joyous countenance that drew everyone towards him, conjoined with his delightful manner. His conversation with everyone he met was full of light-hearted and pleasing phrases, but at the same time whatever he said or did was steeped in holiness, which was a great gift he received from the Lord, a very difficult attainment.

Prudence

227. God adorned Philip with great prudence, which was most noticeable in the things he did for the glory of God, and in giving spiritual advice. In order to conceal this virtue, he pretended to be simple and foolish, to be able to say, like St Paul, 'We are fools for Christ's sake'. [1 Cor 4:10] He made it his endeavour in everything he did to hide his outstanding discernment under the guise of simple stupidity. Men of every type constantly flocked to him as their master, guide and spiritual director. Nobles of the highest rank, members of religious orders and men in authority consulted him over serious and difficult problems, and the advice he gave them was as sound as it was discreet. In his analysis of souls, in directing men to the acquisition of Christian virtue, his prudence was well employed. He could direct anyone, beginning by taking their individual nature into consideration, adapting himself as far as possible to the wishes of each one, that he might draw them all to Christ, fishing for each one with the right kind of bait. He was especially knowledgeable about the discernment of spirits, and the moderation of passions, from which you can see how skilled he was in assessing spiritual matters and directing them, how subtle he could be, and how perspicacious. I could give you plenty of examples of this, but I shall pass them over because it would take too long to tell them.

228. I should become both prolix and tedious if I were to attempt to go through all his virtues in turn, particularly since that would make me repeat much that I know I have already said. So, to avoid that danger, I shall keep silent about Philip's virginal chastity, his

patience under adversity, his perseverance in the projects he undertook, and all the rest of his heroic virtues. One thing I will add about his charity to his neighbour, though I have said quite enough already on his charity towards God – he was so afire with longing to reconcile sinners to Christ that to the very end of his life he was willing to discipline himself and to undertake voluntary penances if only he could win them for Christ. He was so stricken with compassion for sinful men that he was unable to look at them without shedding many tears, as a sure sign of his overwhelming love for them.

229. And now I have said enough about the life of Philip, concluding my work in this year of Jubilee 1600, with the help of God. This year is distinguished above all others, and will long be remembered, partly because every day there is an increase in the works of piety done by the citizens of Rome, her leading men and her highest-ranking prelates, and partly because our Supreme Pontiff Clement VIII has welcomed such a crowd of people flocking to our city from every part of the world, and has relieved the poverty of pilgrims in distress, with the result that the fatherly care which his citizens have known so well is now increasingly becoming known to foreign peoples and nations. For their convenience he has opened a new guesthouse for visiting priests, where he follows the example of Him whose Vicar he is, and frequently washes the feet of his guests, dries them and kisses them, unashamed to give them his blessing as they sit at table. But this is something I must leave to others to describe in greater detail, having touched upon it only in passing.

230. But now, **look down from heaven, holy Father,** for I will address you directly, **from the loftiness of that mountain to the lowliness of this valley; from that harbour of quietness and tranquillity to this calamitous sea.** And now that the darkness of this world hinders no more those benignant eyes of thine from looking clearly into all things, look down and visit, O most diligent keeper, this vineyard which thy right hand planted with so much labour, anxiety and peril. To thee then we fly; from thee we seek for aid; to thee we give our whole selves unreservedly. Thee we adopt for our patron and defender; undertake the cause of our salvation, protect thy clients. To thee we appeal as our leader; rule thine army fighting against the assaults of the devil. To thee, kindest of pilots, we give up the rudder of our lives; steer this little ship of thine, and, placed as thou art on high, keep us off the rocks of evil desires, that with thee for our pilot and our guide, we may safely come to the port of eternal bliss.[295]

---

[295] *This prayer is always known as the 'Prayer of Baronio', for it is recorded that on the day of St Philip's death Baronio tried to say the psalm 'De Profundis' for the dead, but found himself unable to say any psalm other than 79:15, 'respice de caelo, et vide, et visita vineam istam – look down from heaven and see, and visit this vineyard'. From this circumstance it has always been assumed that Baronio wrote the whole of the well-known prayer, though since Gallonio does not give him credit for this, it is possible that Gallonio himself is the true author. The version in the 1601 Italian edition is much shorter. For the translation of this prayer we are indebted to Fr J.H. Newman of the Birmingham Oratory.*

INDEX OF NAMES & PLACES

*All references are to paragraph numbers except where stated;
'n' indicates the note to a paragraph.*

Achillei, Muzio, 104, 127.
Adiuti, Antonino, 107.
Aldobrandini, Cardinal Ippolito,
　see Clement VIII.
Alfonso, 101.
Alluminati, Alessandro, doctor, 169, 174, 180, 184.
Altieri, M. Antonio, 50n.
Altieri, Marzio, 50.
Altovito, Antonio, 5.
Altovito, Giovan Battista, 105.
Ambrogio, 103.
Ames, Louis, 52n, 59.
Ancaiani, Arcangela, 217, 218.
Ancina, Giovan Matteo, 119.
Ancina, Bl. Giovenale, (p. x), 20n, 119, 133.
Anelli, Ortensia, 182, 205.
Anerio, Fulginia, 33, 85n.
Anerio, Giovan Francesco, 33n, 130.
Anerio, Maurizio, 33, 84, 85n.
Anguillara, Lallio, 217.
Animuccia, Giovanni, 101.
Animuccia, Lucrezia, 101.
Antonio, Pietro, 44.
Apicella, Fabio, 215.
Archinto, Filippo, 20.
Arena, Giovan Thomaso, 80.
Ascanio, Cardinal Guido, 59.

Baronio, Cardinal Cesare, (p. x), (p. xii), 18n, 36n, 37, 49, 67, 68, 86, 87, 89, 102, 166–7, 168, 174, 181, 230n.
Barsum, Archdeacon, 172.
Bartolini, Matteo, 109.
Basso, Francesco, 72.
Beier, Girolamo, 113.
Belli, Marc'Antonio, 184.
Benci, Spinello, 179, 184.

Bencini, Francesco, 155.
Bernardi, Giovan Francesco, 135.
Bernardini, Paulino, 97–8.
Bettini, Alessio, 43.
Bianca the Midwife, 77.
Bonardi, Clelia, 207.
Boncompagni, Cardinal Ugo,
　see Gregory XIII.
Bonelli, Cardinal Michele, 35n, 87, 131, 157.
Boniperti, Giovan Battista, 119n.
Bordini, Giovan Francesco, 49n, 86, 87, 89.
Borgo, Massimiano, 40.
Borromeo, St Charles, 42n, 114n, 131.
Borromeo, Cardinal Federico, (p. x), (p. xii), 13, 19n, 39n, 123, 145, 157, 166, 171, 172, 174–5, 189.
Bozio, Francesco, 111, 133.
Bozio, Tommaso, (p. x), 102.
Brissio, Gasparo, 78.
Bucca, Ersilia, 117.
Bucca, Giovan Francesco, 117.
Bucca, Guglielmo, 43.
Buscaglia, Delia, 77.
Buzio, Giacomo, (p. xii), 145.

Caccia, Galeotto, 4.
Caccia, Ippolito and Michele, 4n.
Cacciaguerra, Buonsignore, 14n, 21, 22.
Caetani, Onorato, 106n, 119n.
Calcinardi, Stefano, 198.
Cameroni Oratory, 134.
Camillo, Don, 125.
di Capua, Annibale, 133, 178.
Carafa, Cardinal Antonio, 131.
Carracia, Antonia, 165.
Castiglione, Caterina and Giuseppe, 213.
Caterina, 100.

Ceoli, Tamiria, 140, 142.
Cerasio, Stefano, 83n.
Cesalpino, Andrea, doctor, 185n.
Cesaria, courtesan, 36.
Cesi, Angelo, 123.
Cesi, Cardinal Pietro Donato, 110, 123, 124, 126.
Cheli, Artemisia, 188.
Chimenti (Clement), Maestro, 2.
Cibo, Elena, 140, 142.
Cibo, Vittoria (Vincenza), 160.
Clement VIII, (p. xii), 17, 86, 87, 145, 157, 161, 173, 229.
Colichia, Epifania, 188.
Colonna, Agnesina and Marc'Antonio, 106.
Colonna, Giulio Cesare, 150.
Comparotti, Giovanni, doctor, 155.
Consalvi, Desiderio, 155.
Consolini, Pietro, 12n, 154, 161, 173, 178.
Corcos brothers, 161.
Cordella, Girolamo, 163, 172, 173.
Cordelio, 152.
Corona, Bernadino, 44, 119.
Corteselli, Marco Antonio, 171.
dei Crescenzi, Alessandro, 171.
dei Crescenzi, Costanza, 106, 120, 127, 148, 162, 215n.
dei Crescenzi, Giacomo, 136.
dei Crescenzi, Virgilio, 162.
dei Crescenzi, family, 60, 132n, 199n.
Crescio, Giovan Battista, 93, 112.
Crispi, Pietro, 95.
Cristiano, Lorenzo, 95.
Crivelli, Giovan Angelo, 99.
Crivelli, Prospero, 16, 33, 34.
Curazio, Giovan Paolo, 119.
Cusano, Cardinal Agostino, (p. xii), 37n, 144, 145, 157, 166, 174, 179, 211.

Diaceti (Dicati), Angelo, 66.
Domenico, 72.

Ercolani, Vincenzo, 81.
Eustachio, Bartolomeo, 83.

Fano Oratory, 134.
Fantini, Antonio, 201.
Farnese, Cardinal Ranuccio, 87.
Fedeli, Alessandro, 37n, 86, 87, 114.
Fedeli, Germanico, (p. x), 37n, 87, 95, 104, 109, 118, 176, 177, 178, 184.
Felice di Castelfranco, 66.
Felice, Giovan Battista, 214.
Fermo Oratory, 134.
Ferrara Oratory, 134.
il Ferrarese, Francesco, 47.
Ferrerio, Cardinal Guido, 131.
Florence, 1, 2, 3, 9.
Foligni, Alessandro, 213.
Fortino, Francesco, 43.
Francesca, a maid, 125.
Franceschi, Alessandro, 97–8.
da Francesco, Frà Baldolino, 2.
Francesco of Lucca, doctor, 34.
de Franchis, Antonio, doctor, 201.
Fréjus Oratory, 134.
Fucci, Antonio, 48, 49, 92.
Fugini, Bartolomeo, 147.

Galletti, Tommaso, 133.
Gallonio, Antonio, (p. x), 18n, 37n, 38, 116, 169, 180, 230n.
Gesualdo, Cardinal Alfonso, 145.
Ghettini, Agostino, 48.
Giacomelli, Cesare, 5.
Gigli, Niccolò, 102, 114, 154.
Giovanni di Monaco, doctor, 34.
Girolamo, doctor, 152.
Giulia, a nun, 208.
Giustiniana, Maria, 188.
Gloriero, Alessandro, 123.
Gonzaga, Cardinal Scipio, 145, 157.
Gora, of Corneto, 211.
Gregory XIII, 17, 91n, 107, 110, 116, 126, 131, 143n, 161n.
Gregory XIV, 131, 145, 150, 157.
Grillenzoni, Paolo, 80.
Guerra, Giovan Battista, 143, 178, 184, 190n.
Guerra, Matteo, 158, 182.

INDEX OF NAMES AND PLACES, BY PARAGRAPH NUMBER

Ignatius, St, 10.

Lanciano Oratory, 134.
Lauro, Cardinal Vincenzo, 131, 157.
Lazzarello, Pietro Filippo, 159.
de Lelli, Ortensia, 216.
Lensi, Maddelena, 2n.
Lipomano, Aluigi, 73.
Lorenzi, Marcello, 214.
Lotti, Caterina and Giovan Pietro, 204.
Lucca Oratory, 134.
Luccatella, Teodosia, 219.
Lucci, Giovan Antonio, 110, 112, 132.
Lucia from Bologna, courtesan, 198n.
Lunellio, Giovanni, bishop, 20.
Lupo, Raffaele, 74.

Maffa, Marc'Antonio, 194–6.
Maffei, Mattia, 152–3.
de Magistris, Agostino, Alessandro and Margarita, 187.
Manni, Agostino, 116.
Mansueti, Eugenia, 135, 199.
Manzoli, Giovanni, 14, 152–3.
Manzoli, Giovan Battista, 152.
Margherita, the cook's sister, 15, 44.
Mariotto, Evangelista, 208.
Marmitta, Jacopo, 53n, 55, 79.
Marsuppini, Francesco, 21.
Marzi, Mario, 124.
Massimi, Elena, 168.
Massimi, Fabrizio, 105, 111, 125, 168n.
Massimi, Lavinia, 105, 111.
Massimi, Paolo, 105n, 125.
Massimi, Pietro, 105.
Massimi, Porzia, 41n.
Massimi, Violante, 168n.
Massimi, Virginia, 60.
Mattea family, 60.
Mazzei, Carlo, 122.
Mazzei, Domenico, 142.
dei Medici, Cardinal Alessandro, (p. xi, p. xii), 98, 109, 116, 131, 145, 157, 189.
dei Medici, Catherine, Queen, 41.

Mercati, Michele, 122.
Mercati, Pietro, 122.
Mezzabarba, Fabrizio, 105, 117n.
Mezzabarba, Politonio, 105.
Modio, Ettore, 146.
Modio, Giovan Battista, 44, 45, 48, 49, 146n.
della Molara, Francesco, 128.
Monte Cassino, 3.
Morona, Laura, Girolamo and Giulia, 142.
Morosino, Cardinal Giovan Francesco, 157.
di Mosciano, Lucrezia, 1n.

Nannoni, Fiametta, 203.
Naples Oratory, 102n, 133, 178, 212.
Neri, Catherine, 1.
Neri, Claudio, 164, 192.
Neri, Elizabeth, 1.
Neri, Fausta, Olimpia and Settimia, 207.
Neri, Francesco, 1, 2n.
Neri, Nero, 176.
NERI, Philip, his birth, 1; education, 2, 5; comes to Rome, 4; ordination, 20; temptations, 4, 8, 11, 27, 35, 36, 37, 39, 61–3, 96–8, 129, 165; poverty, 6,7,9; Mass, 23, 24, 25, 29, 30, 150; confessions, 26, 27, 31, 32, 39, 64–5, 74, 104, 119, 126, 149, 163; prayer, 7, 12, 19; visions, 46, 66, 69–71; fasting, 21; almsgiving, 18, 22; cures, 34, 35, 51, 78, 93, 102–6, 112, 120, 128, 130, 132, 141, 142, 143, 147–8, 152–3, 155–6, 160; exorcisms, 100; raising the dead, 125; predictions, 52, 59, 73, 99, 112, 114, 139, 140, 171, 172–3, 176–8; discernment, 71, 72, 113, 117, 121, 135, 136, 146, 148, 158, 159, 164; virtues, 220–9; hospital visits, 9, 32, 151; and the Black Dog, 51, 57, 75–6; and youth, 10; and the Jews, 33, 161; incendium amoris, 12, 13, 14, 24, 28; miraculous preservation,

253

18; Oratory exercises, 28, 49, 60, 89, 107; Congregation of the Oratory, 133–4, 137–8, 166–7; illnesses, 82, 83, 115, 133, 163, 174–5; death, 179–81; burial, 183, 189–90; autopsy, 184–6; apparitions, 118, 182; posthumous cures, 187–8, 191–219.

Orsini, Carlo, 132, 147n.
Orsini, Giulia, 190, 206.
Orsini, Lavinia, 150.
Orsini, Maria Maddelena, 182, 217.
Orsini, Porzia, 156.

Pacelli, Bradamante, 85.
Padua Oratory, 134.
Paganelli, Maria, 148.
Paleotti, Cardinal Gabriele, 131, 145, 157.
Palermo Oratory, 134, 209.
Pamphili, Girolamo, 37n, 159, 179, 197.
Paolo, 80.
Paravicini, Cardinal Ottavio, (p. x), (p. xii), 95, 157.
Parigi, Ludovico, 119.
Parma, Antonio, 210.
Pasquini, Antonio, 165.
Paterio, Pompeo, 105, 114, 116.
Patrizi, Patrizio, 148, 162.
Pellegrini, Prometeo, 146, 154.
Pepoli, Cardinal Guido, 145, 157.
Perrachione, Pietro, (p. x), 114, 116.
Petroni, Alessandro, doctor, 34.
Pierbenedetti, Cardinal Mariano, 145.
Pietra, Henrico, 14, 22.
Pinelli, Cardinal Domenico, 145.
Pius IV, 91, 97–8.
Pius V, St, 93n.
Polanco, Giovanni, SJ, 16.
Poliziani, Cardinal Giovanni, 53.
Porcacci, Drusilla, 200–2.
Porto, Antonio, doctor, 185n.
Pozzo, Pietro, 133, 209.
Priorata, Isabella, 199.

Rangone, Claudio, 206.

Raspa, Theseo, 22.
Rausico, Giovanni, 87.
Raymond, Vincent (the Miniaturist), 46.
de' Ricci, St Catherine, 66n, 146.
de' Ricci, Cardinal Ottavio, 28n, 53n, 79.
de' Ricci, Flaminio, 119, 133, 178.
Ricciardelli, Tiberio, 119.
ROME, Philip arrives, 4; jubilee year, 17.
  Churches:
    the Seven Churches, 6, 7, 40, 60, 93n.
    S. Adriano, 144.
    S. Elizabetta, 124.
    S. Giovanni dei Fiorentini, 50, 86–90, 105.
    S. Giovanni Laterano, 20.
    S. Girolamo della Carità, 21, 23, 29, 79, 94, 95, 101, 106, 126.
    S. Lorenzo in Damaso, 119.
    S. Maria sopra Minerva, 50, 66, 80, 81, 113.
    S. Maria in Vallicella, 50, 91, 107, 109–10, 112, 116, 124, 126, 144–5.
    S. Onofrio, 179.
    S. Pietro in Vaticano, 34.
    S. Salvatore in Campo, 15, 17.
    S. Tommaso in Parione, 20.
    SS. Trinità, 17.
  Confraternities:
    Charity, 21.
    Holy Trinity, 14, 15, 17.
  Hospitals:
    S. Giacomo, 9n, 70.
    S. Maria della Consolazione, 9n, 32, 42.
    S. Salvatore (Lateran), 9n, 32.
    S. Spirito, 9n, 32, 67, 85.
  Monuments:
    Colosseum, 32.
    Baths of Diocletian, 35.
Romolo, Bartolomeo, 3.
Rosa, Persiano, 15, 20, 21, 51.
Rosari, Cardinal Virgilio, 63.
Rositano, Ottavio, 212.

INDEX OF NAMES AND PLACES, BY PARAGRAPH NUMBER

de Rossi, Giovanni, 94.
della Rovere, Cardinal Girolamo, 145, 157.
Ruiz, Caterina, 160.
Rusticucci, Cardinal Girolamo, (p. xii), 145.

Sala, Antonio, 102.
Salort, Jaime, 87.
Salviani, Hippolito, 44, 83.
Salviati, Giovan Battista, 41, 42, 54, 81.
Salviati, Porzia, 81.
de Sanctis, Marc'Antonio, 214.
San Germano, 3.
San Severino Oratory, 134.
Santoro, Cardinal Giulio, 131, 157.
Saraceno, Domenico, 35.
Saraceno, Giovan Battista (Frà Pietromartire), 52, 113.
Savelli, Giacomo, 60n, 124.
Savera, Giulio, 140, 184.
Savioli, Giulio, 111.
Savonarola, Frà Girolamo, 3n, 66n, 146n.
Sebastiano, 75–6.
Sermei, Giuseppe, 216.
Sfrondato, Cardinal Camillo, 157.
Sfrondato, Cardinal Nicolò, *see* Gregory XIV.
Silvestri, Ridolfo, doctor, 169, 197.
Sirleto, Cardinal Guglielmo, 131.
Sixtus V, 144, 145.
de' Soldi, Antonio, Lucrezia, Maddelena, 1.
Somai, Prospero, 139.
Soto, Francisco, 92.
Spadaro, Pietro, 22, 103n.

Talpa, Antonio, 102, 133.
Tana, Gabriele, 53–8.
Tarugi, Cardinal Francesco Maria, (p. x), (p. xii), 23n; 34n, 37n, 41, 48, 49, 54, 63, 69, 70, 73, 83, 87, 105, 107, 114, 115, 133, 167.
Tassone, Costanzo, 42, 95.
Teccosi, Vincenzo, 21n, 29, 30, 35n.
Tommaso, 69.
Tosino, Mario, 46.
Tozzi, Michelangelo, 133.
Tournon Oratory, 134.
Tre Fontane, abbey, 48.
Troiani, Olimpia, 108.

Valdez, Francisco (Juan), 21.
Valentini, Damiano, 59.
Valerio (Valier), Cardinal Agostino, 131, 157, 174.
Varesi, Vittoria, 141, 156.
Velli, Angelo, (p. x), 87, 147, 167.
Vestri, Livia, 147, 149.
Vecchietti, Girolamo, 172.
Vicenza Oratory, 134.
Vipera, Francesco, 52.
Visconti, Cardinal Alfonso, (p. x), 219.
Vito, doctor, 152.
Vittorio, Angelo, doctor, 143, 169, 179, 184–6.
Vittrici, Pietro, 91.

Zazzara, Francesco, 18n, 169, 176, 179, 184.
Zazzara, Monte, 28n, 153, 193.
Zazzara, Frà Simone, 193.
Zerla, Giuseppe, 184–6.

INDEX OF SAINTS IN GALLONIO'S FOOTNOTES

*All references are to paragraph numbers except where stated;
'n' indicates the note to a paragraph.*

Abraham the Syrian, 3n.
Ambrose, by Paulinus, 1n.
Ammon, by Athanasius, 38n.
Anastasius the Martyr, 100n.
Annon the Bishop, 170n.
Ansbert, by Angrad, 190n.
Antoninus, 204n.
Antony, by Athanasius, 1n, 3n, 38n, 39n, 45n, 100n.
  by Osbert the Monk, 8n.
Audoen, 170n.
Augustine, Sermons *de Diversis*, 204n; Tract IX on St John, 8n.
Auxentius, by Surius, 100n, 148n.
Baronio, *Annals*, 100n.
Benedict, in Gregory's *Dialogues*, 8n.
Bernard the Abbot, by William [of St Thierry], 11n, 36n, 59n, 82n;
  by Godfrey, 78n, 101n, 148n.
Bernardine of Siena, by Surius, 4n, 10n, 67n.
Birgitta, by Surius, 39n.
Burchard the Bishop, by Egilhard, 190n.
Cuthbert, by Bede, 46n, 148n.
Cyrus and John, by Metaphrastes, 148n.
Daniel the Stylite, 29n, 36n, 59n, 61n.
Deodatus the Bishop, 110n.
Disibod, by Hildegard, 190n.
Dominic, by Theodoric, 6n, 7n, 190n.
Dositheus, by Dorotheus, 71n.
Dunstan, by Osbert the Monk, 6n, 8n, 35n, 190n.
Ebrulfus, 125n.
Edmund the Bishop, by Surius, 71n.
Elzear the Count, by Surius, 6n.
Equitius, in Gregory's *Dialogues*, 36n.

Euthemius, by Cyril, 39n, 46n, 59n.
Evermodus, by Kranz, 71n.
Francis, 18n, 20n, 96.
Germanus of Paris, 59n.
Giles the Bishop, by Audoen, 18n.
Godefrid, 170n.
Goar the Elder, by Wandlebert, 61n.
Gregory, 96.
Gregory the Great, *Dialogues*, 8n, 18n, 36n, 46n, 71n.
  Register, 8n, 82n.
Gregory of Nazianzen, epistle xliv, 158n.
Gregory of Tours, on Martyrs, 193n.
Hilarion, by Jerome, 3n, 8n, 39n, 100n, 190n.
John the Deacon, in Gregory's *Dialogues*, 18n.
John Moschus, *The Spiritual Meadow*, 46n, 118n, 125n.
John the Silent, by Cyril, 38n, 46n, 59n, 148n.
Lausiacas, by Palladius, 36n, 39n, 100n.
Lidwig, by John Brugman, 190n.
Louis of Tours, by John XXII, 204n.
Ludger (by Gregory of Tours ?), 193n.
Macrina, by Gregory of Nyssa, 205n.
Malachy the Bishop, by St Bernard, 85n, 110n.
Marcellinus and Peter, by Einhard, 100n.
Marcellus the Archimandrite, 59n.
Marcian the Priest, by Metaphrastes (in Surius vol I), 18n.
Marie of Oignies, by J. de Vitry, 57n.
Martin of Tours, by Gregory of Tours, 96, 100n, 193n, 202n, 211n.
Moduald of Trèves, by Stephen, 193n.

Mutius, by Evagrius and Palladius, 125n.
Nicetas by Theosteristus, 96, 148n.
Nicephorus the Archimandrite, by Theosterictus, 9n.
Odilo, 170n.
Othmar by Iso, 190n.
Pachomas, in Palladius' life of Lausiacas, 39n.
Pachomius, by Dionysius Exiguus, 18n, 39n, 110n.
Paul the first Hermit, in Athanasius on Antony, 46n.
Peter of Asturia, 78n.
Peter of Tarentas, by Gaufried, 78n.
Philotheus, by Theodoret, 8n, 67n, 148nn, 170n.
Poppo, by Everhelm, in Surius, 71n.
Porphyry of Gaza, by Mark, 148n.
Radegund the Queen, by Bandomina, 6n, 148n.
Romuald, by Peter Damian, 57n, 71n, 96n, 146n.

Rutilius Benzonus, *On the Jubilee Year*, 193n.
Saba, 20n, 46n, 96, 158n.
Severinus of Noricum, by Eugippius, 125n. (PL 72:1167–1200)
Simeon Salus, by Leontius, 36n, 57n, 59n, 118n.
Stephen, by Evodius, 202n, 204n. (PL 51:821–54)

Theodore the Siceot, by George the Monk, 1n, 8n, 67n, 82n, 110n, 170n, 202n.
Theodosius the Cenobiarch, 59n, 96.
Thomas Aquinas, by Surius, 1n. by John XXII, 190n.
Vincent Ferrer, by Pietro Ranzano, 1n, 11n, 29n, 36n, 38n.

Vide generaliter: Surius, Laurentius, *De Probatis Sanctorum Historiis*, Cologne 1576–81.

INDEX OF SWORN WITNESSES IN GALLONIO'S FOOTNOTES

All references are to paragraph numbers except where stated; 'n' indicates the note to a paragraph.

Achillei, Muzio, 104n, 127n.
Alluminati, Alessandro, 135n, 184n.
Ames, Louis, 52n, 59n.
Anelli, Ortensia, 182n.
Anerio, Giovan Francesco, 130n.
Animuccia, Lucrezia, 101n.
Ansaldi, Orazio, 122n.
Antoni, Francesca, 125n.
Apicella, Fabio, 215n.
Baronio, Cardinal Cesare, 33n, 36n, 37n, 67n, 68n, 71n, 83n, 98n, 102n, 168n, 169n, 171n, 173n, 188n, 203n.

Barsum, Archdeacon, 172n.
Beier, Girolamo, 113n.
Belli, Marc'Antonio, 184n.
Benci, Spinello, 184n.
Bernardi, Giovan Francesco, 135n.
Bordini, Gian Francesco, 45n, 79n, 85n.
Borromeo, Cardinal Federico, 19n, 39n, 46n, 71n, 72n, 149n, 173n.
Bucca, Ersilia and Giovan Francesco, 117n.
Buscaglia, Delia and Gasparo, 77n.
Caetani, Beatrice, 74n, 106n, 156n.

Calcinardi, Stefano, 198n.
Carracia, Antonia, 165n,
Ceoli, Tamiria, 140n, 142n, 160n.
Comparotti, Giovanni, 155n.
Consalvi, Desiderio, 155n.
Consolini, Pietro, 178n.
dei Crescenzi, Costanza, 106n, 120n, 127n, 148n, 162n.
dei Crescenzi, Giacomo, 132n, 136n.
dei Crescenzi, Pietro-Paolo, 132n.
Crescio, Giovan Battista, 93n.
Cusano, Cardinal Agostino, 37n, 169n, 173n.
Fedeli, Alessandro, 37n.
Fedeli, Germanico, 37n, 95n, 104n, 112n, 118n, 148n, 176n, 178n, 184n.
Felice, Giovan Battista, 214n.
de Franchis, Antonio, 200n.
Fugini, Bartolomeo, 147n.
Fuscherio, Giuliano, 103n.
Gallonio, Antonio, 37n.
Giordano, Domenico, 85n.
Giulia, a nun, 208n.
Grazzini, Simone, 50n.
Guerra, Gian Battista, 178n, 184n, 189n.
Guerra, Matteo, 158n, 182n.
Lazzarello, Pietro Filippo, 159n.
Lorenzi, Marcello, 214n,
Maffa, Marc'Antonio, 194n.
Manzoli, Giovanni, 152n.
Mario of the Holy Trinity, 46n.
Mariotto, Evangelista, 208n.
Marmitta, Jacopo, 53n.
Massimo, Fabrizio and Violante, 125n.

dei Medici, Card. Alessandro, 95n, 98n.
Modio, Ettore, 146n.
della Molara, Francesco, 128n, 129n.
Moroni, Girolamo, Giulia and Laura, 142n.
Neri, Claudio, 164n, 192n.
Neri, Nero, 176n.
Neri, Settimia and family, 207n.
Orsini, Carlo, 132n.
Pamphili, Girolamo, 37n, 159n, 197n.
Parma, Antonio, 210n.
Pasquini, Antonio, 165n.
Paterio, Pompeo, 117n, 124n.
Pellegrini, Prometeo, 146n.
Porcacci, Drusilla, 200n.
Pozzo, Pietro, 209n.
Rangoni, Giulia Orsini, 130n, 156n.
Ruiz, Caterina, 160n.
Savera, Giulio, 140n.
Silvestri, Ridolfo, 197n.
Somai, Prospero, 139n.
Tarugi, Cardinal Francesco Maria, 23n, 34n, 37n, 41n, 43n 45n, 47n, 60n, 70n, 71, 73n, 83n, 85n, 93n, 95n, 100n, 101n, 104n, 105n, 114n, 115n, 124n, 158n, 173n.
Teccosi, Vincenzo, 35n.
Varesi, Vittoria, 141n, 156n.
Vestri, Livia, 132n, 147n, 149n.
Vincenzo of the Holy Trinity, 46n.
Vittorio, Angelo, 143n, 184n, 186n.
Vittrici, Pietro, 91n.
Zazzara, Francesco, 176n, 184n.
Zerla, Giuseppe, 184n, 186n.